D1488704

Martin Bormann

Also by James McGovern

NOVELS

The Berlin Couriers
No Ruined Castles
Fräulein

NONFICTION

Crossbow and Overcast

Martin Bormann

By James McGovern

William Morrow & Company, Inc.

NEW YORK   1968

For James Winslow and Elizabeth Laird

CONTENTS

vii

LIST OF ILLUSTRATIONS

Martin Bormann

"The most decisive influence on the Führer during the war, and especially from about 1942 on, after Hess went out in 1941 and a year had elapsed, was exerted by Herr Bormann. The latter had, at the end, disastrously strong influence. That was possible only because the Führer was filled with profound mistrust after 20th July, and because Bormann was with him constantly and presented and described to him all matters."

HERMANN GOERING,
in testimony at the Nuremberg trial of major war criminals.

———

"Bormann remains suspended in limbo, neither dead nor alive: perhaps even more incontestably airborne than before."

H. R. TREVOR-ROPER,
in his preface to the "United States Edition 1962" of his book *The Last Days of Hitler*.

———

"Never hang a man you do not hold."
Old Nuremberg adage.

———

ONE

"The Biggest Unsolved Nazi Mystery"

The night of October 15, 1946, was cold and wet. A piercing wind swept through the shattered walls and broken towers of the ancient city of Nuremberg. Most of its citizens were principally concerned with finding food and shelter from the cold, rather than in the executions of the major Nazi war criminals which were to take place in Nuremberg Prison.

The condemned men housed under maximum security conditions in the warmth of the prison ate their last supper of sausage, cold cuts, potato salad, black bread, and tea. Shortly before one A.M., two white-helmeted American military policemen called for the first man who would be executed. He was the Foreign Minister of the Third Reich, Joachim von Ribbentrop, who was to be followed at short intervals by the others in the cellblock.

Von Ribbentrop offered no resistance as the military policemen led him down a corridor and across a windy courtyard to the prison's small gymnasium. Resistance would have been futile, for the executions had been carefully planned so that they would all follow the same brief, orderly, lethal procedure.

Walking with his eyes half closed and as though in a trance, von Ribbentrop entered the brightly lit gym-

nasium at 1:11 A.M. His manacles were swiftly removed and
his hands tied behind his back with shoelaces. A military po-
liceman was on either side of him as he mounted thirteen steps
to one of three black gallows which had been erected on platforms eight feet high and eight feet apart.

A Protestant chaplain prayed at von Ribbentrop's side as he
stood on a trap door, where a noose was slipped around the
former Foreign Minister's neck by the official U.S. Army
hangman, Master Sergeant John C. Woods of San Antonio,
Texas. An American doctor with a flashlight and a Soviet
doctor with a stethoscope waited at the foot of the gallows as
von Ribbentrop made his final statement: "God protect Germany. My last wish is that Germany's unity be preserved and
that an understanding be achieved between East and West."

Sergeant Woods tightened the noose, then tied a web belt
around the condemned man's legs. There were fifteen official
witnesses: one general from each of the four Allied nations,
the U.S. prison security officer, eight selected foreign corre-
spondents, and two Germans. All stood at attention and removed their hats.

One of Sergeant Woods's two assistant hangmen drew a
black hood over von Ribbentrop's sparse gray hair, covering
his face. Then the other assistant pulled a thin wooden lever.
The trap door rumbled open. Von Ribbentrop fell and vanished, his hooded face concealed by the black curtains which
covered the space below the trap.

As the former Foreign Minister still swung from the taut
rope of the first gallows, Field Marshal Wilhelm Keitel, once
Chief of the Armed Forces High Command, entered the gymnasium. Keitel wore a well-pressed uniform with his decorations and insignia of rank removed. His boots gleamed as he
briskly mounted thirteen steps to the second gallows. Keitel
had appealed to the Allied Control Council "to be granted a
death by firing squad" because he felt that this was the "right
of the soldier in every other army in the world upon whom
sentence of death is pronounced as a soldier." The appeal had
been rejected and now the trap door rumbled open again.

Keitel was followed into the gymnasium in turn by Ernst Kaltenbrunner, Alfred Rosenberg, Hans Frank, Wilhelm Frick, Julius Streicher, Fritz Sauckel, Alfred Jodl, and Arthur Seyss-Inquart. A new rope was used for each man. None had the slightest chance of escaping the end decreed for him. "Ten men in 103 minutes," Sergeant Woods later remarked. "That's fast work," adding that he was ready for a "stiff drink afterwards."

Ten of the twelve major war criminals condemned to death by the International Military Tribunal on October 1, 1946, had thus been executed after a trial of 217 days. But two of the original twelve managed, incredibly, to cheat the gallows. One was Hermann Goering. Like Adolf Hitler, Heinrich Himmler, and Joseph Goebbels, Goering chose his own method of departing a world upon which he and the other Nazi leaders had made such a violent impact.

Somehow a phial of potassium cyanide was smuggled into Goering's cell. The Reich Marshal swallowed its lethal contents two hours before he was to have gone to the gallows. His corpse, tinged green by the poison, was brought on a stretcher to the gymnasium. There it was photographed, both clothed and naked, as were the corpses of the ten who had been hanged, as proof that all of these men were really dead.

There was no such certainty concerning the other condemned man who had evaded the walk up thirteen steps to the noose, the black hood, and the opening trap. He was Reichsleiter Martin Bormann, Head of the Nazi Party Chancellery and Secretary to the Führer.

Bormann had not been hanged for one reason only. He had not been available for hanging. Unlike Goering, he had not been in the cellblock. Nor had he been present in the dock at Nuremberg. Bormann was the only defendant to have been tried and sentenced in absentia. If this absence was both a major mystery and a source of concerned embarrassment to the British and American intelligence services, which had been searching for him in vain since the end of the war, it was consistent with the man.

Bormann was always the most mysterious of the Nazi leaders. He worked in the shadows, despising public recognition and decorations. But he had attained immense power. How real this power was can be gauged by opinions expressed by other Nazi leaders. These men, who were feared and hated by millions of their victims, in turn feared and hated a man virtually unknown to anyone but themselves.

To one of the defendants at Nuremberg, Hans Frank, the Nazi Governor General of Poland, Bormann was an "archscoundrel" and hatred was too mild a word to describe Frank's feelings about him. Another defendant, Hans Fritzche, once a high official in the Propaganda Ministry of Dr. Joseph Goebbels, told the court, "Secondly—and this is something which I cannot express differently under oath—Dr. Goebbels was quite clearly scared of Martin Bormann."

To Count Lutz Schwerin von Krosigk, the Third Reich's last Minister of Finance, Bormann had been Hitler's "evil spirit" and the "Brown Eminence" behind the Führer's throne. In the view of Colonel General Heinz Guderian, once Chief of the Army General Staff, "Next to Himmler, the most sinister member of Hitler's entourage was Martin Bormann." And yet Bormann defeated and humiliated the Reichsführer SS when the two had engaged in a personal power struggle.

The Allies believed that Hermann Goering had been the second most powerful figure in Nazi Germany. But in the last two years of the war Bormann gained that position and thereafter treated the Reich Marshal with contempt and brutality. Goering's feelings about Bormann were expressed when the Reich Marshal was interrogated before the Nuremberg trial by Colonel John Amen of the U.S. Army:

Colonel Amen: "Do you think the Führer is dead?"
Goering: "Absolutely. No doubt about it."
Amen: "What about Bormann?"

Goering threw his hands skyward and replied, "If I had my say about it, I hope he is frying in hell. But I don't know about it."

Albert Speer, the Nazi Minister for Armaments and War Production, knew the reality of Bormann's power and its source. "A few critical words from Hitler," Speer said, "and all of Bormann's enemies would have jumped at his throat." The Führer never spoke those critical words. Bormann remained at his side until Hitler's death. In the bizarre setting of the bunker underneath the Old Reich Chancellery in Berlin, Bormann witnessed the Führer's marriage to Eva Braun and also his will and political testament. The will read, in part, "as my executor I nominate my most faithful party comrade, Martin Bormann."

The executor was the first person to enter the room in which Hitler killed himself. Bormann was also one of the six men who assisted at the funeral pyre of Hitler and his bride. However, Bormann did not follow his Führer into suicide.

As Hitler burned in the garden of the Reich Chancellery with the Red Army drawing ever closer to it, Bormann left the Chancellery. According to those who joined him in the first stages of his flight, Bormann wanted to reach Grand Admiral Karl Doenitz, whom the Führer had appointed the new chief of state.

If Bormann did indeed intend to go to the headquarters of Doenitz in northwest Germany, he did not achieve that goal. That much is certain. After the night of May 1, the man who had lived in the shadows vanished into the shadows at the age of forty-five. It was a situation without parallel. How could the second most powerful figure in a regime whose power had once extended from the Atlantic to the Urals have disappeared without a trace?

The British and American military intelligence services conducted investigations in the immediate postwar period to answer this question, but failed to locate Bormann or any credible evidence of his death. Similar investigations by Soviet authorities led to no announcement that they had solved the mystery. And so, taking the view that Bormann must be considered missing since his death had not been established, the International Military Tribunal tried and sentenced him in his absence. That death sentence was still in effect twenty-two years after the corpses of the eleven other major war criminals were photographed in the gymnasium of the Nuremberg Prison.

Today, there are those who think that the sentence will never be executed, because Bormann was killed on the night of May 1, 1945, and his body buried in some unknown mass grave. Most of these doubters are former Nazis who were with the Head of the Nazi Party Chancellery as he attempted to escape from Berlin. But other people whose opinions must be taken seriously believe that this second most powerful Nazi managed to escape to a hospitable foreign country and is alive today, a ghost from an evil and horrific past.

On April 13, 1961, Dr. Fritz Bauer, Attorney General for the West German State of Hesse, announced in Frankfurt that he was convinced that Bormann was still alive. Dr. Bauer said that a secret international organization might have sent Bormann abroad through an elaborate underground escape system. The Attorney General, who was well known for his prosecutions of Nazi war criminals, opened an active file on Bormann.

The West German government took the many reports of Bormann's survival seriously enough to post, in November 1964, a reward of 100,000 marks ($25,000) for information leading to his capture.

In October 1965, Tadek Tuvia Friedman, Director of the Institute for the Documentation of Nazi War Crimes in Haifa, Israel, told a New York City newspaper reporter that he knew exactly where Bormann was living in Argentina.

In January 1966, Klaus Eichmann, son of Adolf Eichmann, wrote an open letter to Bormann, which was published in a leading West German magazine, asking the Secretary of the Führer to emerge from his South American hiding place and assume responsibility for the crimes "for which my father stood in your place during the trial in Israel."

Dr. Fritz Bauer announced in April 1966 that the search

for Bormann was narrowing down and that he was hopeful that "we are hot on his trail."

On March 27, 1967, Simon Wiesenthal held a news conference in the offices of the Anti-Defamation League of B'nai B'rith in New York City. Wiesenthal was then on his first visit to the United States. This was in connection with the publication of his book, *The Murderers Among Us,* which recounted his experiences since 1945 in locating missing Nazi war criminals. The head of the private Jewish Documentation Center in Vienna told the news conference that "Bormann travels freely through Chile, Paraguay, and Brazil. He has a strong organization dedicated to aiding other Nazi war criminals to evade authorities." Bormann used five or six names, Wiesenthal added, and "has many friends, money. I get reports on him simultaneously from two places too far apart to let there be just one man."

On July 4, 1967, the West German Ministry of Justice renewed its permanent request to the Federal Supreme Court of Brazil for the preventive arrest and extradition of the Secretary of the Führer and Head of the Nazi Party Chancellery. And on December 31, 1967, *The Sunday Times* of London, in a front page story by Antony Terry, its Central European Correspondent, reported that Bormann was living in Brazil in a small Nazi colony located at the southern tip of the border with Paraguay. Terry's informant was Erich Karl Wiedwald, a former SS corporal, who claimed that Bormann traveled along an escape route organized by SS veterans and reached Argentina in 1947. However, according to Wiedwald, Bormann was now unrecognizable because of a botched job of plastic surgery and was moreover dying of stomach cancer. Nevertheless, Bormann's fate or whereabouts continued to remain what Simon Wiesenthal termed "the biggest unsolved Nazi mystery" more than two decades after the demise of the Third Reich.

But there was another puzzle concerning Martin Bormann. Who had he really been? How had he risen from unknown party official to a position of power where, though still largely unknown, he was said by Hermann Goering to have "ruled Hitler's whole existence?" This rise baffled even the few who had known Bormann well during the twelve apocalyptic years of the Nazi regime. One of them was Alfred Rosenberg, the philosopher of the Nazi movement.

As Chief of the *Ostministerium* which administered vast areas of Nazi-occupied Russia, Rosenberg was a frequent victim of Bormann's intrigues. Before walking the thirteen steps to the gallows at Nuremberg, Rosenberg wrote in his memoirs: "Not even the wildest fantast could have foretold Martin Bormann's career."

That career, like Hitler's, began in modest circumstances in a Europe which had the outward appearance of stability and permanence, but which the Nazis would finally destroy.

TWO

The Convict

Martin Bormann was born on June 17, 1900, in Halberstadt, an ancient and picturesque Lower Saxon town of some 40,000 inhabitants. There was nothing in his family background or in his youth, except for his involvement in a brutal murder, to indicate that he would one day be characterized as a major war criminal.

Theodor Bormann, Martin's father, had been a Trumpeter Sergeant-Major in a military band. After retiring from the army, Theodor Bormann, whose own father had owned a quarry, became a post office clerk in Halberstadt and reached the middle grades of the civil service. But he died when his son Martin was four years old, and his widow was quickly remarried to the director of a small bank.

The formal education of Martin Bormann went no higher than the study of agriculture at the American equivalent of a trade high school. This was interrupted when he was attached as a gunner to Field Artillery Regiment 55 from June 1918 to February 1919. But unlike Hitler, who won the Iron Cross, and Goering, who won the Blue Max, Bormann's war service was undistinguished. He did not see action.

In August, 1920, the twenty-year-old former gunner and agricultural student became the manager of a large farm or estate. It belonged to a family of landed gentry named von Treuenfels and was located near the village of Parchim in the northern province of Mecklenburg. To the south, in Munich, an obscure political party adopted at about the same time the name National Socialist German Worker's Party and the swastika as its symbol.

Bormann was probably unaware of the activities of the new Nazi Party or of those of its seventh member, Adolf Hitler. But the young estate manager did reveal his discontent with conditions in postwar Germany by joining the Society Against Presumptuousness of the Jewry and the Rossbach organization.

Originally, the *Freikorps Rossbach,* led by a former lieutenant in the World War, Gerhard Rossbach, was one of the many bands of armed volunteers, of free corps, formed under the patronage of the *Reichswehr.* The regular German Army had been reduced to 100,000 men by the Versailles Treaty and tolerated the use of the free corps, sometimes called the Black Reichswehr, to maintain internal order and to protect the eastern frontiers against the Poles and Bolsheviks. In such capacities, the free corps saw considerable combat action. Soon realizing, however, that these roving bands of disgruntled, rootless ex-soldiers were quite capable of turning their guns on the infant Republic, the government declared them illegal in 1920.

Rossbach refused to disband his organization. He simply changed its name to the Rossbach Labor Community. When this organization was also declared illegal, the name was changed once more to the Union for Agricultural Professional Training. Its members shared the same views: anti-Semitism; discontent with the terms of the Versailles peace treaty; the need to reverse the decision of 1918; overthrow of the Republic; establishment of Germany as the great power of Europe.

This was the sort of organization in which Bormann could

feel at home. He joined the Rossbach group in 1922, too late for him to have seen combat action with it in the immediate postwar period. But he was its section leader and treasurer in Mecklenburg when, on January 9, 1923, the Allied Reparation Commission declared Germany to be in default of her deliveries of timber and coal agreed to under the terms of the peace treaty. French and Belgian troops occupied the Ruhr two days later.

The occupation of the industrial heart of Germany brought her to the verge of political and economic disintegration and hastened the collapse of the mark; by November one dollar was worth 130 million marks. The occupation also encouraged the extremist groups which could thrive only on conditions of insecurity and disorder. The government called for a campaign of passive resistance, while the extremists instigated strikes, guerilla warfare, and sabotage.

The French occupation authorities responded with economic blockade, deportations, the arrests of industrial magnates and trade union leaders alike, and the shooting of saboteurs. On May 23, 1923, Albert Leo Schlageter, a young former officer in the Imperial Army who had fought with the *Freikorps* in Upper Silesia and the Baltic States, was executed by the French for sabotage and industrial espionage. From the French viewpoint, he was guilty and his execution was justified. But to the German nationalist groups he was a patriotic martyr, and it was this feeling that soon involved Martin Bormann in murder.

In February, 1923, Walter Kadow, a twenty-three-year-old elementary schoolteacher, had joined the Rossbach organization. Kadow quickly made himself unpopular. He borrowed money from his comrades without repaying it and pretended to have won many decorations during the war. Perhaps his greatest mistake was in borrowing thirty thousand marks (worth about five dollars) from the treasury of the Rossbach organization.

The treasurer was Martin Bormann. He was now twenty-

three years old, with brown eyes, dark-brown hair, about
five feet seven inches tall, but with a powerful build and
a short thick neck from which derived his nickname, "The
Bull." By German standards, he was not well educated,
but he had a knack for figures and remembering details and he
had an obsession for hard work. He was still a bachelor and he
was losing faith in his Lutheran training and in the social order
into which he had been born at the turn of the century. In this
way, Bormann was no different from thousands of other frus-
trated young Germans of the postwar period. But few of them
came close to reaching the heights that Bormann did, perhaps
because few of them had his talent for shadowy manipulation
and violence. The first recorded victim of this talent was Walter Kadow, who had been in the Ruhr when Schlageter was
arrested and executed.

Bormann gave the order to detain Kadow, should he return
to Parchim in Mecklenburg. Bormann's stated purpose was to
put Kadow to work so that he could repay his debts. But
Bormann also spread the rumor that Kadow was a communist
spy and had probably informed on Schlageter.

Kadow did return to Parchim. On the night of May 31,
1923, he engaged in a long drinking bout with some members
of the Rossbach group in the tavern of a local inn. Toward
midnight, the inebriated Walter Kadow was dragged from the
tavern. He was hustled into a car and driven to a forest outside
the village. There he was beaten senseless with branches and
clubs. His teeth were kicked out and his skull was fractured.
Then his throat was cut.

Two bullets were finally fired into Kadow's head and his
corpse was buried in the forest. The murderers fled, believing
that the martyr Schlageter had been avenged and that an object lesson had been given to other potential traitors.

Political murders were a common occurrence in postwar
Germany. They followed the ancient Germanic pattern of the
Vehmgericht, medieval courts that had sat and passed sen-
tence in secret. But the Weimar Republic was still stable

enough to attempt to bring to justice the perpetrators of such crimes. This it did in the case of Walter Kadow, after a member of the Rossbach group named Berhard Jurisch confessed to his marginal participation. Jurisch had feared that he, too, was marked for execution.

Martin Bormann was arrested in July 1923 and remained under investigative arrest in Leipzig until December of that year. On March 12, 1924, he and other members of the Rossbach group were brought to trial before the State Court for the Defense of the Republic in Leipzig. Neither during this trial, which lasted three days, nor subsequently, was any credible evidence produced that Kadow had been a communist spy or had any connection with the betrayal of Schlageter.

The defendants were found guilty and given jail sentences of varying lengths. The longest—ten years at hard labor—was given to a certain Rudolf Franz Hoess as the probable ringleader. Hoess, the twenty-two-year-old son of a small shopkeeper, here made his first appearance in history. He had once thought of studying for the Roman Catholic priesthood at the urging of his devout parents. But during the war he had served as a machine gunner, and then had seen further action with the *Freikorps Rossbach* in the Baltic States. Hoess would be released after serving four years of his sentence under a general amnesty for persons convicted of political crimes. Still later, he would reappear as the Commandant of Auschwitz, the largest of the Nazi extermination camps.

Martin Bormann was sentenced to one year in prison for his part in the Kadow murder. From the uncooperative attitude of the defendants and the lack of eyewitnesses, Bormann's role in the affair emerged as a hazy one and yet one that would later prove typical for him. He appears to have been the one who urged the killers on, provided them with a car, helped to hide them, but who took no direct part in the murder.

Bormann and the other defendants were defiant as sentence was pronounced. As they were hustled into a paddy wagon to

be driven from the court to the prison, one man began to sing
and Bormann and the others joined in vigorously:

> "If you're run through by the sword, keep
> fighting nevertheless
> Give yourself up for lost, but not the flag
> Others will wave it when they bury you
> And win the glory that hovered over you."

Bormann served his full term under the harsh discipline of
the Prussian prisons of the time. Upon his release in March
1925 he returned to his job as general manager of the estate in
Parchim. Here he was little more than a hired hand supervis-
ing peasant farmers on property belonging to members of the
aristocratic class. Bormann was far from being a member of
this class, which he both envied and hated. But a job was a
job, and an ex-convict was fortunate to have one at all in a
country with millions of unemployed.

Bormann's prison term did nothing to make him abandon
his extreme nationalistic views, for he soon joined the *Front-
bann*. This was a successor organization to the *Deutscher
Kampfbund* (German Fighting Union), units of armed ex-
soldiers, which had been dissolved by the Weimar Republic
after supporting Adolf Hitler's disastrous putsch of 1923 in
Munich.

Hitler himself had served almost fourteen months in prison
because of the putsch. Upon being released on December 20,
1924, he found the Nazi Party a moribund, divided organization which had been declared illegal by the government. The
ban was lifted in 1925 and Hitler resurrected his party in that
year. But few people believed that this slightly comic, minor
Bavarian politician would ever become a major factor in
German, much less world, affairs. For the conditions of inflation, unemployment, and general discontent upon which the
Nazis depended to draw mass support were largely corrected
as Germany began a remarkable economic recovery.

There seemed to be no significant future for Adolf Hitler in

1925. This was even more true for a man Hitler was yet to meet. Martin Bormann in that year was not even a member of the Nazi Party. He was an unknown estate manager and, moreover, an ex-convict, and his prospects appeared dim.

But conditions would change, the night of the drums and torchlights would come, and in that night Bormann's star would rise, precisely and ironically because he had been sent to jail for his part in one brutal murder.

THREE

The Unknown
Reichsleiter

Shortly before dusk of January 30, 1933, drums began beating in the depths of the wooded Tiergarten in the heart of Berlin. Tens of thousands of Nazi Storm Troopers assembled there picked up torches filled with fuel and lit them. Then they formed into disciplined columns and marched out of the Tiergarten, through the Brandenburg Gate and down Unter den Linden, waving their flaming torches in the darkening winter air.

The Storm Troopers swung right at Wilhelmstrasse and marched down that broad avenue, their jackboots striking the pavement "with steady, quiet tread," in the words of the Horst Wessel Song, the Nazi anthem which they sang. Drums thundered and martial music blared from scores of bands as the massive torchlight parade flowed like a river of fire past cheering crowds, silent foreign embassies, and the Presidential Palace. From a window in the Palace, Field Marshal Paul von Hindenburg, then eighty-six and almost senile, watched stoically as the marchers continued on past the nearby Reich Chancellery. Standing at one of its open windows, Adolf Hitler—smiling, laughing, tears of joy occasionally filling his eyes— gave them the Nazi salute.

Hitler had been appointed Chancellor of the German Reich that afternoon by von Hindenburg, the President of the Republic. "Fourteen years of hard work has been crowned with victory," Joseph Goebbels later wrote. Through a microphone installed in the Reich Chancellery, Hermann Goering roared at the Storm Troopers and the assembled crowds:

"January 30, 1933, will be recorded in German history as the day when the nation was restored to glory once more, as the day when a new nation arose and swept aside all the anguish, pain and shame of the last fourteen years . . . There stands the renowned Field Marshal of the World War, and by his side the young Führer of Germany, who is about to lead the people and the Reich to a new and better era . . ."

There is no record of where Bormann was standing. He was not important enough to have his whereabouts noted on this long and fateful day, which was largely a by-product of the worldwide economic depression. The Nazis had exploited the severe crisis it caused within Germany to recover their fading strength and become the country's single largest political party.

Within a year of having been legally appointed Chancellor, Hitler had smashed all effective opposition to him, completed the Nazification of Germany, and become the country's dictator. And Martin Bormann was among those washed up out of obscurity on the tide of Hitler's triumph. Bormann, however, played no significant role in the maneuverings which enabled Hitler to become Reich Chancellor.

For Bormann was a latecomer to the Nazi movement. He had not joined the party until February 17, 1927, as party member number 60,508. From then on his rise was steady, rather than swift like that of the men who had been with the Führer since the Munich beer-hall days of the early 1920's.

In 1927, Bormann served as press chief of the Party *Gau** of Thuringia. On April 1, 1928, he became district leader in

---

* The Nazis divided Germany into major administrative regions, roughly resembling states, which they called *Gaue*.

Thuringia and business manager for that *Gau*. On November 15, 1928, he was appointed to the staff of the Supreme Command of the *Sturmabteilung*, or S.A., whose rank and file, commonly known as Storm Troopers or Brown Shirts, offered battle in the streets to those who opposed the Nazis.

On April 25, 1930, Bormann left the Storm Troopers to become *Leiter der Hilfskasse* (Leader of the Aid Fund of the Nazi Party). The purpose of the Aid Fund was to provide financial assistance to the families of men who had been killed or wounded while fighting for the Nazi cause. It became an important undertaking as the depression worsened. While directing the Aid Fund, Bormann placed hundreds of future Nazi officials in his personal debt.

Six months after Hitler came to power, Bormann was rewarded for his faithful service. In July 1933, he was appointed a *Reichsleiter** and Chief of Staff to Rudolf Hess, the Deputy Führer. Bormann's rise from party latecomer to *Reichsleiter* was greatly aided by his part in the Kadow murder. To the Nazi leaders, any young man who had served time in the political jails of the Weimar Republic was to be trusted, admired, and rewarded. A coveted Nazi medal, the *Blutorden* (Order of the Blood) was struck for this purpose. Bormann duly received it.

Bormann's marriage also set him apart from other deserving but obscure Nazis. On September 2, 1929, he had married Gerda Buch. She was then twenty, nine years younger than her husband. Gerda Bormann was a sturdy, rather plain blond girl with an avid interest in German folklore and a great admiration for Adolf Hitler. Her father, Walter Buch, a former major in World War I, was chairman of the Nazi Party Court responsible for maintaining party discipline.

Walter Buch was an influential and powerful figure in Nazi

---

* The *Reichsleiter* (National Leaders) of the Nazi Party were the highest office holders in the party. Hitler appointed the *Reichsleiter* and they were directly responsible to him. However, their duties had only to do with party, as distinct from military, international, or SS, affairs.

circles. Hitler served as witness to Gerda Buch's marriage, and thus became personally acquainted with the bridegroom. The first Bormann child was born on April 14, 1930. The father did not look long for a name for the boy. He was christened Adolf, after his godfather, Hitler.

Once the Nazis had gained control of the government, Bormann proved to be a tireless and devoted worker for the party and its Führer. This was understandable, from Bormann's viewpoint. His life was typical of the men of his generation who had joined the Nazi Party and become its administrators. Born in rural areas or small towns and cities, of fathers with modest incomes and prestige, the Nazi administrators had acquired little formal education and, after the First World War, had faced a future which held scant hope for advancement or personal satisfaction.

To Bormann and thousands of rootless, discontented young Nazis like him, the years of the Weimar Republic seemed riddled with disruption and disaster. The Armistice, the Versailles Treaty, the red flags of the Workers' and Soldiers' Councils, the Kapp Putsch, the occupation of the Ruhr, the inflation of 1923, and the depression of 1929, with its millions of unemployed, followed each other in quick succession. Hitler and the Nazi Party offered a seemingly feasible solution to Germany's difficulties and a sense of purpose to men like Bormann. The Führer wanted to establish a new kind of government which would no longer be based on the leadership of the aristocratic classes, the business elite, or the "November criminals" of the Weimar Republic. And after Hitler became Reich Chancellor in 1933, his program did at first bring work and hope to those who had brought him to power. No one could foretell at that time that the Führer's bloody thoughts would end in monstrous deeds. Martin Bormann did know what his devotion to the Führer had done for him. The son of a minor post-office official, a former agricultural student, convict, and estate manager was now a *Reichsleiter* and Chief of Staff to the Deputy Führer, Rudolf Hess, who was charged with deciding all questions of party leadership in Hitler's name.

The Führer maintained four separate chancelleries. One handled his purely personal affairs. Another dealt with routine matters such as the granting of pardons which came to him as chief of state. The third, the Reich Chancellery, administered matters that devolved upon Hitler as Chancellor of the Reich. The fourth, the Office of the Deputy Führer, handled all Nazi Party matters.

Outwardly, it would have seemed that the Reich Chancellery was the most important office and the one offering the greatest hope of advancement for an ambitious young man. But Hitler had made it plain that there was a difference, when he said at the 1934 Nazi Party rally in Nuremberg: "The State does not command us, rather we command the State."

Bormann saw the difference. Leaving the center of the stage to others, he quietly and industriously set out to gain control of the working machinery of the Office of the Deputy Führer. Here is where the real power in Germany resided, since, legally, the Nazi Party was the only political party in the country, and Hitler wanted the party to command the state. Hess was constantly seen at Hitler's side at parades and party rallies. But the rank-and-file party members soon came to realize that it was the unknown Martin Bormann who was the man to see when a job or a favor was needed.

Nothing was so insignificant that Bormann allowed it to escape his personal attention. When the *Gauleiter** raised the question of whether the Nazi salute should be accompanied by the salutation "Heil Hitler" or simply "Heil," Bormann resolved it. After solemn consideration, he duly informed the *Gauleiter* that either form was acceptable.

Bormann also made it a practice to single out for advancement people whom he considered to be truly convinced Nazis

---

* Subordinate to Bormann as a *Reichsleiter* (National Leader); the *Gauleiter* were leaders of the *Gaue*, the major administrative regions into which the Third Reich was divided.

who appeared to possess future potential. For old-line Nazis who seemed unable to keep pace with the changing times, he displayed impatience bordering on contempt. No gratitude was to be shown for past service; those who could not understand that Hitler was not the legal Chancellor of a legal government and that the old street-brawling days were over had to be dealt with ruthlessly.

By the spring of 1934, the S.A. and its Chief of Staff, Ernst Roehm, had in particular become both an embarrassment and a threat to the Führer. It counted for nothing that Hitler had once largely based his power on the Storm Troopers' intimidation of the public. There was now no further use for the unruly Brown Shirts, many of whose leaders were, like Roehm, notorious homosexuals given to a disorderly and luxurious way of life. For his future purposes, Hitler required a disciplined *corps d'élite* totally obedient only to him. He found the nucleus of it in the SS, the black-shirted *Schutz Staffeln* (Protective Squadrons) organized by Heinrich Himmler. Hitler also needed the backing of the officer corps of the *Reichswehr,* if he were ever to rearm Germany along professional lines.

But the aristocratic officer corps was both contemptuous and fearful of Roehm and his force of nearly three million Storm Troopers. For Roehm wanted to absorb the professional army into his S.A. As long as this possibility existed, Hitler knew that the *Reichswehr* officers would withhold their support. He also realized that if Roehm had his way, the S.A. would dominate the army and through it the State, possibly eclipsing the Nazi Party and its Führer.

Bormann understood the problem. For a year and a half he had been on the staff of the Supreme Command of the S.A. He knew its leaders well. He had enjoyed their confidence. But now they were expendable; they had failed to fit into the New Order.

Beginning in the early hours of June 30, 1934, one of Hitler's oldest supporters and closest friends, Ernst Roehm, was suddenly arrested along with other unsuspecting S.A. leaders.

Over the following three days they were liquidated by SS gunmen. So were others Hitler professed to believe were plotting against him, such as his predecessor as Reich Chancellor, General Kurt von Schleicher.

The purge eliminated the S.A. as a rival to the SS, gave the latter control of all police organs, and won for Hitler the support of the regular army. It also gave evidence and warning of the murderous lengths to which the Führer was prepared to go to attain absolute power. During this "Night of the Long Knives," as it came to be known, Bormann played a role that had been and would continue to be uniquely his.

Bormann was not one of the gunmen. He remained in the background, collecting complaints and evidence of scandals about Roehm and the "gang of fairies" around him. This material was communicated to Bormann's father-in-law, Walter Buch, and to Rudolf Hess, who in turn passed it on to the Führer. Bormann did not hesitate to provide information about his former colleagues which would give the gunmen a pretext for action. It did not disturb him that many of those killed were guilty only of having become detrimental to the Führer's larger purposes. They had not been able to keep pace with the changing times, to fit into the New Order.

But there were those who had no difficulty finding their place in the new Germany. In 1936, two years after the "Night of the Long Knives," Bormann and a large group of party officials were given an inspection tour of the Dachau concentration camp near Munich by Heinrich Himmler. At Dachau, Bormann encountered an old friend, Rudolf Franz Hoess. Once of the Rossbach organization, Hoess had become a *Rapportführer,* the SS official who had the most direct contact with the prisoners.

Hoess later recalled his thoughts at the time of this inspection: "The Dachau concentration camp is also going well at the moment. The prisoners are well fed, clean and well-clothed and housed. Most of them are busy in the workshops, and the number of sick is hardly worth mentioning. The total strength of about 2,500 is accommodated in ten brick-built huts. The sanitary arrangements are ample. There is a plentiful supply of water. Underwear is changed once a week and bed linen once a month. One-third of the complement consists of political prisoners and two-thirds of professional criminals, asocials and forced labor prisoners, homosexuals, and about two hundred Jews."

The thoughts of those under inspection were not recorded.

Hoess seemed quite self-satisfied at the orderly way in which he was handling the prisoners in the first large concentration camp. Himmler and Bormann, too, appeared to be impressed. They asked Hoess if he were satisfied with his job and asked after his family. Shortly thereafter, Hoess was promoted to *Unterstürmführer* (Second Lieutenant). Here was the type of man whom Bormann believed could be of use to the future purposes of the New Order.

Hoess continued to receive promotions in the SS. These would culminate in his appointment as the commandant of a camp whose purpose was not to "concentrate" people but to kill them. It would be in Poland, at Oswiecim, better known under its German name, Auschwitz.

Heinrich Himmler recognized Martin Bormann as a man who might have some influence in the future course of the Third Reich, and decided to recruit him for his growing SS. Bormann avoided close personal relationships, but he did maintain a tenuous friendship with Himmler. To Bormann, the *Reichsführer SS* was "Uncle Heinrich," because he was the godfather of the fourth Bormann child, Heinrich Ingo, who was born on June 13, 1936. Himmler, in his letters to Bormann, addressed him as "Lieber Martin."

Himmler granted Bormann a commission as an *SS-Gruppenführer* (Major General) on January 30, 1937. Bormann accepted it, but if Himmler thought that this meant that Bormann would thereafter regard himself as a subordinate of the *Reichsführer SS,* he was due for a surprise.

All SS officers, of course, were Nazi Party members. But

not all of the latter belonged to the SS. There was a distinction here, and Bormann believed that the Nazi Party must be the more dominant organization. The Party, of course, was his particular province. He treated his commission as an *SS-Gruppenführer* as a sort of honorary degree. To Himmler, he made it plain that he would not march with SS leaders at the party rallies in Nuremberg. Bormann would be in the reviewing stand, near Rudolf Hess and the Führer. And indeed, "Dear Martin" was in the reviewing stand at the November 1937 rally. From this vantage point, Bormann looked down as the SS columns executed their *Vorbeimarsch* (March Past).

Bormann continued to concentrate on the domestic affairs of the Nazi Party. He played no significant role in the remilitarization of Germany, the occupation of the Rhineland, the annexation of Austria, the Munich crisis, the invasion of Czechoslovakia, or any of the major events and decisions which followed the Nazi seizure of power. More in Bormann's line was the formulation of internal Nazi policies and the transmission of them in the form of "Decrees of the Deputy of the Führer" to Nazi officials. One decree which he sent out over his signature from the party headquarters in Munich, the Brown House, on January 8, 1937, was typical of his activity:

SUBJECT: Refusal of financial assistance, etc. to patients of Jewish physicians, etc.

At my instigation the Reich and Prussian Minister of the Interior has issued the following circular decree, which I transmit to you herewith for your information:

(1) Financial assistance, including payments on account or relief payments will no longer be paid to civil service employees for expenses that have arisen because they employed the services of Jewish physicians, dentists, pharmacies, medical personnel, hospitals, sanitoria, lying-in hospitals, funeral parlors, lawyers, etc. Exceptions will only be made in very exceptional individual cases (i.e. when

imminent danger to life made the calling-in of a Jewish
physician inevitable).

*   *   *   *   *   *   *   *

In this connection I would like to remark that negotiations concerning further-reaching stipulations are already
progressing.

Bormann, like Stalin during Lenin's lifetime, occupied himself with a routine administrative job: solidifying control of
the party machinery, gathering unto himself all personnel files;
deciding on promotions, demotions, and appointments within
the party. And also like Stalin during Lenin's lifetime, Bormann remained in the background. He was unknown to the
German public and to the foreign press.

But Bormann preferred to work behind the scenes. He once
told his wife that Dr. Robert Ley, the head of the German
Labor Front, was well known to the mass of the German
people, "while I have deliberately avoided this type of notoriety." As for medals, decorations, titles, and all the visible
trappings of power, Bormann instructed his wife that "if ever
there is a memorial ceremony after my death, there must
under no circumstances be a cheap exhibition of cushions with
rows of medals and so on. These things give a false impres-
sion. Any nitwit who has been chasing after that sort of trash
can have several cushions covered with it. . . ."

But if Bormann despised the symbols of power, he was
deeply interested in its reality. His chances of becoming anything more than a highly placed bureaucrat, however, seemed
slim in the years before the war. That he could ever displace
his immediate superior, the Deputy Führer Rudolf Hess, in
Hitler's favor was unthinkable.

No Nazi had known Hitler longer and on more intimate
terms than Hess. His father had been a German merchant with
a wholesale business located in Egypt. There, Rudolf Hess had
spent the first twelve years of his life before being sent to
school in Germany. He volunteered for the army during the

World War and served in the same infantry regiment with
Hitler on the Western Front, although the two did not meet at
the time. As an infantryman, Hess was shot in one lung and
hospitalized. Later, he transferred to the Imperial Flying
Corps as a pilot. After the war, Hess studied economics at the
University of Munich, but spent much of his time distributing
anti-Jewish and anticommunist pamphlets. He first heard Hitler speak in 1920. Hess was overwhelmed by Hitler's elo-
quence, joined the Nazi Party as its sixteenth member, and
thereafter was the Führer's close friend and private secretary.

In November 1921, more than a hundred anti-Nazis attempted to break up a Hitler meeting in a Munich brewery.
Hess was one of about fifty Nazis who threw the intruders into
the streets through doors and windows. In this fray, he took a
blow from a beer mug aimed at Hitler. Hess suffered a life-
long head scar as a result. He also marched at Hitler's side in
the beer hall putsch of 1923. After its failure, Hess gave himself up to the police to spend a jail term with Hitler in Landsberg Prison. There Hess took most of the dictation for *Mein
Kampf.*

The bonds between Hitler and Hess appeared to be un-
breakable. Certainly, as a relative latecomer to the Nazi
movement, Bormann had nothing approaching the close relationship to Hitler that the Deputy Führer did. And Hitler maintained his own curious loyalty to the *alte Kämpfer,* the Old
Fighters who had supported him in his early struggles.

To rise higher, Bormann was thus faced with surmounting a
formidable obstacle. That this could ever happen was considered so unlikely that it was not even discussed in the early
years of the Nazi ascendancy. Hess, a tall man with thick dark
hair, bushy eyebrows, and deepset, intense dark eyes was a
popular figure in Germany. Despite his high office, he led an
unpretentious middle-class family life. He rarely plagued
subordinates about details, and his loyalty to the Führer was
unquestioned and appeared to be returned in kind. Though a

somewhat dull and rambling public speaker, he could on such occasions as introducing the Führer at party rallies evoke a tumultuous response from his audience.

Bormann was incapable of making a public speech. Even in private his rasping voice uttered only curt sentences. His short, stocky body, rounded shoulders and bull neck made his appearance disquieting. As one Nazi described him, "His head was always pushed forward a little and cocked slightly to one side, and he had the face and shifty eyes of a boxer advancing on his opponent." Another thought that he looked like a wrestler, and that "his round face with its strong cheekbones and broad nostrils has an expression of energy and brutality. His black straight hair is parted backwards. His dark eyes and the play of his features reveal slyness and cold ruthlessness."

Bormann's manner was equally disturbing. He confided in no one. Getting the job done seemed to be his only concern. He was brusque to subordinates in the best of times, and brutal to those who displeased him. The marginal comment he scribbled in the file of a higher SS leader gave a fair example of his approach: "It is not my habit to have relations with idiots."

But popularity, or even elementary pleasant relations with his colleagues, was not Bormann's goal. Power was, despite his inability to become a popular leader. Thus, to achieve power, Bormann set out on a course of action whose aim was startlingly simple, so simple that the other Nazi leaders seem to have overlooked it.

The only real source of power in the Third Reich was Hitler. The other Nazi paladins, who would have been a gross collection of misfits in any other society, owed everything to this unique historical phenomenon and demonic figure. Nevertheless, while paying allegiance to the Führer, his early intimates now began to carve out their own private empires. Himmler had the SS, Goebbels the Propaganda Ministry, von Ribbentrop the Foreign Office, Reich Marshal Goering the

Luftwaffe and a score of other concerns. These pursuits meant that the men undertaking them could no longer find time to be constantly at the Führer's side.

Reichsleiter Martin Bormann, unknown and content to be so, left to the others the decorations, the international fame or notoriety, the jeweled marshals' batons, the resounding official titles. His goal was both more simple and more ambitious: to make himself *unentbehrlich*—indispensable—to the Führer.

FOUR

Chief of Staff to the Deputy Führer

Hitler was a man of few material needs. He ate very little, never touched meat, and neither smoked nor drank any kind of alcoholic beverage. He was indifferent to the clothes he wore, and his uniforms were simplicity itself compared to the splendid attire of Reich Marshal Goering and the other Nazi leaders. As for women Hitler seemed at times to enjoy their company, but marriage was out of the question because it would interfere with his mission.

In 1936, Eva Braun had been installed in the Berghof as its *Hausfrau.* She was a blond, moderately attractive girl from a lower-middle-class Bavarian family who seemed interested mainly in sports and cheap novels. She was twenty years younger than Hitler, who had first met her when she was employed in the shop of his personal photographer, Heinrich Hoffmann. The physical nature of the relationship between Eva Braun and Hitler was known only to them, but it was certain that he kept her in the background and never permitted her or any other woman to influence his policy decisions.

Hitler also cared nothing for money itself. After he became Chancellor, someone had to manage his private finances. This was a dull, obscure job, and the Nazi leaders evaded the drudgery of taking it on. Bormann saw the opportunity.

Beginning in 1933, a number of leading German industrialists, among them Krupp, had placed at Hitler's personal disposal a yearly contribution of several million marks. The *Adolf-Hitler-Spende der deutschen Industrie* was donated in grateful recognition for his smashing communists, socialists, and the free trade unions. No accounting of these funds was asked for. Bormann took over their management for the Führer, as he did the royalty income from *Mein Kampf,* which came to some $300,000 in 1933, and Hitler's salaries from his various state offices.

The former estate manager handled all of this money capably and in a manner calculated to gain him Hitler's favor. Beyond servicing the living requirements of the Chancellor of the Reich, Bormann saw to it that the money was used to bring to reality Hitler's dearest dreams, in particular the Berchtesgaden project.

Hitler had first been introduced to Berchtesgaden as a summer retreat for himself and his friends in 1923. He fell in love with this small market town and its picturesque valley enclosed by a belt of snow-capped mountains at the southeastern tip of the Bavarian Alps.

In 1928, Hitler rented the Villa Nachenfeld on the Obersalzberg above Berchtesgaden. After he became Chancellor, the villa was bought for him through Bormann, rebuilt on a vast and lavish scale, and reopened in 1936 as the Berghof. It was in the Berghof, with its big rooms, thick carpets, tapestries, and terrace with magnificent views over the mountains that Hitler spent much of his time. Here he received foreign dignitaries and made some of his most important decisions.

Bormann then gradually bought up all the parcels of land around the Berghof, forcing the local peasants to sell until none were left on the Obersalzberg. He also dispensed the funds for the construction of a vast complex of additional buildings. These included SS guard posts, greenhouses to supply the vegetarian Hitler with fresh fruit and vegetables, and the *Kehlsteinhaus,* an aerie perched on a mountain peak above the Berghof which could only be reached by means of an elevator constructed inside the mountain.

To supervise this work, Bormann would naturally have to be on the scene. As Chief of Staff to the Deputy Führer, he worked at Party Headquarters, the Brown House in Munich, and lived in a Munich suburb, Pullach, some one hundred miles from Berchtesgaden. Now he had constructed for himself Haus Göll, named after a nearby mountain, the Hoher Göll, on the Obersalzberg; the house was within the shadow of the Berghof.

Bormann did not restrict himself to the Obersalzberg in his efforts to make himself indispensable to the Führer. Through his agents he bought, in 1938, the house at Branau on the Inn River where Hitler had been born. Its owner, a party member named Pommer, had not been anxious to sell but he eventually yielded to Bormann's persuasion. Bormann also acquired the house where Hitler had spent much of his youth in the village of Leonding near Linz and where his parents had passed their last years.

Hitler considered Linz, the dowdy capital of upper Austria, to be his home town. The personal project closest to his heart, next to the Berghof, was the transformation of Linz into the cultural center of the western world. The new Linz would surpass Paris, Rome, and especially the Vienna in which he had once as a vagabond painted crude little picture-postcards of the spire of St. Stephan's Cathedral and advertising posters for such products as Teddy Perspiration Powder.

Plans for the new Linz were conceived by Hitler personally, for he maintained a keen interest in architecture and always thought of himself as an artist by nature. At the heart of Linz would stand a massive array of public buildings; separate museums for armor, rare coins, furniture, tapestries, sculpture, objets d'art; a library containing a quarter of a million rare books; a large theater. Biggest of all would be the *Führer-*

museum, containing the greatest single collection of paintings the world had ever known.

Bormann knew and cared nothing about art. But he grasped the emotional importance that the Linz project held for the Führer. So Bormann took a personal interest in it.

The artistic treasures necessary to transform Linz could only be obtained from countries which would be occupied by the Nazis. To prepare for this, Hitler created the *Sonderauftrag* (Special Mission) *Linz,* a vast organization of art experts headed by Dr. Hans Posse, Director of the Dresden Art Gallery. On June 26, 1939, Dr. Posse would be commissioned by Hitler to "build up the new art museums for Linz."

Bormann required all correspondence concerning Special Mission Linz to pass through his office. He treated it as top priority, dealt with much of it personally, and kept a watchful eye on the activities of Dr. Posse. In particular, Bormann made it his business to see that Dr. Posse and his staff were not outdone in their search for the choicest works of art by the rival agents of Reich Marshal Hermann Goering.

Contrary to popular belief, Goering did not become the greatest Nazi plunderer of art. Though his celebrated acquisitions were immense in scope, they were outdistanced by those of the little-known Special Mission Linz. By forced sale or direct acquisition, Dr. Posse and his experts, with Bormann's interested support, eventually amassed for Hitler some 100,-000 works of art worth an estimated 300 million dollars. These included 10,000 paintings, half of them old masters, including the Ghent altarpiece by the van Eycks, Michelangelo's "Madonna and Child," the great Czernin Vermeer, and works by Breughel, Goya, Rembrandt, and Leonardo da Vinci.

Construction of the museums to house these masterpieces had to be postponed because the necessary materials were needed for military purposes. Bormann continued his efforts to ingratiate himself with the Führer in many other ways. In his shadowy maneuverings to gain favor, he was greatly aided by the behavior of the man who stood in his path, the Deputy Führer, Rudolf Hess.

The seemingly powerful and impregnable Hess began to develop some disturbing eccentricities, even for Nazi circles. He had always been a solemn, moody man, but now he behaved as though his brain had been affected either by his war injuries or the head blow he had taken from the beer mug in the 1921 brawl.

Hess took to reading books dealing with visionary revelations and prophecies. Nostradamus was a particular favorite. Hess also enjoyed consulting old horoscopes, seeking in them knowledge of his own fate and that of Germany. Astrologers, seers, mediums, and nature therapists were among the people he saw frequently. He remained under the influence of one of his old professors from the University of Munich. This was the well-known proponent of geopolitics, Dr. Karl Haushofer, whose strongly nationalistic philosophy had been embraced by the Nazis as a rationale for a German-controlled Europe. One of his ideas, however, they rejected: that Germany should never make war upon England, because the peoples of both nations came from a common Germanic strain. In this matter, Hess privately preferred Dr. Haushofer's theory to official Nazi thinking.

Hess, though remaining blindly devoted to the Führer, became less available to him. He was frequently away, indulging his hobby of flying his private plane, driving his magnificent Mercedes-Benz sports car on the Autobahn and country roads, where it was recognized because of its distinctive brown color, or skiing with his family.

While Hess was away, Bormann maneuvered closer to the Führer, missing no opportunity to do so. One warm summer afternoon, Bormann was standing on the terrace of the Berghof with Hitler and his personal driver, Erich Kempka. Hitler paused, enjoying the view of the wide green expanse below him. It was unfortunate, he remarked, that this splendid panorama was broken by an old peasant's house.

Kempka drove Hitler to Munich. They returned to the Berghof twenty-four hours later. Kempka could not believe his eyes at the sight which greeted them. The old peasant's house had vanished. In its place was a broad meadow, upon which cows grazed. Bormann had found other quarters for the peasant farmer and called in hundreds of workers who, overnight, tore down the house which had blocked the Führer's view.

It was Hitler's habit to stand, sometimes for hours, in the open air in front of the Berghof, greeting the hundreds of people who came to the Obersalzberg to see him. After a hot summer afternoon spent greeting a long file of adulatory subjects, Hitler remarked that it had tired him; he did not tolerate the sun very well.

The next day, when the Führer returned to the accustomed spot, he was speechless. There stood a huge shade tree. During the night, the tree had been torn up from its original site and replanted in front of the Berghof on Bormann's orders.

Because Hitler abstained from nicotine, liquor, and the eating of meat, Bormann followed suit, at least in the Führer's presence. Erich Kempka noticed him enjoying beef steaks and chops when the Führer was absent. Hitler often worked and talked almost until dawn, not arising until midday. Bormann adjusted his schedule accordingly so as to be always available.

Gradually, Bormann worked his way into the intimate circle of people who lunched with the Führer every day. He sat on the right side of Eva Braun, who sat next to Hitler. Bormann arranged to have one of his adjutants call him away from the table frequently on the pretext of pressing and unavoidable business. Observing this, Hitler must have thought that Bormann was the hardest-working man in the Third Reich.

The Führer read widely, if haphazardly, and often astonished his aides by his ability to retain much of what he had read. His fields of interest were many: books on art and architecture; the philosophical works of Nietzche and Schopenhauer; Greek, Roman, and Germanic history; Goethe; Ibsen; the librettos of Wagner's operas; Nordic mythology; works on military and naval history and technique. Noting Hitler's interest in certain types of books, Bormann detailed some of his staff to screen all newly published books and summarize their contents for him on a single sheet of paper. Bormann was thus able to interject into a conversation a reference to almost any kind of book and to recommend suitable ones to the Führer. Hitler may have wondered how this hard-working man also found time to read so widely.

Bormann's methods gained ground, in part because of the character of the Führer himself. Hitler was eccentric and somewhat slovenly in his work habits. Lost in the dreams of his messianic mission, he hated systematic work and submission even to self-imposed discipline. He needed someone close at hand who could handle details for him and relieve him of administrative burdens. This vacuum was filled by Bormann.

Hitler hated to have his intuition subjected to analysis. His anger was easily aroused by reasoned criticism of any kind. Those who were not prepared to follow him blindly must go. Bormann was the most faithful of followers. And since he had few original ideas of his own, he never irritated the Führer by trying to outshine him or by disagreeing with him. This hard-working man who seemed to want no grandiose titles, medals, or rewards and who masked his own ambition under the guise of only wanting to serve the Führer gradually became indispensable.

Too late, the older Nazi leaders noticed what had happened. The Reich Minister of Economics, Walter Funk, remarked to Erich Kempka: "You can't imagine, Erich, how unbelievably difficult it has become to have a reasonable word with the Führer. Bormann always sticks his nose between us. He interrupts me, he makes every serious discussion impossible."

Alfred Rosenberg, one of Hitler's earliest mentors, was known as the philosopher of the Nazi movement because of

his 700-page book, *The Myth of the Twentieth Century* and
hundreds of other writings which bore such titles as *Im-
morality in the Talmud* and *Plague in Russia: Bolshevism, its
Leaders, Handymen and Victims.* Rosenberg noticed that
Bormann was now always present whenever he called on the
Führer. This had become standard practice. No matter how
important the caller, be it Goering, Goebbels, or Himmler,
Bormann hovered at the Führer's side, often to the intense
annoyance of the guest. Hess, observed Rosenberg, was rarely
around anymore because, Rosenberg thought, he "had obviously got on the Führer's nerves."

Rosenberg was astonished by Bormann's rise. "In Munich
I had hardly ever heard his name," he later wrote. Now
Rosenberg had a chance to observe Bormann in action and to
gauge his indispensability to the Führer. "If, during our dinner
conversation, some incident was mentioned, Bormann would
pull out his notebook and make an entry. Or else, if the Führer expressed displeasure over some remark, some measure,
some film, Bormann would make a note. If something seemed
unclear, Bormann would get up, leave the room, but return
almost immediately—after having given orders to his office
staff to investigate forthwith and to telephone, wire, or write.
Then it might happen that before dinner was over Bormann
had an explanation at hand."

Bormann did not think much of Rosenberg's abilities, as
was the case with most people who had preceded him in Hitler's favor. This antagonism was reciprocated. "Whenever I
talked to him personally, no coherent statement ever passed
his lips," Rosenberg later wrote.

The Nazi "philosopher" searched for some reason for Hitler's growing dependence on Bormann, finally settling for the
obvious one: "Everybody agreed that he was an unbelievably
energetic and tireless worker. He was always with the Führer,
made notes of everything, dictated, kept voluminous records
—always in a much vulgarized form—carried on constant
telephone coversations with the various Gauleiter, and often

hauled his co-workers in Berlin and Munich out of their beds in the middle of the night to check on something in the files."

To Bormann, all of this work must have seemed worthwhile. For while it furthered his own ambition, his motives were not limited to that. To him, the Nazi cause was great and so was the leader in whose shadow he desired to work.

"He really is the greatest human being we know of, not only the greatest German. Really, I was incredibly lucky to be called to his side."

This, as Bormann informed his wife, was his opinion of Adolf Hitler.

By August 1939, this "greatest human being" found himself at the center of a crisis. Danzig, inhabited mostly by Germans but essential to the economy of Poland, had been made a Free City by the Versailles Treaty. Hitler wanted it returned to the Reich. The Poles stubbornly refused to permit this, or to consider German claims for other territory which had been given to Poland after the First World War. France and Great Britain, after having previously yielded every position where Nazi Germany might have been checked, now agreed to defend the integrity of Poland should she be attacked. But the Soviet Union signed a nonaggression pact with Nazi Germany: eastern Europe was divided into zones of influence that cut Poland in two by its secret clauses.

Long months of diplomatic negotiations had brought the Polish matter to a stalemate. Bormann played no part in these negotiations. He was still solely concerned with the internal affairs of the Nazi Party, and for all his personal usefulness to Hitler, not even Bormann had any influence on the Führer as he dealt with a crisis that involved the peace of Europe. His own ministers and generals had no better idea of what was really on the Führer's mind than did foreign statesmen. But Hitler's manner of resolving the Polish stalemate would open the door for Bormann's further rise to a unique position of influence. The Führer would also shatter the world as it then existed.

FIVE

Hitler summoned the senior commanders of the Armed Services to the Berghof on August 22, 1939. They listened to a secret briefing in which he told them: "The destruction of Poland stands in the foreground . . . I shall give a good propaganda reason for starting the war, whether plausible or not."

Shortly after eight P.M. of August 31, the German radio station at Gleiwitz near the Polish frontier was seized by seven armed men dressed in Polish Army uniforms. They broadcast a short speech in Polish over an emergency transmitter, declaring that the hour of the Polish-German war had sounded and that the united Poles were to crush all resistance on the part of the Germans. Then they fired a few random pistol shots and departed, leaving behind a dying, blood-smeared German in civilian clothes.

The seven men were members of the Security Service of the SS. Their uniforms, the script for the broadcast, and the German civilian "casualty"—a concentration camp prisoner—had been supplied by the Gestapo. The faked attack on the radio station and other staged incidents of Polish provocation were the excuses used by Hitler to unleash an assault already planned down to the most minute detail.

As the broadcast came from Gleiwitz, German forces were already moving toward the Polish frontier through a clear, beautiful night. At dawn of September 1, screaming Stuka dive bombers, mechanized infantry, self-propelled rapid-firing guns, and whole divisions of tanks struck the Poles with a speed and concentrated fury such as the world had never seen.

The Poles resisted bravely. But they were divided internally. They also lacked modern fighting equipment and were outnumbered. Neither France nor Great Britain made a single move while Poland was smashed within two weeks.

Hitler came to Poland on the "Führer Special" to observe mopping up operations. Later he moved from this train to the Headquarters of the Army High Command at the Casino Hotel in Zoppot. Bormann came there to look after the interests of the Nazi Party in a time of triumph for the German Army and its devastating new tactics of *blitzkrieg*—lightning war.

Because they all wanted to be near the Führer, civilian visitors like Bormann presented a problem to the Headquarters Commandant and the commanding officer of the security battalion responsible for guarding Hitler. He was Erwin Rommel, who hit upon a solution of having the civilians seated in two cars before they were driven to a battlefield. The cars would be level with each other and behind the Führer's car. Thus, none of the bureaucrats could feel slighted.

This plan worked until one morning when the cortège approached a battlefield. Then it had to go down a narrow dirt road where it was no longer possible to maintain the two-abreast formation. The car in which Bormann was riding was held up, and he was left behind as the Führer was driven on.

According to Colonel Walter Warlimont of the Operations Staff of the Army High Command, Bormann "made a fearful scene and cursed General Rommel in outrageous language because of the supposed slight inflicted upon him. There was nothing Rommel could do to answer such insolence." The

incident illustrated Bormann's rough way of treating professional officers whose actions displeased him. It certainly did
not endear him to Rommel, who would later gain fame as the
Desert Fox, be made a Field Marshal, and finally be forced by
the Nazis to kill himself with poison after being implicated in
the anti-Nazi plot of July 20, 1944.

Hitler returned to Berlin on September 26, and the next day
he informed the senior commanders of the Armed Services at
a meeting in the new Reich Chancellery of his intention to
take up an offensive in the West. "All, including even
Goering, were clearly entirely taken aback," according to
Colonel Warlimont. But no one uttered a word of protest. On
September 29, the "German-Soviet Boundary and Friendship
Treaty" was signed. The two unnatural allies proceeded to
divide Poland between them, and Hitler was relieved for the
present of the threat of an attack from the east.

There was now an interlude. The largest army in Europe
did not attack Germany. For the French, as well as their British allies, still seemed to think that another big war could be
avoided. Hitler paused. OKW (Armed Forces High Command) repaired the damages of the first blitzkrieg.

There was, however, some German activity in Poland.
What was going on there was later summarized by Bormann.
He recorded a conversation that took place in Hitler's Berlin
apartment on October 2, 1940.

"The conversation began when the Reich Minister, Dr.
Frank, informed the Führer that the activities in the Government General [of German-occupied Poland] could be considered very successful. The Jews in Warsaw and other cities had
been locked up in the ghetto; Cracow would very shortly be
cleared of them. . . . The Führer further emphasized that the
Poles, in direct contrast to our German workmen, are especially
born for hard labor; we must all give every possibility of advancement to our German workers; as to the Poles—there can
be no question of improvement for them. On the contrary, it is
necessary to keep the standard of life low in Poland and it

must not be permitted to rise. . . . The Führer stressed once more that there should be one master only for the Poles—the German; two masters, side by side, cannot and must not exist; therefore all representatives of the Polish intelligentsia are to be exterminated. This sounds cruel, but such is the law of life. . . ."

Hitler resumed his military activity in early April 1940 by occupying Norway and Denmark. Three hours after midnight of May 10, the Nazis swept across the borders of the Netherlands, Luxembourg, and Belgium and quickly finished these three countries before attacking France.

On June 22, 1940, the French surrendered in a railway carriage set in a clearing in the Compiègne forest northeast of Paris. In that same carriage, the French had witnessed the signing of armistice terms by German emissaries on November 11, 1918.

The improbable had happened. The half-educated son of a petty Austrian customs official, the drifter of the Vienna Home for Men, the slightly comic rabble-rouser with the odd moustache and the lock of hair plastered over his forehead had kept the promise he had made while haranguing Munich audiences in 1920. He had avenged the humiliation of 1918.

The Führer was now at the peak of his power. An unchecked series of brilliant political and military triumphs had made him the master of most of Europe. From Martin Bormann's point of view, he had every reason to believe that Hitler was the greatest human being that he knew of. He had seen the look of almost crazed adulation which the Führer evoked as he walked past solid phalanxes of wildly cheering Nazis at the Nuremberg Party Rallies. Bormann had witnessed Hitler gauge and then outmaneuver his seemingly more powerful political adversaries, first within Germany and then on the international level. The Führer had persisted in undertaking the Polish military campaign and then the offensive in the west against the advice of many of his generals. Bormann could note that France, supposedly the possessor of the world's best army, had now fallen almost as easily as Poland.

And it had all happened so quickly. Only eight years before, Hitler had been merely the Führer of one of the many political parties contending for power in Germany. Bormann had been an obscure party official, collecting money for the Aid Fund in a bleak time of economic depression. Now the prospect of a Nazi New Order extending from the North Cape to the Nile, from the Atlantic Ocean to the Ural Mountains of Russia loomed as almost certain. This prospect gave even greater importance to the question of who would emerge as the Führer's closest confidant and right-hand man.

That this man might be Bormann appeared highly unlikely on June 22, 1941. Bormann was not even present at Compiègne, as were Hess, Goering, Field Marshal Wilhelm Keitel, Foreign Minister von Ribbentrop, General Jodl and other members of Hitler's inner circle. For all his progress in making himself indispensable to the Führer, Bormann was still only Hess's deputy in the Nazi summer of victory. And there were several other men more ruthless than Hess who stood between Bormann and the source of power, Hitler. The most formidable of these appeared to be Reich Marshal Hermann Goering, whom Hitler had officially designated as his successor as head of state on the day Poland was attacked.

Goering, the son of a former cavalry officer who later became a member of the German consular service, had served as a fighter pilot in the First World War and as the last commander of the famed von Richtofen squadron. He had shot down twenty-two Allied planes and won Germany's highest decoration, the *Pour le Mérite* or "Blue Max," awarded not for a single action but for continuous courage in action.

After the war, Goering worked for aircraft companies in Scandinavia. In 1921, he returned to Munich and enrolled as a student of political science at its university at the age of twenty-eight. In October 1922, he first heard Hitler speak, agreed with his ideas, joined the Nazi Party and was made commander of the S.A.

On the bleak morning of November 9, 1923, Hitler, Goering, Rudolf Hess and certain other Nazi leaders left the *Bur-
gerbräukeller* beer hall in Munich and marched at the head of
some three thousand Storm Troopers toward the center of the
city and the War Ministry. Their objective was to occupy the
ministry and overthrow the Bavarian government. As they
reached the end of a narrow street leading to the War Ministry, their progress was blocked by armed government police.
Shots were fired. Hitler fell to the pavement and dislocated his
shoulder, but escaped in a waiting car only to be caught and
sentenced to five years in Landsberg prison. Goering, too, fell
to the pavement, badly wounded in the groin. He was carried
into a nearby house and then smuggled into Austria, where his
serious wounds were treated by doctors who prescribed morphine to ease his pain.

Unable to return to Germany, where he was a wanted man
because of his part in the unsuccessful beer-hall putsch,
Goering wandered around Europe and eventually went to live
in Sweden. There he was supported by his wife, a wealthy
member of the Swedish nobility, and there he continued to use
morphine. In September 1925, he was certified as a dangerous
drug addict and confined to a violent ward in the Langbro
asylum. Slowly, under psychiatric care, he regained his health,
but it was not until the autumn of 1927 that he returned to
Germany under a political amnesty proclaimed by the newly
elected President von Hindenburg and resumed his activities
for the Nazis.

By 1940, Goering was not only Hitler's successor, but the
only Reich Marshal in the Third Reich, Commander in Chief
of the Air Force, Minister for Air, President of the Reichstag,
Minister President of Prussia, Plenipotentiary for the Four
Year Plan and the holder of a score of other offices. His position seemed unassailable. And yet once Goering had attained
tremendous power and influence, he increasingly exhibited
qualities of sloth, vanity, and a love of luxury. He spent a
great deal of time hunting and feasting at his great country
house of Carinhall, where his fabulous collection of art works

looted from every part of Europe was displayed. He amused himself by designing fantastic uniforms to fit his various offices and by entertaining guests at Carinhall dressed in outfits that struck most of them as weird. After one visit to Carinhall, Ulrich von Hassell, a career diplomat who had been the German ambassador to Italy from 1932 to 1937, noted in his diary that Goering "changed his costume after the day and appeared at the dinner table in a blue or violet kimono with fur-trimmed bedroom slippers. Even in the morning he wore at his side a golden dagger, which was also changed frequently. In his tiepin he wore a variety of precious stones, and around his fat body a wide girdle set with many stones—not to mention the splendor and number of his rings."

Goering allowed his weight to reach 280 pounds. He also never completely mastered his drug addiction. It was an open secret that he daily consumed about one hundred tablets of paracodeine, a mild derivative of morphine, for he popped the tablets into his mouth and chewed them like gum even during important conferences. Such eccentricities were tolerated, but they dulled the natural abilities of Hitler's designated successor and left him vulnerable to attacks by his enemies. The most implacable of these was Martin Bormann.

Another Nazi leader who stood between Hitler and Bormann was Joseph Goebbels. The idea of signing the 1940 armistice in the same railway car where the French had dictated surrender terms in 1918 stemmed from Goebbels, Minister for Propaganda and Public Enlightenment, who had been rejected as physically unfit for military service in the First World War. Infantile paralysis had left Goebbels with steeply sloping shoulders, a slight, gnomish build, and a left leg that was shorter than his right and caused him to walk with a noticeable limp. He was a few inches over five feet in height, weighed little more than a hundred pounds, and his black hair and dark brown eyes gave him a swarthy appearance in marked contrast to the blond "Aryan" ideal which his propaganda so vigorously espoused.

Goebbels, the son of pious Catholic working-class parents in the Rhineland, had spent an embittered, poverty-stricken youth in which he had nevertheless managed, with the aid of loans and scholarships, to attend several German universities, where his marks were excellent, and to acquire a doctor of philosophy degree from the University of Heidelberg. He thus qualified as the only intellectual in Hitler's court. A failure as a novelist and playwright, he proved to be a genius as a propagandist after joining the Nazi Party in 1925. Goebbels was the first person in the twentieth century who understood how the minds of the masses could be influenced through the instruments of modern power propaganda—radio, films, the popular press, sound trucks, loudspeakers, posters, and mass demonstrations. His mastery of propaganda techniques, and his own abilities as an orator, played a decisive role in bringing Hitler to power in 1933 and in continuing to delude most of the German people into following him.

As one of the original Nazi leaders, and as the absolute dictator of all forms of expression in the Third Reich, Goebbels possessed enormous influence and power. And yet, like Goering, his personal idiosyncrasies made him vulnerable to those who would supplant him in Hitler's favor.

Goebbels' cynical intelligence, combined with a biting wit which he made no attempt to hide, made him unpopular in the party and caused Hitler to treat him with some mistrust and coolness after the Nazis had consolidated their control over the state. More serious were the scandals caused by Goebbels' love affairs. Though married and the father of six children, he carried on numerous liaisons with young actresses and secretaries who were dependent on the propaganda ministry for employment. One affair with the well-known Czech actress, Lida Baarova, caused Goebbels' wife to demand a divorce. Hitler himself, who was remarkably tolerant of the personal conduct of his close associates unless it tarnished the image of his regime, ordered Goebbels to sever his relationship with Lida Baarova. Such cracks in the armor of the powerful prop-

aganda chief were duly noted by the patient Martin Bormann.

Still a third man to become a Bormann enemy, Heinrich
Himmler, was not as powerful and well-known in 1940 as
were Goering and Goebbels. His father had been a teacher in
Munich and once had served as private tutor to Prince Heinrich of Bavaria. Like Bormann, Heinrich Himmler served in
the army during the last months of the First World War, but
saw no combat duty. Then he studied agriculture at the University of Munich. He graduated in 1922, became interested
in the Nazi movement, and played a minor role in the beer-
hall putsch of 1923.

Himmler remained a loyal, insignificant Nazi until 1929.
Then, while he was operating a small poultry farm outside of
Munich, Hitler appointed him Reichsführer (Reich Leader)
of the SS, an auxiliary of the S.A. numbering some 200 men.
After the Storm Troopers were broken by the Night of the
Long Knives, Himmler set out to build up the SS. Eventually,
he would command his own private army of half a million
men, the *Waffen* (Armed) *SS,* as well as the Secret State
Police (Gestapo), the Criminal Police, the Security Service
(SD), the Intelligence Service, and, through other SS organizations, the concentration and extermination camps. And
eventually, "Uncle Heinrich" and "Dear Martin" would come
into conflict; only one of them could be the second most powerful man in Nazi Germany.

But Bormann could tolerate Himmler, in 1940, much better than he could either Goering or Goebbels. Perhaps he realized that the Reichsführer SS was actually a man of rather
limited intelligence who consulted astrologers and spent a
great deal of his time in attempting to organize the SS along
the romantic lines of a knightly order of the Middle Ages.

To Albert Speer, Minister for Armaments and War Production, Himmler was "half schoolmaster, half crank." The man
eventually responsible for executing Hitler's racial ideas about
the Jews and the Slavs could ask an aide who had a passion for

shooting deer, "How can you find any pleasure in shooting from behind cover at poor creatures browsing on the edge of a wood . . . Properly considered, it's murder."

Himmler, in addition to being rather hesitant and unrealistic, was not as robustly healthy as was Bormann. In fact, the Reichsführer SS felt the need to employ Felix Kersten, a Finnish masseur, to massage away his severe, constant stomach cramps. Kersten thought of his employer as "a narrow-chested, weak-chinned, spectacled man with an ingratiating smile."

The other members of the Nazi hierarchy who ranked above Bormann also had personal deficiencies which made them vulnerable to an ambitious man who could exploit their shortcomings. Joachim von Ribbentrop, the former wine dealer who was Foreign Minister, was described by his Italian counterpart, Count Galeazzo Ciano, as being "vain, frivolous, and loquacious." Ciano added in his diary, "The Duce says you only have to look at his head to see that he has a small brain."

Robert Ley, a chemist by profession and the boss of the Labor Front, was a drunkard. Alfred Rosenberg was a dull, ineffectual bumbler, and his major book, filled with half-baked ideas about Nordic supremacy, was so muddled that the ultimate critic, Hitler, confessed that he had never been able to finish reading it.

None of his generals would ever have any real influence on Hitler. The Austrian ex-corporal mistrusted the aristocratic Prussian officer corps as a bulwark of conservatism, and merely used the professional expertise of its members as it suited his purposes. Only two general officers would remain with Hitler from the beginning of the war to its end: Field Marshal Wilhelm Keitel, Chief of the Armed Forces High Command (OKW) and General Alfred Jodl, Chief of Operations of OKW. Neither man was a Prussian. Both survived in their positions by never crossing Hitler.

Thin-lipped, tall, and taciturn, Keitel was a rigid, literal-minded soldier whose great aim in life was to be a farmer and manage the family estate at Brunswick. He believed that he was bound by the strictest tenets of honor to serve and obey the head of state. And so he carried out the Führer's orders with diligence, no matter how crazy or criminal they were.

Alfred Jodl had more ability and was somewhat less subservient than Keitel, who was known as Hitler's *Lakaitel* (little lackey). But although he and Keitel were in almost daily personal contact with Hitler, neither officer was equipped by training or disposition to maneuver within the political jungle that grew so lushly within the Nazi hierarchy. Thus, neither presented a serious obstacle to anyone ambitious to become Hitler's right-hand man.

Easily the most bizarre member of Hitler's court continued to be Rudolf Hess. It was not necessary for Bormann actively to subvert Hess's position in order to sidetrack his superior. Bormann had merely to continue working his way into the Führer's confidence, while allowing Hess's own odd behavior to undermine the influence he once had had. Walter Schellenberg, the head of Himmler's Foreign Intelligence Branch, observed the Deputy Führer and later wrote: "It was astonishing how Hess, with the complete assurance of a fanatic or a madman, believed in old prophecies and visionary revelations. He would recite whole passages out of books of prophecies, such as Nostradamus and others I cannot remember . . . At times there were signs of uncertainty which must have represented a change to a depressive state. All this he expounded time and again in the most elaborate manner to his wife."

Hitler declined to downgrade Hess officially, however. This would have harmed the public image of the Nazi regime. But then, in 1940, Hitler could afford to be tolerant. He had, thus far, made no major mistakes. He did not really seem to need an efficient deputy. And as useful to him as the loyal workhorse Bormann was, not even he was totally indispensable. The Führer seemed sufficient unto himself. "He towered over the rest of us," Bormann later informed his wife, "like Mount Everest."

Hitler's summer of victory was flawed only by the escape of the British Expeditionary Force from Dunkirk and the abandonment of Operation Sea Lion, the poorly planned cross-channel invasion of England. More serious in the fall and winter was the failure of the Luftwaffe to knock England out of the war in the aerial Battle of Britain. This was the first setback for Reich Marshal Goering, and from this point on his influence with Hitler began to diminish.

In the spring of 1941, Hitler decided not to bother with England any longer. Time, he felt, was running out. Operation Barbarossa, the long-planned invasion of Soviet Russia, a major goal of Nazi policy and an event which, in Hitler's words, would "make the world hold its breath," could no longer be postponed. But in May, an event occurred which caused Hitler himself to hold his breath. It also gave Bormann the opportunity for which he had so patiently waited.

SIX

The Opportunity

The second spring of the war brought still more Nazi triumphs. If Hitler thought that he was invincible and incapable of error, and if Bormann also believed this, the facts supported these judgments.

By the middle of April 1941, Rommel and the Afrika Korps captured Tobruk and struck to within a few miles of the Egyptian border, threatening the entire British position in Egypt and in particular the Suez Canal. On April 17, the Yugoslav Army capitulated to invading German troops. Ten days later, Nazi tanks rolled into Athens.

On May 4, the Führer presented his report on the Balkan campaign to a cheering Reichstag. Then he retired to the Berghof to complete the planning for the attack on Russia. The original invasion date of May 15 had been postponed only so that Hitler could vent his fury on Yugoslavia, where certain military officers had dared to oust a regime friendly to Nazi Germany. Now the Führer set a new date for Barbarossa. This operation would begin a year from the day the French had capitulated at Compiègne: June 22, 1941.

That Barbarossa was going to be more than a military operation had been indicated in a secret special directive issued by Field Marshal

Keitel to the senior officers of the Army on March 13. It provided that "in the area of operations, the Reichsführer SS is entrusted, on behalf of the Führer, with special tasks for the preparation of the political administration, tasks which result from the struggle which has to be carried out between two opposing political systems. Within the reach of these tasks, the Reichsführer SS shall act independently and under his own responsibility."

Shortly, Keitel would issue two more directives. One ordered that excesses committed by German troops against the civilian populations of the eastern territories were not normally to be made the subject of courts-martial. The other decreed that communist political commissars were to be sorted out from the bulk of Russian prisoners of war and killed.

All of these directives constituted revolutions in conventional warfare. Many senior army generals privately opposed them, but did nothing actively to have them countermanded. Field Marshal Keitel admitted that they were "highly controversial" innovations. But Hitler wanted them introduced, and the Chief of the Armed Forces High Command felt that he was bound by honor and loyalty to carry out the Führer's every wish.

The "special tasks" entrusted to Himmler included the use of *Einsatzgruppen* formed from the SS Security Service. These "Action Groups" would move in behind the victorious regular army to deal with Jews, gypsies, Soviet commissars, and others whom the Nazis classified as their racial and ideological enemies. In brief, the SS Action Groups would kill as many of these people as they could find and the army was not to interfere with their operations.

To direct the civilian agency responsible for governing those Russians who were not targets of the Action Groups, Hitler appointed Alfred Rosenberg as Reich Minister for the Occupied Eastern Territories. This seemed like a logical choice. The son of a German shoemaker, Rosenberg had been born in a Baltic town which was then part of the Russian

Empire. Though reared as a German, he was equally at home with Russian culture and customs. Rosenberg received a degree in architecture from the University of Moscow in 1917, lived through the Bolshevik Revolution, and did not come to the Reich until 1918. There, in Munich, he joined the Nazi Party as one of its earliest members.

But while Rosenberg was the only Nazi leader with a first-hand knowledge of Russia, he was not a practical politician. And he would have to compete for authority not only with the army and the SS; Martin Bormann had decided to assert his right to have an important voice in the affairs of a conquered Russia on behalf of the Nazi Party.

Rudolf Hess by now had all but disappeared from the inner councils of the Third Reich. In particular, he was not brought into the planning for Barbarossa. The former pilot of the First World War whiled away much of his time in the apparently harmless hobby of flying a plane put at his disposal by the Messerschmitt Works in Augsburg. His Chief of Staff, Bormann, had worked his way into the Führer's confidence and was now largely running the Nazi Party. Hess had good reason to brood and to feel neglected. Hitler did not replace him, but he had no time for him, either. Barbarossa, a truly staggering undertaking, completely dominated the Führer's thoughts.

When he was an unsuccessful Bavarian politician and a resident of Landsberg Prison in 1924, Hitler had dictated these words for *Mein Kampf* to his faithful secretary, Rudolf Hess:

> We [National Socialists] take up where we broke off six hundred years ago. We stop the endless German movement toward the south and west of Europe, and turn our gaze toward the lands of the east. At long last we put a stop to the colonial and commercial policy of prewar days and pass over to the territorial policy of the future. But when we speak of new territory in Europe today we must think principally of Russia and her border vassal states. Destiny itself

seems to wish to point out the way to us here. . . . The colossal Empire in the east is ripe for dissolution, and the end of the Jewish domination in Russia will also be the end of Russia as a state.

Now the time to put these ideas into effect had almost come. As three million German troops moved eastward, Hitler had to keep his intentions secret from the Russians, who were still his allies as they had been for the past twenty-one months of the German-Soviet Pact. He and his ministers also engaged in deceptive diplomatic maneuverings with Germany's other major allies. The Italians would not be told about Barbarossa officially until the day before it was launched. The Japanese were also kept uninformed, while being urged to attack Singapore and thus destroy Great Britain's position in the Far East.

Preoccupied as he was with all of the many details involving Barbarossa, Hitler still had to contend with those who counseled the abandonment of the operation. Remembering the First World War error of fighting on two fronts, some German generals and diplomats objected to the invasion of Russia while Britain continued to resist in the West. Hitler had encountered reservations about his aims before. He had always ignored them. His decisions had proved to be as spectacularly right as the judgment of his professional military and diplomatic advisers had been wrong. Now he was determined to hold to June 22 as the date for Barbarossa, whatever happened to Britain.

Hitler, in May 1941, considered Britain to be defeated for practical purposes; an isolated island with no foothold on the continent. There would be time enough to return and finish her off, once the grander scheme of Barbarossa was completed. Hitler confidently expected to require no more than three months to defeat Russia. A longer campaign was not contemplated or planned for; German combat troops were not issued winter clothing. It was assumed that their tasks would be accomplished well before the onset of the Russian winter.

After that, Russia would be dealt with by Himmler and the SS and Alfred Rosenberg's *Ostministerium*.

Still, Britain did possess a certain nuisance value for Hitler. What he wanted was a completely free hand from the West to deal with the East. To this end, he permitted tentative peace feelers to be put out to Britain through sympathetic neutral sources, and was surprised when no response was forthcoming. So the aerial blitz continued. On the night of May 10, the largest air raid of the war was launched on Britain, devastating hundreds of acres of London at the cost of thirty German bombers.

On that same night, as Hitler was deep in his planning for Barbarossa at the Berghof, a single plane, coming from Augsburg near Munich, flew through the mists above the North Sea and headed not for London but for the Scottish coast. Men of the Royal Observer Corps identified the plane as a Messerschmitt 110 when it crossed the coast and flew west. This struck the spotters as odd. There was no logical reason for a lone German plane to be flying toward the west of Scotland, and it was known that aircraft of its type could not carry enough fuel to return to the continent.

A Spitfire on coastal patrol gave chase, but was not fast enough to catch and shoot down the Messerschmitt. But ten miles west of Glasgow, above Dungavel House, the pilot tumbled out of his plane, his parachute billowing as the Messerschmitt crashed and burned in a field near the stone mansion belonging to the Premier Duke of Scotland, the Duke of Hamilton.

David McLean, the head plowman of Floors Farm near Dungavel House, heard the crash as he was preparing for bed. He looked out of a window of his farmhouse and saw the white cloud of a falling parachute. McLean dashed into the night to where he thought the parachute might land and soon found the pilot on his hands and knees, struggling to slip the catches of the parachute's harness. He then stood up, favoring his right ankle which had been injured in the fall.

In the silvery moonlight, McLean saw a well-built man in his late forties, dark-faced and beetle-browed, dressed in a field-gray uniform of fine soft cloth and magnificent flying boots. Because of his age, splendid attire, and apparent lack of resistance to being captured, the plowman sensed that the parachutist was not an ordinary Luftwaffe pilot. When Mc-Lean asked him who he was and if he were a German, he answered slowly, in English: "Yes. I am a German. My name is Captain Alfred Horn. I want to go to Dungavel House. I have an important message for the Duke of Hamilton."

When Captain Horn was eventually brought to the Duke and his true identity established, Winston Churchill was quickly notified. "I thought this was fantastic," the Prime Minister later wrote.

For the middle-aged parachutist had turned out to be Reich Minister without Portfolio, member of the Ministerial Council for the Defense of the Reich, member of the Secret Cabinet Council, and Deputy Führer of the Third Reich, Rudolf Hess. He had flown from Germany to offer peace to Great Britain in a mission described by Churchill as a "completely devoted and frantic deed of lunatic benevolence."

The news of what the Deputy Führer had done "burst into the Berghof like a bomb," according to Dr. Paul Schmidt, Hitler's interpreter. The Führer first learned of it in a manner that accorded with the bizarre nature of the entire episode.

Hess had written a letter and then given it to one of his adjutants, Captain Karlheinz Pintsch, shortly before the Deputy Führer took off from Augsburg around six P.M., Saturday, May 10. Pintsch was instructed by Hess to go from Augsburg to the Berghof in his private train and deliver the letter to Hitler personally, which Pintsch managed to do the following noon.

After waiting while the Führer dealt with several scheduled appointments, Pintsch was received by Hitler in his study, a wide room in light wood with a red marble floor and large windows that offered breathtaking views of snow-capped mountains. The peaceful atmosphere of the study was shattered when Hitler read the letter, which gave a long, rambling account of Hess's purpose in flying to England. Shaken, the Führer immediately sent for Goering, von Ribbentrop, Bormann, and Keitel in order to determine how this sensational event could have taken place and how to deal with it.

"Hitler was walking back and forth with me in his big study," Keitel later recalled, "and he talked, and he was touching his forehead and he said, 'Hess must have had a mental derangement. He must have had some sort of mental disturbance, and that I can see also in the letter he wrote to me.' Hitler also said, 'Well, the letter that he has written, in it I can't recognize Hess. It is a different person. Something must have happened to him.' "

Since there had been no announcement from the British of Hess's arrival, Hitler, according to Keitel, asked Goering: "Did he ever get there? Did he have enough gasoline to make the trip, to bridge the gap between the continent and England? Goering, how is this business? Can he do it with this type of plane?" The Commander in Chief of the Luftwaffe, not knowing at the time that Hess had fitted the Messerschmitt 110 with two extra gasoline tanks, reasoned that the Deputy Führer could not have reached Scotland and had probably crashed in the North Sea.

Hitler ordered that Hess be shot or confined in an insane asylum should he return to Germany. Martin Bormann meanwhile had the unfortunate Captain Karlheinz Pintsch placed under arrest by two captains of Hitler's personal guard as an intensive investigation of Hess's flight was launched.

It was determined that Hess had made thirty practice flights from Augsburg. On two previous occasions he had actually tried to fly to Scotland, but had been forced to turn back, once because a fault developed in his plane and once because of bad weather. The big question was how he could have obtained the use of a specially equipped ME 110 from its designer, Dr. Willi Messerschmitt, and made the complicated arrangements for his flight from the Messerschmitt airfield without his true intentions being discovered and reported.

"Well, I remember that was the question that occupied Hitler immediately, too," Field Marshal Keitel later testified, "and I remember, I was pretty sure that right away Hitler ordered that Professor Messerschmitt was to be locked up. On the other hand, Hess had free access to all plane factories, and experimental airdromes and training airdromes; and he was an old flyer himself, and I know that he was absolutely free to come and go as he pleased. It could not be proved of Messerschmitt that he had the slightest inkling or knowledge of the plans. That was definitely established, and his wife, that is Mrs. Hess, didn't know either."

Hess's thinking had undoubtedly been influenced by the astrologers he frequently consulted and by his old mentor, Dr. Karl Haushofer, head of the Geopolitical Institute in Munich, who considered Britain and Germany to be Nordic nations who should live together in peace. The German investigation, however, indicated that Hess had planned his flight on his own.

But how to present this bizarre event to the German public and to the world? For Hess was no ordinary Nazi. He was probably Hitler's oldest and closest personal friend. The Führer himself had chosen him to be his deputy as leader of the Nazi Party and his successor as head of state after Goering. The Nazis would have to acknowledge his flight with an explanation designed to soften its impact.

Two days after Hess had taken off from Augsburg, the British had still not announced that he was in their custody. So on May 13, all German newspapers printed this story:

"Party Member Hess, because of an illness of many years standing which was becoming worse, and who had been forbidden by the Führer to do any flying, went against this order and obtained an airplane on Saturday, May 10th. At 6.00 he left Augsburg in the plane and has not been heard from since.

A letter which he left behind shows from its confused writing the unfortunate traces of mental derangement, and it is feared that Party Member Hess sacrificed himself to a fixed idea. It is felt that somewhere on this trip he has crashed and probably perished. The Führer has ordered the immediate arrest of Hess's adjutants, who alone knew of the flight and of the fact that such flights had been forbidden by the Führer."

The British responded with their first announcement that the Deputy Führer was in their hands. Before the British could obtain damaging revelations from him or invent them for propaganda purposes, the Nazis were obliged to issue another and stronger statement:

"As far as it is possible to tell from papers left behind by Party Member Hess, it seemed that he lived in a state of hallucination as a result of which he felt that he could bring about an understanding between England and Germany. It is a fact that Hess, according to a report from London, jumped from his airplane near the town to which he was trying to go and was found there injured. The National Socialist Party regrets that this idealist fell as a victim to his hallucinations. This however will have no effect on the continuation of the war which has been forced upon Germany."

Hess was thus dismissed as a mentally unstable crank. Foreign Minister von Ribbentrop gave a blunter explanation when he was flown to Rome to tell Mussolini what had happened. "He's crazy," von Ribbentrop said, according to his interpreter, Dr. Paul Schmidt. Upon returning to Berlin, Dr. Schmidt was asked by an old man who helped him tend his garden, "Hadn't you already known that we are governed by madmen?"

This was a natural reaction. For if Hess were of unsound mind, and yet had been permitted to continue as the Deputy Führer, what did this strange state of affairs reflect on the other Nazi leaders and their regime? The episode was intensely embarrassing to Hitler, the more so because it had happened with Barbarossa close at hand.

There were those who wondered if the Führer's judgment, heretofore excellent to an uncanny degree, had not failed him in publicly labeling his deputy as mentally unbalanced, with the consequent damage which this characterization did to the prestige of the Nazi regime. Walter Schellenberg, the head of Himmler's Foreign Intelligence Branch, told the Reichsführer SS that he considered the German people much too intelligent for the story of Hess's mental illness.

"That was Bormann's influence," Himmler replied quickly. He looked at Schellenberg for a long time, then added, "It is too late to do anything about it now."

Himmler offered no specifics. Bormann's ability to influence Hitler was now a generally accepted fact in the highest Nazi circles, but rarely was it possible to pinpoint exactly what Bormann had done. His methods were shadowy: the subtle hint, the well-timed innuendo, the conversations that took place with no one else present.

Bormann, however, set down his thoughts on the Hess flight in a letter which he sent to Himmler: "Even in the earliest statements by the adjutants Pintsch and Leitgen, and by General Haushofer, as well as in one of the first letters of Frau Hess herself, there is a possible explanation of the flight—R. H. wanted to shine because he suffered from an inferiority complex. In the opinion of the Führer, these are in fact the real causes. Only now has it become known that R. H. has been treated again and again for impotence, even at the time when the son called Buz was produced. Before himself, before his wife, and before the Party and the people, R. H. believed that by this undertaking he could prove his virility . . ."

The British meanwhile confined their strange prisoner first in a military hospital near Loch Lomond, then in the Tower of London, and finally in a heavily guarded country house called Mytchett Place near Aldershot. The wreckage of the ME 110 from which Hess had parachuted was exhibited on Trafalgar Square to help the sale of War Savings Certificates.

The lengthy British interrogations of Hess indicated that

while he was suffering from some form of mental disturbance, he had nevertheless been sincere in undertaking his peace mission. He had sought out the Duke of Hamilton, whom he had met briefly at the 1936 Olympic Games, because he felt that the Duke could put him in touch with influential government figures who would listen to his ideas. The Deputy Führer told the Duke that he was on "a mission of humanity," and that he was convinced that Hitler could destroy Great Britain but was reluctant to do so. The Führer preferred to negotiate a peace settlement with Great Britain which would give him a free hand in continental Europe.

In making his proposals, Hess undoubtedly felt that he understood Hitler's thinking as no one else could. If his dramatic mission were successful, he would have accomplished the Führer's real wishes and also would have restored himself to the position from which Bormann had displaced him. The British were determined, however, to fight the Nazis and were not prepared to accept any negotiated settlement which Hess could offer. "I never attached any importance to this episode," Churchill later wrote. No attempt was made to use Hess either as a bargaining tool or for propaganda purposes. After his interrogations were finished, he was confined as an ordinary prisoner of war.

In Germany, Hess's Office of the Deputy Führer was abolished. No one replaced him as Hitler's successor as head of state after Goering. His name was removed from streets and public buildings. Hess was soon forgotten and his sensational adventure had but one tangible result.

On May 29, 1941, a special Hitler directive announced that the former Office of the Deputy Führer would be designated the Party Chancellery and would be under his personal command. The Leiter (Leader) of the Party Chancellery would be Martin Bormann.

At the age of forty-one, Bormann now had the official power for which he had patiently waited. Hitler had said that he would resume personal direction of the Nazi Party, the instrument he had forged and used to attain power. But he was much too preoccupied with his new role of Supreme Warlord to do this. Soon the Führer would admit that he had "totally lost sight of the organizations of the party."

In reality, Bormann assumed control of the entire Party machine throughout the Reich and the occupied territories. Every party official was either appointed by him or continued to serve at his pleasure, and all were under his orders. He could advance or ruin almost any career within the Party and also with the military and the government of the state. In wielding this enormous power, Bormann was answerable to Hitler alone. Only the Führer could countermand his orders or dismiss him.

Bormann also succeeded in gaining another and less definable type of power. This would not be formalized until April 12, 1943, when he would officially be appointed *Sekretär des Führers*. The title of "Secretary of the Führer" was modest. But Bormann was not concerned with titles. He was concerned with the reality of power. And the crucial importance of the Secretary of the Führer in a dictatorship like that of the Third Reich could hardly be overestimated. The holder of this position was far more influential than any Reich Marshal, Foreign Minister, Field Marshal, or Reichsführer SS. For the Führer was the ultimate authority in Nazi Germany. The source of this authority could not be defined in rational terms, but rested on the assertion that he possessed qualities lacking in ordinary humans.

Below Hitler, a continuous struggle for power went on among various individuals, offices, and factions within the Party, the ministries of the national government, the army, the judiciary, and the SS, many of whose areas of competence overlapped. These struggles were resolved in the end by Hitler, who thus retained for himself control over everything of importance that was done in the Third Reich.

But to reach Hitler and present a proposal for his decision it was necessary to go through Bormann. First without official authority and then as Secretary of the Führer, it was he who decided what reports Hitler should read and which people he should see. Bormann was present at nearly every interview, and then drafted the only instructions resulting from them that counted, those of the Führer.

The other Nazi leaders came to fear and hate Bormann. They could never be certain what he was telling the Führer about them or which of their personal projects he considered worth bringing to the Führer's attention. And those who fell into Bormann's disfavor were effectively barred from the source of ultimate authority.

For those peoples who were still to be overrun by the Nazis, Bormann was an even more sinister figure. He was no right-hand man prepared to modify the Führer's military adventures or murderous racial ideas. Had he tried to do so, of course, he would not have survived in his unique position. But the evidence is that Bormann was not an opportunist motivated solely by ambition and a desire to retain personal power. He was also genuinely and fanatically dedicated to what passed for the ideology of National Socialism and to its leader, Adolf Hitler.

This ideology, which defied scientific definition, held that the principal goal of nature, and therefore of human activity, was the procreation and perfection of biologically higher forms of life. The most valuable races of mankind must be increased and advanced. Here, Bormann made a personal contribution: he and his wife eventually produced ten children.

The Bormann children were members of one of the two main racial groups recognized by the Nazis—the Aryan race, loosely represented by the Germanic and Nordic peoples. To Nazis like Bormann, the second group included all other races, such as the Mongoloid, Negroid, Semitic, and Slavic peoples, who were inferior and fit only to serve the Aryan race. The Jewish race, in particular, was an implacable enemy and would have to be eliminated.

As noted earlier, Bormann gave vent to his anti-Semitic sentiments as far back as 1920, when he joined an obscure organization called the Society Against Presumptuousness of the Jewry. Now, as Head of the Nazi Party Chancellery, he would have the opportunity to indulge his long-held prejudice in a direct and sinister fashion. So, too, would he have the opportunity to indulge his hatred of Christianity. Like many of the Nazi leaders, Bormann styled himself *Gottgläubig,* a believer in God but an opponent of organized religion. Even as an obscure party official in the thirties, he had done everything he could to harass both the Roman Catholic and Protestant Churches. He despised Christianity as a corrupting and softening influence, interfering with the creation of the new Nordic man.

One of Bormann's first actions after being appointed Head of the Nazi Party Chancellery was to send, on June 6, 1941, a secret decree to his Gauleiter in which he defined his views on the "Relationship of National Socialism to Christendom."

"National Socialist and Christian concepts are irreconcilable," Bormann explained in his blunt and graceless bureaucratic style. "Christian churches build on the uncertainty of human beings and attempt to preserve the uncertainty of as wide segments of the population as possible, for only in this way can Christian churches keep their power . . . Our National Socialist ideology is far loftier than the concepts of Christianity, which in their essential points have been taken over from Jewry. For this reason also we do not need Christianity . . . No human being would know anything of Christianity had it not been drilled into him in his childhood by pastors. The so-called dear God in no wise gives knowledge of his existence to young people in advance, but in an astonishing manner in spite of his omnipotence leaves this to the efforts of the pastors. If therefore in the future our youth learns nothing more of this Christianity, whose doctrines are far below ours, Christianity will disappear by itself . . . For the first time in German history the Führer consciously and com-

pletely has the leadership of the people in his own hand. With
the party, its components and attached units the Führer has
created for himself and thereby the German Reich leadership
an instrument which makes him independent of the church.
All influences which might impair or damage the leadership of
the people exercised by the Führer with the help of the
NSDAP [Nazi Party] must be eliminated. More and more the
people must be separated from the churches and their organs,
the pastors. . . ."

This decree was not followed by any specific instructions for
implementing it. For Bormann's extremism had led him into a
blunder. The Führer decided that he wanted no violent assault
launched when millions of members of the armed forces were
still so misguided as to belong to Christian churches. The im-
plementation of Bormann's ideas, which Hitler shared, would
have to await the establishment of the Nazi New Order
throughout Europe.

The full text of Bormann's decree somehow eventually became known to church authorities, to the irritation of the
Reich Minister for Propaganda and Public Enlightenment.
The realistic Goebbels wrote in his diary: "Our enemies
abroad have unfortunately got possession of a circular letter
by Bormann on the church question. Why does Bormann at
this time have to let loose a pronouncement on the church
question anyway? It is not a problem of any decisive importance in winning the war."

The incident only went to illustrate Bormann's extremism.
Ironically, this quality would prove disastrous to the Nazis
themselves. If Hitler were to succeed over the long term, he
really needed a close adviser who could manage at least to
modify his own radicalism. Though such an adviser would not
have been tolerated for long, he still might have pointed out to
the Führer the impracticality of ruthless brutality toward "inferior" peoples and the immediate execution of the Nazis' racial and religious ideas. These approaches only provoked
resistance and wasted manpower that could be usefully em-

ployed elsewhere. More importantly, there were serious flaws in the military position of Nazi Germany on the eve of Barbarossa which endangered the operation's chances for ultimate success.

Neither the German economy nor armed forces was ready for an extended war. Great Britain still held out, as the Luftwaffe was withdrawn from the aerial blitz in June to prepare for the invasion of Russia. The Royal Navy remained strong and battle-ready. Large quantities of weapons were reaching Britain from the neutral United States.

"Operation Punishment," the Nazi assault on Yugoslavia, had caused a delay in the start of Barbarossa; four weeks of good weather, the only kind in which blitzkrieg tactics were effective, had been lost. And in attacking their Russian ally, the Germans would be engaging a population which outnumbered their own by three to one.

Now that he had won so much at so little cost, Hitler could have profited from the counsel to modify his mission to find more living space for the Germanic race in the east, to postpone to a more favorable time an adventure which would "make the world hold its breath."

Certainly no such advice was forthcoming from Bormann. But then the former gunner who had seen no combat action in the First World War could have had little comprehension of global military strategy. The former estate manager and leader of the party Aid Fund possessed scant understanding of the enormous economic requirements needed to sustain a major war. And the bureaucrat who had concentrated on the internal affairs of the Nazi Party and never traveled outside of countries occupied by the Nazis could not perceive that even those Russians who detested communism might resist a brutal invader of their homeland.

Bormann did understand one thing: the Führer had always been right. During dinner on June 20, 1941, the new Head of the Nazi Party Chancellery found him in a contemplative mood. And so Bormann said to Hitler: "You are burdened with great worries just now—the successful conclusion of this great campaign depends on you alone. Providence has appointed you as her instrument for deciding the future of the whole world. No one knows better than I do that you have devoted the whole of yourself to this task, that you've studied every conceivable detail of this problem. I am convinced that you have planned everything thoroughly, and that your great mission will surely succeed."

On June 22, three hours before the sun rose over the long frontier dividing Nazi Germany from Soviet Russia, the "great mission" was undertaken. More than three million German troops struck eastward, into the endless space of Russia: Army Group North toward Leningrad, Army Group Center toward Moscow, and Army Group South toward the Ukraine and the Caucasus Mountains.

SEVEN

Brown Eminence

Stalin had made no plans to meet an invasion, despite numerous indications of Hitler's decision. The Red Army, which had been purged of many of its best generals by Stalin for political reasons and which was engaged in routine border exercises, was smashed back by the sudden German onslaught.

General Franz Halder, Chief of the Army General Staff, confidently expected to be in Moscow by August. He noted in his diary for July 3: "It may be said even now that the objective of shattering the bulk of the Russian Army this side of the Dvina and Dnieper Rivers has been accomplished . . . It is thus probably no overstatement to say that the Russian campaign has been won in the course of two weeks."

As the rapid German advance continued according to plan, there was only elation and optimism in official German quarters. By July 8, General Halder considered it time to begin preparations for billeting German forces in Russia for the coming winter as occupation, not combat, troops.

On July 14, Hitler himself felt that "the military rule of Europe after the conquest of Russia permits the substantial demobilization of the army."

The Führer, it appeared from all

the evidence, had been as uncannily right in ordering the attack as he had been in making all of his other major decisions. By July 16, German troops had captured Smolensk; this was 450 miles from their starting point and only 200 miles from Moscow. On that date, Hitler called a conference to restate his views concerning Russia. There was no longer any question that Russia would be conquered. The question was how it would be administered after it became part of the Nazi Empire.

The conference was held in the Führer's private train near his new field headquarters, *Wolfsschanze* (Wolf's Lair), at Rastenburg in East Prussia. Wolf's Lair was hidden in a dimly lit forest in one of the most remote parts of the Reich. Its buildings resembled Alpine chalets, and they were protected by heavy antiaircraft batteries and a triple ring of SS guards. A sense of unreality pervaded this gloomy fortress, cut off as it was from the outside world.

Bormann was present at the conference, to which Hitler also summoned Rosenberg, Keitel, Goering, and Hans Heinrich Lammers, Head of the Reich Chancellery. It lasted from three in the afternoon until eight o'clock, but Hitler's views could be summed up in a portion of the confidential minutes which were kept by Bormann:

> While German goals and methods must be concealed from the world at large, all the necessary measures——shooting, exiling, etc.——we shall take and we *can* take anyway. The order of the day is
> first: conquer,
> second: rule,
> third: exploit.

Some of the "necessary measures" were already being taken by the SS Action Groups which followed the advancing German Army. Action Group D, commanded by Dr. Otto Ohlendorf, who held university degrees in economics and law, operated in the southern sector. In its first year of operation, Action Group D would collect and shoot some 90,000 men, women, and children. Most of the victims were Jews.

This new type of warfare was so ghastly that it had a debasing effect on the men who conducted it. Eventually, after one mass shooting at Minsk, SS General von dem Bach-Zelewski told Himmler to look at the eyes of the men of the Action Group to "observe how badly shattered they are. These men are through with their nerves for the rest of their lives. We are raising neurotics or savages here."

Himmler then told the assembled commandos that he understood how repulsive their duty was, but that it was a necessity which should not affect their consciences. "A bug or a rat has a right to live," the Reichsführer SS explained, "as a thistle has a right to grow. Yet men exterminate vermin and weed out thistles. This is in self-defense, otherwise vermin will kill men and thistles will destroy the crop."

The killings continued. The army command, as ordered, did not intervene although it did instruct its soldiers not to "gaze curiously at such procedures" and forbade the "distribution of photographs and the spreading of reports about such events." One old-time Nazi found the mass shootings so loathsome that he was moved to protest. He was Wilhelm Kube, District Commissioner for White Russia. Kube was an early anti-Semite and a bearer of the Nazi Blood Order of 1923. He had fallen into disfavor in 1936 after it had been discovered that he had written an anonymous letter to the President of the Party Court, Walter Buch, insinuating that Buch's wife was partly Jewish. Frau Buch was the grandmother of Martin Bormann's children, and Kube found himself for a short time in a concentration camp. He was eventually rehabilitated by Himmler, but even so staunch a Nazi as Kube was shaken by the wholesale slaughters executed by the SS Action Groups in his district. "With these methods we will not achieve peace and order in White Russia," he wrote to his superior, Hinrich Lohse, the Reich Commissioner for Ostland. "To bury alive

seriously wounded people, who crawl out of their graves, is
such a bottomless piece of vileness that it ought to be reported
to the Reich Marshal [Goering]."

Goering could have done nothing about the SS methods,
even if he had wanted to. The Führer had ordered the killings
as necessary for clearing the way for the Nazi New Order, and
that settled the matter. Meanwhile, the German military advance into the east continued, despite the onset of heavy rains
which turned the hard, dry ground into mud which slowed the
tanks and other vehicles used in the blitzkriegs. In September,
the Germans claimed the capture of 600,000 prisoners in one
engagement alone, the rout of Red Army forces in the Kiev
pocket. On October 3, Hitler proclaimed in a speech: "I can
tell you now—and I could not say this until now—that the
enemy has been struck down and will never rise again." One
week later, the Führer authorized Dr. Otto Dietrich, Under-
Secretary at the Propaganda Ministry, to announce that the
outcome of the war had been decided.

By this time, the Nazis had taken more than three million
Russian prisoners. They were regarded as *Untermenschen*
(subhumans). While they were not liquidated as were Jews
and communist functionaries, the prisoners were given the
barest minimum of food and medical attention. Goebbels
noted in his diary that the Russians "are not a people, but a
conglomeration of animals."

But as the Nazi armies drove deeper into the Soviet Union,
some OKW officers noted uneasily that Russian resistance was
at times strong and skillful. Nevertheless, it did seem that
Barbarossa would soon succeed. And when it did, the Nazi
New Order would be permanently established. Great Britain
alone could not hope to defeat the Nazis. The United States
was still neutral, but even if she did enter the war on the side
of Britain, these Allies would face an almost impossible task in
overcoming a Nazi Empire of some four hundred million
people embracing most of Western Europe, North Africa, and
the vast eastern spaces of conquered Russia.

Martin Bormann's particular obsession was to make certain

that this New Order would be ruled by the Nazi Party machine which he headed, and not by the Army, the SS, or any other agency. To prevent Himmler from gaining too much power in the east, Bormann had used his influence with Hitler to secure the appointment of Alfred Rosenberg as Reich Minister for the Occupied Eastern Territories, realizing that Rosenberg was a weak man who could be manipulated.

Goebbels noted in his diary that Rosenberg was "a good theoretician but no practitioner, he is completely at sea as far as organization is concerned, besides having rather childish ideas." These ideas evolved from the fact that many Ukrainians initially welcomed the invaders as friends who had come to liberate them from Stalinist oppression. Rosenberg wanted to foster this good will as support against the Kremlin regime. Rather than to follow an inflexible policy of terror and oppression, he advocated a middle course of enrolling the support of Ukrainian, Turkic, Caucasian, and other non-Russian peoples against the Great Russians. He proposed to do this through the abolition of the hated collective farms, the establishment of religious freedom, the granting of a measure of local self-government under Nazi-sponsored regimes, and the cessation of terror methods unless the targets were communist officials and Jews.

To all of this, Bormann, gripped by the fantasy of a master race, was implacably opposed. The Slavs were subhumans, and were to be treated as such without exception. So Bormann, having diluted Himmler's power by backing the appointment of Rosenberg, now set out to undermine the latter's authority. This he did by securing the appointment from Hitler of Erich Koch as Reich Commissar for the Ukraine.

Though he was nominally Rosenberg's subordinate, Koch was Bormann's man. The two had been on intimate terms since the days of the Rossbach organization. Koch had served as one of the pallbearers at the funeral of the Nazi martyr, Albert Leo Schlageter. He had joined the Nazi Party as its ninetieth member. Koch was short with a bull neck like Bormann's, his round pink face was adorned with a Hitler mous-

tache. Now forty-five years old, he was the Gauleiter of East
Prussia, and the kind of man Bormann could depend on as the
instrument for his own ideas.

The Ukraine was the largest Soviet Republic occupied in
full by the Germans, it contained many anticommunist factions, and it was the greatest supplier of manpower and food
of any of the eastern territories. When a press officer at the
Rosenberg Ministry congratulated Koch on his appointment
as Reich Commissar, characterizing it as "the undertaking to
bring back a sense of nationality to so strong and valuable a
race as the Ukrainians," Koch retorted: "My dear sir, you
must have read that in some local newspaper. Let me tell you
one thing. The Ukrainians will be handled with cheap tobacco
stalks for them to smoke, with vodka and the whip, while you
are sitting in some place, discovering the Slav soul."

At the inaugural speech to officials of his staff, Koch said:
"Gentlemen; I am known as a brutal dog; for that reason I
have been appointed *Reichskommissar* for the Ukraine. There
is no free Ukraine. We must aim at making the Ukrainians
work for Germany and not at making people happy."

Koch lived up to his promise. The more moderate Rosenberg was prevented by Bormann from expressing his own
views to Hitler. Thus, the Nazis lost all chance of gaining the
cooperation of the Ukrainian population in a struggle against
the Kremlin. To Bormann, it could not have mattered very
much that the Russians were now countering savagery with
tenacious resistance. The country could be dealt with in any
way its new masters saw fit once the Red Army was finally
broken. And this moment did not seem far off.

At the Führer's side in the austere, remote fortress of Wolf's
Lair, Bormann, using Hitler's maps, followed the progress of
Barbarossa. Though he understood little about military strategy, he could see plainly enough that Army Group Center,
under Field Marshal Fedor von Bock, was within forty miles
of Moscow by October 20. Stalin remained in the capital, but
the main ministries and the diplomatic corps had been evacuated a week earlier, as German Intelligence accurately re-

ported to Wolf's Lair. And the Führer had already said that the outcome of the war had been decided.

German officers and men in the field, however, were not as certain of this as were those studying maps at Wolf's Lair. Despite the staggering losses it had taken, the Red Army somehow kept throwing fresh divisions into the battle. And its equipment was better than German Intelligence had predicted; the T-34 tank, which was superior to anything the Nazis possessed, came as a particularly unpleasant surprise. German supply lines had become extremely long, and they were continually harassed by partisan bands. In early November, light frosts set in and snow began to feather down.

"Then the weather suddenly broke," according to the Chief of Staff of the Fourth Army, General Günther Blumentritt, "and almost overnight the full fury of the Russian winter was upon us. The thermometer suddenly dropped to thirty degrees of frost . . . With steadily decreasing momentum and increasing difficulty the two Panzer groups continued to battle their way towards Moscow."

The mechanized summer army was now attacked by icy blasts that scythed across the snowy countryside. Automatic weapons froze, oil congealed in tank motors, artillery could not be fired. Hundreds of thousands of skilled, irreplaceable soldiers who had not been issued winter clothing were maimed by frostbite or frozen to death by the intense cold. The breath of those who continued to attack seemed to hang in the air; icicles hung from their eyelashes and nostrils. The penalty for losing four good weeks of weather in the "Operation Punishment" diversion was now being exacted in full.

Still, to Hitler and Bormann in Wolf's Lair, it must have seemed that Barbarossa would succeed by the narrowest of margins. On December 1, Germany army groups began an attack on Moscow from points within thirty miles of the capital. The next day, an infantry reconnaissance battalion actually penetrated into a Moscow suburb from which the Kremlin spires could be seen.

The main attack on the 200-mile front north, south, and

west of Moscow was halted, however. On December 6, one hundred divisions of the Red Army, whose strength the Nazis had underestimated, launched a massive counterattack before Moscow. German troops for the first time in the war were beaten back along a broad front.

Hitler's generals advised him to retreat, establish a tenable winter line, and regroup. He would have none of this and ordered that the freezing, exhausted troops "must hold fast, regardless, in every position and in the most impossible circumstances." This order was obeyed in most areas, probably averting a catastrophic rout.

Hitler now began looking for scapegoats for what had happened to Barbarossa. His fury and frustration were directed against his generals. On December 19, he quickly accepted the resignation of Field Marshal Walther von Brauchtisch as Commander in Chief of the Army, characterizing him as "a vain, cowardly wretch . . . a nincompoop." Hitler assumed the post of Commander in Chief himself. Three army group commanders and more than half of the army commanders were banished to retirement. The confident expectation of a blitzkrieg victory gave way to the possibility of an extended war.

The year 1941 ended with the New Order still unachieved. Instead, Nazi Germany was confronted by three major allies: Britain, the Soviet Union, and the United States, upon whom Hitler had declared war four days after Pearl Harbor.

Nevertheless, the Nazis retained possession of huge blocks of eastern territory. The snow and cold had hampered the Red Army, too; it was unable to encircle and destroy any large part of the invading forces. Hitler was convinced that a new offensive launched after the coming of the spring thaws could finish Russia off. The German Army remained a formidable striking force, despite the humiliation and sacking of so many of its experienced generals and its total casualties of well over a million men.

But one man profited from the failure of the first phase of Barbarossa. At Compiègne, Hitler had seemed all-powerful and sufficient unto himself. Now, he increasingly sought the support of someone who never questioned his judgment and who carried out his orders quickly and energetically. In this winter of frustration and waiting, Martin Bormann came to be called, although never in his presence, the "Brown Eminence" behind the Führer's throne.*

This position still held limitless possibilities, despite what had happened, as the warm early summer of 1942 arrived. The Nazis retained control of most of continental Europe, which the British and Americans were not strong enough to invade. U-boats were sinking more ships in the Atlantic than could be replaced by Allied shipyards. Rommel and his Afrika Korps seemed on the point of taking the Nile Delta.

But it was Russia that the Führer regarded as the main theater of operations. And here he resumed his ambitious planning. The northern front before Leningrad and Moscow would be held. A main attack would be launched in the south, through the corridor between the Donetz and Don Rivers. The objective was to cripple Russia's capacity to fight by capturing the industrial complex around the Donetz River basin, the oil fields of the Caucasus Mountains, the wheat fields of the Kuban region, and Stalingrad. The capture of Stalingrad would seal off the last main route by which crucial oil supplies were shipped to central Russia.

In early June 1942, the German Army resumed its attack with a speed and fury reminiscent of the first blitzkriegs. On July 16, Hitler moved from Wolf's Lair in East Prussia to a new field headquarters near Vinnitsa in the Ukraine. Here, on maps, he followed the swift progress of the renewed offensive with mounting optimism and excitement. With him were offi-

---

* Father Joseph (1577-1638) was the confidant and adviser to the powerful "Red Eminence," Cardinal Richelieu, chief minister to King Louis XIII of France, who was completely under the Cardinal's control. A shadowy figure, adept at secret diplomacy and power politics, Father Joseph, a Capuchin monk, gained the sobriquet of *Éminence Grise* (Gray Eminence) from the color of his habit. The color of Bormann's Nazi Party uniform was, of course, brown.

cers of the Armed Forces High Command, the Army General Staff, and Martin Bormann.

Bormann was the only Nazi leader permanently stationed at "Werewolf," as the Vinnista headquarters was called. Himmler was eighty miles away in his own SS headquarters in a former Soviet military academy near Zhitomir. Goebbels was in Berlin, occupied with his Ministry for Propaganda and Public Enlightenment. Goering stayed away from Werewolf as much as he could. The Führer was already displeased with him because of the failure of the Luftwaffe to subdue Britain. The displeasure turned to anger after the Royal Air Force delivered its first thousand-bomber raid on Cologne during the night of May 30.

The other Nazi leaders had business which kept them distant from Werewolf. There, Hitler concentrated almost totally on military matters. Bormann dealt with the way in which those Russians living in areas held by the German Army should be handled. Assiduously pouring fire on the oil of the Führer's hatred and contempt for the Slavs, Bormann continued to support the brutal policies of Erich Koch over the more moderate approach of Alfred Rosenberg.

Neither Bormann nor Koch had learned anything from the experience of the previous year; no attempt would even be considered of driving a wedge between the occupied peoples, in particular the Ukrainians, and the Soviet government. On one occasion, Koch declared: "If I find a Ukrainian who is worthy of sitting at the same table with me, I must have him shot." When Rosenberg reproached him for the common practice of whipping Ukrainians, Koch replied: "True enough, once . . . about twenty Ukrainians were whipped by the police because they sabotaged important bridge construction across the Dnieper. I knew nothing of this measure. Had I known what a chain of reproaches this act would unleash, I probably would have those Ukrainians shot for sabotage."

Bormann himself motored through the villages and collective farms around Vinnitsa on July 22. The large numbers of

blue-eyed, chubby-faced children he saw surprised and depressed him. Upon returning to Werewolf in the evening, he
told the Führer, "In comparison, our children look like totter-
ing little chicks. It really is curious to think that these children
will become Ukrainian adults, with their vulgar, inexpressive
faces. I was much struck by the fact that in these huge open
spaces one saw so many children and so few men. Such pro-
lific breeding may one day give us a knotty problem to solve,
for as a race they are much hardier than we are. . . . If these
people are allowed, under German supervision—that is, under
greatly improved conditions—to multiply too quickly, it will
be against our interests, for the racial pressures which these
damned Ukrainians will exercise will constitute a real danger.
Our interests demand just the reverse—namely, that these territories, hitherto Russian, should in time be populated by a
larger number of German colonists than local inhabitants."

Hitler agreed with Bormann and set off on a rambling
monologue concerning the manner in which he felt that the
Slavs should be handled. Bormann, in his now familiar fashion, edited these remarks and sent a summary of them the next
day to Rosenberg as a policy directive from the Führer's
Headquarters. Bormann wrote, in part:

> The Slavs are to work for us. Insofar as we don't need
> them, they may die. Therefore compulsory vaccination and
> German health services are superfluous. The fertility of the
> Slavs is undesirable. They may use contraceptives and prac-
> tice abortion, the more the better. Education is dangerous.
> It is sufficient if they can count up to a hundred. At best an
> education is admissible which produces useful servants for
> us. Every educated person is a future enemy. Religion we
> leave to them as a means of diversion. As to food, they are
> not to get more than necessary. We are the masters, we
> come first.

This effectively settled the issue between Koch and Rosenberg. Eventually, Bormann succeeded so adroitly in under-

mining Rosenberg's position with Hitler that the latter refused
to have any dealings at all with his Reich Minister for the
Occupied Eastern Territories. Meanwhile, another Bormann
favorite was at work. This was Fritz Sauckel, a former sailor
and worker in a ball-bearings factory, who had been Gauleiter
of Thuringia since 1927.

In March 1942, Sauckel, through Bormann's influence, had
been appointed Plenipotentiary General for Labor Allocation.
This title masked the true nature of Sauckel's function, which
was to direct the rounding up of Russians and their shipment
to Germany as slave laborers.

There were some 50,000 *Ostarbeiter* (Eastern Workers) in
the Reich when Sauckel was appointed. Before he was finished, the number would reach nearly three million. Recruit-
ment of the Eastern Workers recalled the days of the slave
trade. Russian civilians were rounded up at random in their
homes, on the street, in market places, and in churches. Man
hunts were conducted in the literal sense of the term. Failure
to comply with demands for manpower were met with whip-
pings, the burning down of homes and even of entire villages.

The plight of the Eastern Workers, however, was not as
grim as that of the prisoners of war. The workers were useful
to the Nazis and, however barbarous their treatment, most of
them would survive the war. Of the more than five million
soldiers captured by the Germans, barely one million would
survive. One of those who did not was Stalin's eldest son,
Jacob.

Reich Marshal Goering, in discussing the Russian prisoners
with Count Ciano, complained to the Italian Foreign Minister
that ". . . after having eaten everything possible, including the
soles of their shoes, they have begun to eat each other, and
what is more serious, have also eaten a German sentry."

The catastrophe that befell the prisoners was not deliberately planned, however. Expecting a short campaign, the
Nazis had not made plans to care for millions of prisoners, the
majority of whom perished through hunger, disease, inade-

quate shelter, and general neglect rather than by design. This was not the case with another segment of the eastern peoples.

In his diary entry for March 27, 1942, Goebbels had written: "Beginning with Lublin, the Jews in the General Government [of Poland] are now being evacuated eastward. The procedure is a pretty barbaric one and not to be described here more definitely."

As the "procedure" continued, so did the renewed blitzkrieg. By the third week in August, the German Sixth Army reached the Volga River just north of Stalingrad. It had driven 500 miles from its starting point in the Ukraine. At the same time, Army Group A fought to within fifty miles of the main Soviet oil centers in the Caucasus.

Behind the lines, the Action Groups went about their grisly tasks; thousands of Russian prisoners died each day under open skies, and Eastern Workers were rounded up and shipped in crowded freight cars to the Reich. As a result, any one who could now sought salvation by joining the struggle against the Nazis. There were even some Nazi officials who doubted, from a practical standpoint, the wisdom of the brutal approach. The armament inspector for the Ukraine wrote to his headquarters: "If we shoot the Jews, let the prisoners of war die out, expose the urban population to starvation and are about to lose part of the rural population next year owing to hunger, the question is: Who is going to produce anything in this area?"

Such objections could not have mattered much to Hitler and Bormann at Werewolf. They followed the military maps and on them could see that a decisive victory was near which would lead to the establishment of the Nazi New Order. On August 21, the Nazi flag was raised on Mount Elbrus, the highest peak in Europe. Two days later, the Sixth Army was at the gates of Stalingrad. The Führer ordered that the great industrial city, stretching for thirty miles along the Volga River, be taken by August 25.

EIGHT

Rumors About
the Position
of the Jews

Some of his generals had attempted to make Hitler realize that the German forces, after their losses of the previous winter, were not strong enough to succeed in carrying out two powerful offensives in the different directions of Stalingrad and the Caucasus at the same time. The generals counseled that a single main objective should be concentrated upon. In particular, Franz Halder, Chief of the General Staff, attempted to point out the growing danger of a Soviet counterattack across the German north flank, which was stretched out for hundreds of miles from the Ukraine to Stalingrad. This long flank was held only by Italian, Rumanian, and Hungarian divisions.

But supported by Bormann, the Führer would have none of the generals' advice. ". . . his decisions had ceased to have anything in common with the principles of strategy and operations as they had been recognized for generations past," Halder noted in his diary. "They were the product of a violent nature following its momentary impulses, a nature which acknowledged no bounds to possibility and which made its wish the father of its deed."

Army Group A had not taken the oil centers of the Caucasus by September 10, and on that date Hitler dismissed its commander, Field Marshal Wilhelm List. This disturbed Field Marshal Keitel. "I never found out who had been stirring things up against List," he later wrote, "an army commander of the highest calibre who had particularly proved his value in France and in the Balkans. It is my belief that the witchhunt started on the political side, with Himmler or Bormann; otherwise it is inexplicable."

Keitel himself, the senior officer of the Armed Forces, complained that he was "unable to issue an order to anybody . . . apart from my driver and my batman." The Führer, he felt, was suffering from a "pathological delusion that his generals were conspiring against him and were trying to sabotage his orders on what were in his view pretty shabby pretexts."

Stalingrad was still in Russian hands on September 24. Hitler reacted to this by dismissing the Chief of the General Staff. "You and I have been suffering from nerves," the Führer told General Halder at their last meeting. "Half of my nervous exhaustion is due to you. It is not worth it to go on. We need National Socialist ardor now, not professional ability. I cannot expect this of an officer of the old school such as you."

Shortly after this, the Führer refused to continue his previous practice of dining with his staff officers at a common table. He took his meals alone, or with Bormann. No record of what was said or done during these meals would survive, but it was apparent to those at Werewolf that Bormann was the one man in whom the Führer now put any trust.

The battle for Stalingrad continued, block by block, house by house, through cellars, sewers, blasted factories, and enormous clouds of burning, blinding smoke. By early October, the Nazis controlled most of the central parts of the city, all of its southern parts, and were smashing through the rubble toward the industrial section in the north.

Bormann observed the progress of the battle on maps at Werewolf, but he also had other matters to deal with. One of them concerned the "procedure" which Goebbels had noted in his diary. Though it was a secret undertaking, rumors about it had begun to spread throughout the Reich. To clear up any misunderstandings and to assist his party leaders in dealing with the rumors, Bormann issued another of his innumerable decrees. It was dated October 9, 1942, and entitled: "Preparatory Measures for the Solution of the Jewish Problem in Europe—Rumors About the Position of the Jews in the East."

Bormann wrote that "In the course of the work on the final solution of the Jewish problem discussions about 'very strict measures' against the Jews, especially in the Eastern territories, have lately been taking place within the population of the various areas of the Reich. Investigations showed that such discussions—mostly in a distorted and exaggerated form— were passed on by soldiers on leave from various units committed in the East, who had the opportunity to eye-witness these measures.

"It is conceivable that not all 'Blood Germans' are capable of demonstrating sufficient understanding for the necessity of such measures, especially not those parts of the population which do not have the opportunity of visualizing bolshevist atrocities on the basis of their own observations.

"In order to be able to counter-act any formation of rumors in this connection, which frequently are of an intentional, prejudiced character, the following statements are issued for information about the present state of affairs:

"For approx. 2000 years, a so-far unsuccessful battle has been waged against Judaism. Only since 1933 have we started to find ways and means in order to enable a complete separation of Judaism from the German masses. . . .

"Since even our next generation will not be close enough to this problem and will no longer see it clearly enough on the basis of past experiences and since this matter which has now started rolling demands clearing up, the whole problem must still be solved by the present generation.

"A complete removal or withdrawal of the millions of Jews residing in the European economic space is therefore an urgent need in the fight for the security of existence of the German people.

"Starting with the territory of the Reich and proceeding to the remaining European countries included in the final solution, the Jews are currently being deported to large camps which have already been established or which are to be established in the East, where they will either be used for work or else transported still farther to the East. The old Jews as well as Jews with high military decorations, Iron Cross First Class, Golden Medal of Valor, etc., are currently being resettled in the city of Theresienstadt which is located in the Protectorate of Bohemia and Moravia.

"It lies in the very nature of the matter that these problems, which in part are very difficult, can be solved only with ruthless severity in the interest of the final security of the people."

This was Bormann's way of explaining a "matter" of whose true nature he was fully aware. He knew what such deceptive phrases as "or else transported still farther to the East" really meant and what was being done to implement the "Final Solution of the Jewish Problem" as the battle for Stalingrad approached its climax.

The majority of Austrian and German Jews had been stripped of their civil rights by the Nazis and forced to emigrate before the war. After that, many thousands who could not emigrate died in concentration camps. But the East, which to the Nazis meant Poland, the Baltic States, and occupied Russia, was the center of the prewar Jewish population of Europe. There were more than three million Jews in Poland, and one and a half million in occupied Russia. Mass shootings of these Eastern Jews by the Action Groups had been going on since the conquest of Poland. In Russia, another technique had been introduced: mobile gas vans, into which Jews were herded and killed with exhaust fumes on their way to burial pits. But the decision to adopt genocide as an active and fully organized Nazi policy does not appear to have been made until the summer of 1941.

Conversations concerning the decision were top secret, apparently never committed to paper, and were probably taken part in only by Hitler, Goering, Bormann, Himmler, and Reinhard Heydrich, head of the SS Main Office for State Security, who was to be the central authority for the Final Solution.

On July 31, 1941, undoubtedly after having been given verbal instructions by Hitler, Goering had sent a written directive to Heydrich: "Supplementing the task that was assigned to you on 24 January 1939, to solve the Jewish problem by means of emigration and evacuation . . . I herewith instruct you to make all the necessary preparations as regards organizational, financial, and material matters for a total solution [*Gesamtlösung*] of the Jewish question within the areas of German influence . . . I instruct you further to submit to me as soon as possible a general plan showing the measures for organization and for action necessary to carry out the desired final solution [*Endlösung*] of the Jewish question."

Heydrich took up his assignment with his customary administrative skill, imagination, and fierce driving energy. Within six months, an organization and the physical facilities necessary to carry out the "desired final solution" were fully operative. A number of *Vernichtungslager* (Extermination Camps) were established in the East. Auschwitz, thirty-seven miles west of Cracow, was the largest. Jews were transported to the extermination centers, where those not selected to work as slave laborers were sent immediately to gas chambers. There they were killed with Zyklon B, a crystallized prussic acid which was dropped into death chambers camouflaged as shower rooms. Eventually, most of the slave laborers were also sent to the gas chambers. Zyklon B, which was quicker and more efficient as a killing device than mass shootings or the carbon monoxide of the mobile gas vans, was introduced by the Commandant of Auschwitz, Rudolf Franz Hoess, Bormann's old friend from the days of the Rossbach organization and the Kadow murder.

Each of the two larger gas chambers at Auschwitz alone

could accommodate up to three thousand persons every day. Heydrich had done his work well. But then, he was efficient in anything he attempted. Physically a sound "Nordic" specimen, as the other Nazi leaders were so notably not, Reinhard Tristan Heydrich was thirty-eight years old, tall, lean, and blond, with light blue eyes that were piercing and hypnotic. He was a skilled pilot and athlete, and an expert fencer. His father had been a distinguished teacher of music and Heydrich, who had been brilliant at school, was an accomplished classical violinist.

Bormann had originally been one of Heydrich's staunchest supporters. This enthusiasm waned, however, when he began to recognize in Himmler's calculating, coldly efficient second in command a more dangerous rival than the Reichsführer SS himself. On September 27, 1941, Heydrich had been appointed Acting Reich Protector of Bohemia and Moravia (the greater part of prewar Czechoslovakia), in addition to his other duties. This was another appointment which Bormann had influenced Hitler to make. All of Heydrich's reports from the Reich Protectorate went through his ally Bormann to the Führer. But Heydrich was so successful in administering the Final Solution and the Protectorate that he won Hitler's admiration to the point where Bormann's envy and jealousy were aroused. The result was typical.

Heydrich, accompanied by Walter Schellenberg, head of the SS Foreign Intelligence Branch, went to Werewolf to report to Hitler in person on the economic problems of the Protectorate. They were obliged to wait for a long time outside of Hitler's bunker. Finally, the Führer emerged. He was accompanied by Bormann. Heydrich greeted Hitler with the Nazi salute, then waited for him to ask for the report. But Hitler only stared at Heydrich for a moment. Then an expression of distaste appeared on his face. Bormann took the Führer's arm and with a confident and easy gesture drew him back into the bunker. Heydrich waited for Hitler to return. He did not do so.

The next day, Bormann met Heydrich and told him that the

Führer was no longer interested in his report. Observing this encounter, Schellenberg thought that while Bormann delivered the rejection in a most amiable tone, "Heydrich sensed his implacable hatred."

Upon his return to Prague, Heydrich was being driven on the warm, sunny morning of May 27, 1942, from his chateau outside of the city through its suburbs to its airport. The route taken was his usual one. His low, green, two-door Mercedes-Benz roadster was easily recognizable. A pennant flew from each of its front fenders, one representing the Reich Protectorate, the other the SS. Heydrich was notably careless about security precautions, and the convertible was open. He sat in the front seat next to Sergeant Klein, his driver. As the latter slowed the car to take a hair-turn curve, a man suddenly appeared and attempted to fire a Sten-gun through the windshield.

The weapon jammed. Instead of speeding off, Klein brought the car almost to a halt as Heydrich reached for his revolver. A second man then rolled a large gray metal ball underneath the back of the car. The ball was a Mills grenade of a special type, and its explosion wrecked the back of the Mercedes-Benz and brought it to a bumping halt.

Klein jumped out of the smoking car and pursued one of the assailants in vain. Heydrich ran after the other one, firing his revolver at him until it was empty. The man escaped, thinking that the Reich Protector had survived the attempt on his life. Then Heydrich walked back to the car and suddenly slumped against its hood. He was, in fact, seriously wounded. The grenade had exploded upwards fine splinters of steel, as well as horsehair and material from the car's seat. These had penetrated deeply into Heydrich's lumbar regions and spleen. The police arrived and drove him to a hospital. Despite the finest medical attention the Third Reich could offer, Heydrich died after nine days of considerable agony. He would be the only Nazi leader assassinated during the entire twelve years of the Third Reich.

Walter Schellenberg's first reaction to the assassination was that it had been plotted by Bormann. But this only illustrated what even knowledgeable Nazis were prepared to believe Bormann capable of doing to eliminate his rivals. For the deed had actually been done by two Free Czech agents. They had been trained, equipped, and dropped by parachute by the British. Later, they were among 120 members of the Czech resistance who were discovered hiding in a church by the SS. The SS killed them all.

Himmler waited for eight months after the death of the ambitious Heydrich to appoint his successor as head of the SS Main Office for State Security, and then the man was a mediocrity who could be effectively controlled. Dr. Ernst Kaltenbrunner was a lawyer and veteran Austrian Nazi of disquieting appearance. He stood nearly seven feet tall. His massive broad shoulders and huge arms ended with hands that were small, delicate and stained brown with nicotine. His long impassive face was slashed with scars received in student duels. He was a chain smoker who began to drink early in the morning, achieving incoherency before he tumbled into bed at night. He resembled the coldly intelligent Heydrich only in the zeal with which he pursued the goals of the Final Solution. He was not a man whom Bormann need fear.

Heydrich's work survived his death. So well had he functioned as the engineer of the Final Solution that its machinery was working smoothly and in high gear by the time Bormann felt obliged to issue his decree aimed at counteracting the rumors about "the position of the Jews in the East."

Gerda Bormann, who was as ardent a Nazi as her husband, once wrote to him that "Every single child must realize that the Jew is the Absolute Evil in this world and that he must be fought by every means, wherever he appears." To which Martin Bormann replied, "Quite true."

But Bormann never bothered to observe at first hand the end results of this kind of thinking. At Auschwitz, thousands of Jews were daily being led into the "shower rooms." An SS guard would call out reassuringly: "Put your shoes right next to your clothes, so that you can find them again after the bath." Then the doors were locked, the seals of apertures on the ceiling were removed, and a head wearing a gas mask appeared at each aperture. A loud cry of horror was suddenly heard as the men wearing gas masks emptied cans filled to the rim with blue pellets the size of peas through the openings, which were quickly closed again. The Zyklon B pellets did their work usually within four minutes, for by then the screaming stopped.

At other places in Auschwitz, inmates were killed by having phenolic acid injected into their hearts. Babies were tossed into the air as shooting targets, or hurled alive into the crematory fires. Other inmates were trampled to death or subjected to a "rigorous interrogation" on the "Boger swing." The latter was a form of torture. The victim was ordered to place his bound hands on his bent knees. Then a rod was inserted between elbows and knees, and the ends of the rod placed on tables. The prisoner swung helplessly, head down, between the tables, and as he swung, the soles of his feet, his buttocks, and his genitals were beaten with a bullwhip.

Neither Hitler nor Bormann witnessed any of these scenes. There is no record of either of them ever having visited Auschwitz or any other extermination camp. Once having set the Final Solution in motion, Hitler left the execution of its machinery to underlings. He was much too preoccupied with his role of Supreme Warlord and gaining a decisive victory at Stalingrad to bother with inspection tours of a problem that seemed well on its way to being solved. And Bormann, as usual, stayed close to the Führer.

On the last day of October 1942, Hitler, Bormann, the Army General Staff and the Armed Forces High Command left Werewolf in the Ukraine and returned to Wolf's Lair in East Prussia. Nine-tenths of Stalingrad was now in German hands. Though Hitler was aware of the danger posed by the long, exposed north flank of the German Sixth Army, he had convinced himself that the Russians would not counterattack across it and that a Russian winter offensive was more likely to take place on the north and central fronts. He could handle this problem better from East Prussia.

So heedless was Hitler of intelligence reports that the Russians were indeed readying a counterattack across the Don River flank in the rear of the Sixth Army that he entrained on November 7 for Munich. There, on the evening of November 9, he was scheduled to deliver his annual address to the old Nazi Party members on the anniversary of the beer-hall putsch.

Hitler did deliver a ringing speech in the *Löwenbrau* beer hall. He spoke confidently of the situation at Stalingrad. Then he and Bormann, with the generals of the Armed Forces High Command and the Army General Staff tagging along, went to Berchtesgaden. This gave Bormann a welcome opportunity to spend some time with his wife and family. He might also have reflected on the news that British and American forces under General Eisenhower had landed in French North Africa on November 7, and were pushing toward the Tunisian border. In the Western Desert, the British 8th Army under General Montgomery was well into the destruction of Rommel's exhausted Afrika Korps. And to the disgust of Hitler and Bormann with Reich Marshal Goering, the Luftwaffe could do little to stop the bombing raids of the Royal and American Air Forces on German cities and industrial targets which were daily mounting in intensity. Hitler's insistence upon attacking Russia before Britain was eliminated was now revealed as a crucial blunder.

But there was worse news to come, news bad enough to shake the faith in the Führer and the establishment of a Nazi New Order of even so devoted a disciple as Martin Bormann. In the Berghof on November 19, Hitler learned that three Red Army groups had attacked on a huge front north and south of Stalingrad. He returned with Bormann to Wolf's Lair on November 22 and that evening learned that the Red Army had encircled twenty-two German and two Rumanian divisions between the Volga and the Don.

There was now only one way in which the 230,000 men of
the Sixth Army could be saved. That was for them to break
out of Stalingrad and join up with the Fourth Panzer Army
thirty miles away. Hitler would have none of this, although
another bitter Russian winter had set in. He ordered the
hungry, exhausted troops who had no winter clothing to stand
and fight to the last man. The result was inevitable.

"We are entirely alone, without help from the outside. Hitler has left us in the lurch," a German soldier wrote in a letter
carried on the last Nazi plane to fly out of Stalingrad in January 1943. Another wrote, "The truth is the knowledge that
this is the grimmest of struggles in a hopeless situation. Mis-
ery, hunger, cold, renunciation, doubt, despair, and horrible
death." And still another wrote, "I believed in the Führer and
his word. It is terrible how they doubt here, and shameful to
listen to what they say without being able to reply, because
they have the facts on their side."

On February 3, 1943, Second Lieutenant Herbert Kuntz
flew his Heinkel bomber over Stalingrad. He was the last German pilot to fly over the city. As he dropped down through a
dense fog to an altitude of 300 feet, the mist suddenly parted.
Kuntz saw clearly the wrecked and rubble-strewn city in
which only a few walls and chimneys still stood. But he saw no
signs of fighting anywhere.

That same day, the German radio was interrupted by a long
roll of muffled drums. Then an announcer solemnly read a
special communiqué from the Armed Forces High Command:

"The battle of Stalingrad has ended. True to their oath to
fight to the last breath, the Sixth Army under the exemplary
leadership of Field Marshal Paulus has been overcome by the
superiority of the enemy and by the unfavorable circumstances confronting our forces."

This announcement was followed by the playing of the second movement of Beethoven's Fifth Symphony and the proc-
lamation of four days of national mourning.

The total loss of the Sixth Army had a profound and shattering effect on Hitler. But the catastrophe, as had earlier been the case in the narrow failure of Barbarossa's first phase, did not shake Martin Bormann's faith in the Führer and again had the curious side effect of increasing Bormann's power.

Hitler became a recluse after Stalingrad. The spell-binding orator made just four more speeches in public. He rarely ventured outside his remote fortress of Wolf's Lair. There he listened only to those who told him what he wanted to hear and shielded him against reality.

Bormann, Keitel, and Jodl were the only important Nazis who saw Hitler regularly. Himmler, Goebbels, Goering, and various military commanders made occasional visits to Wolf's Lair, as did a very few other people who had business which Hitler could not avoid dealing with personally.

All visitors first had to be granted an audience by Bormann. Then the procedure was to arrive at the electrified barbed-wire fence of *Sperrkreis III* (Security Ring III), where credentials were examined by SS guards. If these were in order, the visitor drove down a narrow asphalt road through a forest so deep and dark that even in midsummer sunlight rarely penetrated it. From late fall to early spring, either snow or a damp gray mist hampered visibility. On either side of the road, pillboxes and SS men patrolling with dogs were much in evidence. Land mines were not.

After two miles, the visitor arrived at Security Ring II, where he

was anticipated because of a telephone call from Security
Ring III. Passing through a second electrified barbed-wire
fence, the visitor soon saw the first signs of human habitation.
To the right of the road, expertly camouflaged by paint and
bushes planted on their roofs, were some low concrete huts.
These had replaced the earlier Alpine-type chalets because of
the threat of air raids. The huts contained the information
office of the Reich Press Chief, the radio and telephone exchange, and the living quarters of Keitel, Jodl, and lesser officers. To Jodl, the general atmosphere of the entire area was a
mixture of cloister and concentration camp.

To the left of the road were two more concrete huts. One
housed the SS men whose duty it was to safeguard the Führer.
The other housed Martin Bormann. From his hut, it was only
a few hundred yards to Security Ring I. This was another
electrified barbed-wire fence, seven and one half feet tall. The
few people permitted beyond it saw three buildings only.

One was a large single-story wooden structure reinforced
with a concrete shell. This served as Hitler's map or situation
room, and in it his daily military conferences were held. Then
there was a large wooden kennel. Here lived Blondi, the Alsatian bitch given by Bormann to Hitler to cheer him up after
Stalingrad. The dog appeared to be the one living thing
toward which the Führer was capable of displaying genuine
affection.

The last building was *Führerbunker I,* a bombproof shelter
imbedded in the ground with concrete walls eighteen feet
thick. Its three rooms were sparsely furnished with the sim-
plest wooden furniture. Here dwelt the man who had come so
close to becoming the master of Europe and who persisted in
his designs for a Nazi New Order.

A visitor who had seen Hitler only in his days of triumph
would have been shocked by his appearance. In 1943 he was
fifty-four, but looked at least ten years older. His face was
ashen and haggard. His eyes, covered by a slight film of exhaustion, stared fixedly at the visitor, but still projected their

strange magnetism. He walked with a stoop, dragging his left foot upon the ground. His left leg and arm trembled. To control this trembling, he braced his left foot against any convenient object and held his left hand in his right. His rages were sudden, frequent, and terrible.

General Heinz Guderian endured one of them and later described it: "His fists raised, his cheeks flushed with rage, his whole body trembling, the man stood there in front of me, beside himself with fury and having lost all self-control. After each outburst of rage Hitler would stride up and down the carpet edge, then suddenly stop immediately before me and hurl his next accusation in my face. He was almost screaming, his eyes seemed to pop out of his head, and the veins stood out in his temples."

The strains and pressures on Hitler would have broken most men, but he compounded them with his unhealthy way of life. He left his underground bunker only for his military conferences or for short walks with Blondi. The walks were his only exercise. Late in the evening, a few intimates joined him in the Führerbunker for tea and cakes. Hitler then informally held forth for hours on a wide variety of subjects such as his youth in Vienna, the early years of struggle of the Nazi Party, the meaning of history, the destiny of man, the music of Wagner, race. No mention of the war was permitted.

Bormann saw to it that this "table talk" was recorded by shorthand stenographers he selected. As the only reliable interpreter of the Führer's thought, Bormann read through the recordings of the monologues, sometimes correcting them or adding his own comments before preserving them in his personal custody. Eventually, the "table talk", officially known as the *Bormann-Vermerke* (Bormann Notes) filled 1,045 typed pages at the head of which he wrote: "Notes of fundamental interest for the future. To be preserved with the greatest care."

Hitler often talked on until dawn. Then he slept until it was time for the military conference at noon. To keep going, he became totally dependent on his quack physician, the gross and cringing Dr. Theodor Morell, who prospered by manufacturing patent medicines under the Führer's patronage.

Morell used at least twenty-eight mixtures of drugs on his patient, some of them worthless, some of them harmful. A group of conventional doctors felt that one of Morell's drugs, compounded of belladonna and strychnine, was slowly poisoning the Führer. Hitler dismissed them and continued to rely on Morell, who obligingly dispensed his concoctions to most of the other members of the inner circle at Wolf's Lair. Bormann was not one of them. Still robust and healthy at forty-three despite occasional headaches, the Head of the Party Chancellery stayed clear of the grotesque quack who ministered to the failing Führer.

Despite the drugs he constantly took and the unhealthy way of life which he led, it was probable that Hitler's mental and physical deterioration stemmed principally from a prosaic malady that afflicts, without warning or known cause, millions of people in the fifth or sixth decade of life. Of the scores of doctors who attended Hitler at one time or another, none was ever permitted to give him a thorough clinical examination. But some thought that he displayed the obvious external symptoms of *paralysis agitans* (Parkinson's disease).*

Its specific cause is entirely unknown. The disease is not limited to any type of occupation or particular continent or race, and its onset is slow and insidious. As it progresses, it is characterized by trembling of the limbs and the rigidity of certain muscles. The victim's affected lower limb drags if he attempts to run. He suffers from bouts of anxiety and nervous depression, and frequently gives way to hysterical outbursts. Rigidity affects the facial muscles in particular, causing an unnatural stillness recognized as the staring "parkinsonian mask." The disease is seriously disabling, but seldom fatal. No

* In 1963, Dr. Johann Recktenwald published a clinical study of Hitler based on a variety of symptoms: *Woran hat Hitler gelitten?* (What Did Hitler Suffer From?) (Munich; Reinhardt). Dr. Recktenwald's diagnosis is postencephalitic Parkinson's disease. Hitler, of course, was never examined by a psychiatrist.

known form of therapy will alter its course or cure it.

Whether Hitler had fallen victim to Parkinson's disease, or whether his troubles had an unknown hysterical origin, he was no longer the man the world had known. And the sicker he became, the more he resigned himself into the hands of his energetic secretary. Bormann's dominance at Hitler's court was now complete. Either constantly at the Führer's side, or else immediately available to be so, Bormann was the sole channel of approach to him, the keeper of his secrets, the man charged with issuing his orders.

"Bormann's proposals are so exactly worked out," Hitler once remarked to an aide, "that I need only say yes or no. With him I despatch in ten minutes a pile of papers over which other men take hours of my time. When I tell him to remind me in six months' time of this or that business, I can be sure that he will do so."

Walter Schellenberg, head of the SS Foreign Intelligence Branch, while recognizing Bormann's talents, took a cynical view of the way he exercised them. "He had the ability to simplify complicated matters, to present them concisely, and to summarize the essential points in a few clear sentences," Schellenberg later recalled. "So cleverly did he do this that even his briefest reports contained an implicit solution."

Was Bormann maneuvering the Führer into doing what he, Bormann, wanted done? Hitler did not think so. He would tolerate no complaints about his secretary. "I know that he is brutal," Hitler said, "but what he undertakes he finishes. I can rely absolutely on that. With his ruthlessness and brutality he always sees to it that my orders are carried out." The Führer must have felt that Bormann was the one man upon whom he could always count. His oldest friends and supporters had failed to live up to his expectations, and some had fallen by the wayside.

Ernst Roehm had been murdered on Hitler's orders. Julius Streicher, the lecherous, sadistic, Jew-baiting Gauleiter of Franconia, who had marched with Hitler, Hess, and Goering

in the 1923 beer-hall putsch, had to be removed from office in
1940 when his conduct became too scandalous even for the
Nazis. Hess was a prisoner in England. Goering had become
grossly fat and self-indulgent. His costumes grew more bizarre. On a visit to Italy, he was described by Foreign Minister
Ciano as appearing in a "great sable coat, something between
what motorists wore in 1906 and what a high-grade prostitute
wears to the opera." Goering was no longer taken seriously
after the Luftwaffe was unable to deliver relief supplies to
Stalingrad, and he knew it. But he continued his luxurious
way of life and Bormann, living in the austerity of Wolf's Lair,
despised him for it. Frau Goering was convinced that Bormann had tapped the Goerings' telephones in Berchtesgaden
and was listening in on their private conversations.

Military officers were now merely Hitler's puppets or the
objects of his vindicative spite. Himmler, the "loyal Heinrich,"
retained favor to a degree, but even his position was not secure. SS Lieutenant General Gottlob Berger, Head of the SS
Main Office, thought that he knew why. "In 1942, this terrific
distrust of Hitler's started," Berger later said, "and into the
range of this distrust he also included Himmler. Bormann was
carrying on an unheard-of policy. Some people called it
clever, but I say an absolutely disgraceful policy, and he managed everything so cleverly by feeding things to Hitler around
many back ways. Before that time, Himmler had felt himself
to be a very strong man and now, suddenly, he felt that this
wasn't true at all. . . . He was so unsure of himself at that time
that he wanted to create a liaison with Bormann in some way,
or rather, make himself subordinate to Bormann."

The realistic Goebbels had begun to suggest seeking a compromise peace, obviously because his faith in final victory had
weakened. "I noticed for the first time," Rudolf Semmler,
Goebbels' secretary, confided in his diary, "that Goebbels now
admits to his intimates his weakness as against Bormann. He
will not allow the slightest ill feeling to arise between himself
and the head of the Party Chancellery. How inconsequent he

can be! The day before yesterday he referred disparagingly to
Bormann's moderate intellectual ability. He called him 'a
primitive Ogpu* type.' Today he shows that he is frightened of
him."

Less highly placed figures than Goebbels learned not to
cross Hitler where Bormann was concerned. One was Heinrich Hoffmann, Hitler's personal photographer and the man
who had introduced him to Eva Braun. Hoffmann was an
old crony from the happier prewar days. To his intimates, the
Führer was then a charming fellow who was loyal to his
friends, loved dogs and children, and had a passion for simple
pleasures like Viennese pastry and candy.

As the military situation worsened, Bormann decided that
the jovial Hoffman was taking up too much of Hitler's time
and got rid of him by making the hypochondriac Führer believe, falsely, that his court jester was the bearer of a conta-
gious disease. But on one occasion, Hoffmann came to Wolf's
Lair from Vienna, where he had dined with the Gauleiter of
that city, his son-in-law Baldur von Schirach. The photographer relayed a message to Hitler from von Schirach. Its import
was that Bormann had taken it upon himself to instruct the
Gauleiter to forget about organizing antiaircraft defenses for
Vienna, as such a step would alarm the population unneces-
sarily.

"Hitler seemed to regard this message as an implied criticism of Bormann," Hoffmann would later write, "for he
rounded on me sharply. 'Get this quite clear in your own
mind, Hoffmann, and tell it to your son-in-law, too,' he cried.
'To win this war I have need of Bormann! It's perfectly true
that he is both ruthless and brutal . . . but the fact remains,
one after the other, everybody has failed in their implicit obedience to my commands—but Bormann, never!'

"His voice rose to a scream; he looked searchingly into my

---

* OGPU (United State Political Administration) was an early Soviet
agency assigned to the task of fighting counterrevolution, including counter-
espionage.

face, as if his words held some special application to me personally. 'Everyone, I don't care who he may be, must understand clearly this one fact: whoever is against Bormann is also against the State! I'll shoot the lot of them, even if they number tens of thousands, just as I will shoot those who babble of peace! Far better that a few thousand miserable and witless nincompoops should be liquidated, than that a people of seventy millions should be dragged down to destruction.'

"Never had I heard Hitler talk in such tones, and never in my life had I seen such wild and hate-filled eyes."

From early 1943, Bormann was a member of the "Committee of Three," whose other members were Keitel and Hans Heinrich Lammers, Head of the Reich Chancellery. All proposals concerning the war effort had first to be submitted to the "Three Wise Men from the East," as Goebbels referred to them, who then decided which proposals should be put before Hitler.

Goebbels had little use for any of the "Three Wise Men," and he attempted without success to push Goering into using his still existing titular powers to overcome their influence. On March 2, 1943, Goebbels noted, in his diary, Goering's opinion of those who had replaced the latter in the Führer's confidence: "He hates Lammers from the bottom of his soul. He regards him as a bureaucrat who is attempting to get the leadership of the Reich back into the hands of the ministerial bureaucracy . . . Keitel, in Goering's opinion, is an absolute zero who need not be taken seriously . . . As regards Bormann, Goering is not quite certain about his true intentions. There seems to be no doubt that he is pursuing ambitious aims. . . ."

Neither Goebbels nor Goering nor anyone else could figure out Bormann's "true intentions." He confided in no one but Hitler. The frequent discussions between himself and the Führer were private and not committed to record. Thus, Bormann and Hitler were the only two people who could accurately describe Bormann's role in the Third Reich—whether he was simply a fanatically dedicated right-hand man or whether he was pursuing a purpose all his own. Only Bormann could really know if he had gained such influence over his master that he could manipulate him to his own purposes and whether, working behind the scenes and through the failing and often hysterical dictator, he was now the true ruler of the Third Reich.

It was not Bormann's nature to reveal any hint of his personal feelings, except to his wife. She lived in their comfortable house near the Berghof on the Obersalzberg while he was with the Führer. To his wife, Bormann did not appear to be a sinister intriguer, but a model husband and father who was devoted to her and to Hitler.

Gerda Bormann was a loyal Nazi wife who produced ten children, one of whom died during infancy. She agreed with her husband that the Jews were responsible for most of the troubles of the world. She also agreed with him that their children must never be allowed to become infected with the "poison" of Christianity.

The Bormanns exchanged letters during his long absences, and in them she could read of his admiration and devotion. He addressed her by various terms of endearment: "My darling girl," "My Gerda darling," "Beloved, sweet, darling wife," "Mummy girl." She could read that she was the "loveliest" of women and a "glorious and wonderful woman, infinitely loveable."

There was no reason for Gerda Bormann to suspect that her husband was anything but faithful and devoted as he professed to be. And there was no reason for her to suspect that he was guilty of "filthy, deceptive, secret carryings on with the Führer," as Hermann Goering would later describe them.

In June, Hitler came to the Berghof for a few weeks. Bormann of course accompanied him. When they returned to East Prussia, Gerda Bormann wrote to her husband of "the beautiful weeks we were allowed to have together. . . . We love you so, all of us. Your Mummy and all your children."

Bormann might well have remembered those weeks with fondness, too, for once back in East Prussia, he and Hitler

Martin Bormann in the early 1930's, when he was a young Nazi official.

UPI Photo

Above, Martin Bormann in 1935, after he had become Head of the Nazi Party Chancellery, during a reception for party officials in the Reich Chancellery, Berlin. *Below,* Martin Bormann in 1944, Head of the Nazi Party Chancellery and Secretary of the Führer.

Above, Bormann's wedding, 1929. Back seat, left to right: The father of the bride, Major Walter Buch, the bride, Gerda Buch, the bridegroom, Martin Bormann. Front seat, next to driver, the witness. *Below,* Hitler and Bormann in front of Bormann's house on the Obersalzberg sometime before the war.

Martin Bormann and Rudolf Hess in 1935.

Above, a pause during the Munich Conference, 1938. Front, Hitler and Bormann. Rear, dark uniform, Himmler. *Below,* left to right: Bormann, Hitler and Joachim von Ribbentrop, Foreign Minister of the Third Reich, probably during the war.

Left to right: Bormann, General Karl Bodenschatz, Hitler's Luftwaffe adjutant, and Goering at Wolf's Lair in East Prussia, 1944.

Left to right: Goering, Hitler and Bormann at Wolf's Lair in East Prussia in July 1944, shortly after the unsuccessful attempt by a group of Army officers to kill the Führer with a bomb.

Left to right: Bormann, Field Marshall Wilhelm Keitel, Chief of the Armed Forces High Command, and Hitler, at Wolf's Lair, East Prussia, 1944.

were confronted with increasingly bleak military news. The Afrika Korps had already been destroyed in May and 275,000 Axis prisoners taken by British and American forces. Now, in July, the latter conquered Sicily and prepared to invade southern Italy. Another blitzkreig was launched in Russia on July 5. It quickly petered out, and the Red Army went over to the offensive. But on August 9, Bormann wrote to his wife: "Marvelous to see the Führer's poise in the face of the fantastic complications in the East, the South, and so on and so forth! The coming months are bound to be very difficult, now is the time to hold out with iron resolution. . . ."

Now was really the time to seek an end to the war, before Germany itself was destroyed. But Hitler, lost in his own private world of fantasy, still believed victory possible. And Bormann appeared still to believe in the Führer. Both of them remained isolated in the remote fortress of Wolf's Lair. They made no inspection visits to the front lines or to the smoking ruins of German cities which were being destroyed by air raids which the Luftwaffe could never again be strong enough to stop.

Bormann, however, was aware in an impersonal way of the destruction that the air raids were causing, for on August 2 he had written to his wife: "I have seen an enormous number of really horrifying photographs from Hamburg*, which show how the whole catastrophe happened. People could no longer stick it in the smoke-filled shelters—such a city is turned into a veritable sea of smoke—and rushed into the streets where the smoke was equally dense; there the women's silk stockings and dresses caught fire and they were burnt or choked to death, with the children . . ."

Bormann's reaction to such photographs was to advise his wife how to seek shelter on the Obersalzberg should an air raid alert ever sound there. The war continued. So did the air raids. And so did the Final Solution. Freight and cattle cars packed with Jews rounded up under the direction of SS Lieu-

---

* Some 700 Royal Air Force bombers had attacked Hamburg on the nights of July 24, 27, and 29.

tenant Colonel Adolf Eichmann, a minor bureaucrat whose identity could hardly have mattered to one so highly placed as Bormann, arrived regularly at Auschwitz, Treblinka, Sobibor, and the other death camps in the East. In them, the "shower rooms" continued to operate. From their crematories, fatty dark smoke wafted across the sky, carrying with it the stench of burning flesh. At Auschwitz, one Jew, realizing that he was doomed, wrote with his blood on the barracks walls: "Andreas Rapaport—lived sixteen years."

On October 28, Bormann wrote to his wife: "My dear little Gerda, My fondest thanks for the beautiful days you and your children gave me. I am full of happiness because of you all, because of you and each one of your children. Keep well, all of you."

One month after writing this letter, Bormann sent a directive to the Armed Forces High Command complaining about its treatment of Russian prisoners of war. The Army was not severe enough. Some of its guards had even developed attitudes of being the protectors of the captives. This was intolerable. Eventually, Bormann had the prisoners removed from Army supervision and turned over to the care of the SS.

On November 28, the day Bormann sent his directive to OKW, Stalin, Roosevelt, and Churchill began the first Big Three conference at Teheran. They knew that a difficult struggle lay ahead, but that its outcome had already been decided. The Big Three discussed the future of eastern Europe and agreed that Anglo-American forces would invade the French coast in the coming spring. A sidelight to the Teheran discussions was what to do with the Nazi leadership after the war.

Stalin's solution to the problem was simple. He favored shooting fifty thousand key officers and technicians. Churchill bridled at mass executions, but Stalin persisted. "Fifty thousand," he said, "must be shot." Perhaps forty-nine thousand would do, Roosevelt suggested, probably facetiously in an effort to relieve the tension.

No specific decision was made at Teheran concerning the postwar treatment of the Nazi leaders. But that some form of punishment awaited them was clear. The Big Three had already signed the Moscow Declaration, largely written by Churchill, which contained the warning: "Let those whose ranks are not yet stained with the blood of the innocent avoid joining the ranks of the guilty, for the three Allied powers will definitely pursue them to the furthest corners of the earth and deliver them to their judges so that justice may be done."

The Moscow Declaration further stated that:

1. War criminals who have perpetrated their crimes in a limited area will be handed over to the country concerned to be judged according to its laws.
2. War criminals whose acts cannot be localized geographically because they effect several countries will be punished by a common decision of the Allies.

The Moscow Declaration had no effect whatever on the activities of Martin Bormann. As 1944 arrived, the crucial year for the war and for Nazi Germany, he continued to behave like a man who believed that the Third Reich would survive. On May 30, 1944, he issued a secret letter to party officials prohibiting any police measures or criminal proceedings against German civilians for lynching or otherwise murdering Allied airmen who bailed out and landed on German territory.

During 1944, Bormann also turned his attention to two personal problems. One concerned Heinrich Himmler, whose growing SS empire was threatening the supremacy of Bormann and the Nazi Party. A confrontation between the two leaders was inevitable, and its result would determine who was really the second most powerful figure in the Third Reich.

Bormann's other problem concerned his "beloved, sweet, darling wife."

TEN

"Our Unshakeable Faith In Ultimate Victory"

Bormann occasionally found it necessary to leave the Führer's side in East Prussia and fly to Berlin to attend to business there at the Party Chancellery building. During one such trip, in October 1943, he had become involved with a young and minor motion-picture actress whose fiancé had been killed in action. She was acquainted with both Bormanns. Upon meeting her again in Berlin, Martin Bormann felt attracted to her. The result of this attraction was, eventually, described to his wife in a letter which he wrote to her on January 21, 1944:

> I kissed her without further ado and quite scorched her with my burning joy. I fell madly in love with her. I arranged it so that I met her again many times, and then I took her in spite of her refusals. You know the strength of my will, against which M. was of course unable to hold out for long. Now she is mine, and now —lucky fellow!—now I am, or rather, I feel doubly and unbelievably happily married . . . What do you think, beloved, of your crazy fellow?

Gerda Bormann responded to this news three days later like a model Nazi wife: "I am so fond of M. myself that I simply cannot be angry with you, and the children too love her very much, all of them." Frau Bormann considered it a "thousand pities" that M. should be denied children because her fiancé had been killed. She felt that her husband would be able to alter this situation. "But then," she wrote, "you will have to see to it that one year M. has a child, and the next year I, so that you will always have a wife who is mobile."

Bormann found this a "wild idea," but his wife was serious. "We'll put all the children together in the house on the lake," she wrote, "and live together, and the wife who is not having a child will always be able to come and stay with you in Obersalzberg or Berlin." To this proposal, Bormann replied: "That would never do! Even if the two women were the most intimate friends. Each stays by herself. Visits, all right, but even that without exaggeration."

So understanding was Gerda Bormann, and so imbued was she with the Nazi doctrine of producing large numbers of suitably Aryan children, that she made a further proposal to her husband on February 10. She did not want the mothers of illegitimate children to have a status inferior to that of legally married women, and proposed that her husband should contract a *Volksnotehe* (National Emergency Marriage) with M. This was a scheme conjured up by Frau Bormann to legalize bigamy, as she believed had been done during the Thirty Years' War because of manpower losses.

Martin Bormann did not act on his wife's proposal, but it did serve to increase her esteem with him. When she wrote to ask if M. really loved him, he replied: "I believe she loves me very much. Of course it doesn't go so deep as our love does; fifteen years of one's youth, rich in shared experience, and ten children weigh heavily in the scales."

Almost to the end of the war, when time infrequently permitted, Bormann would maintain his relationship with M. But she disappointed him in many ways, as his wife did not. M. was fuzzy on the principles of National Socialism, displayed unfortunate leanings toward Christianity, was frightened by air raids, and showed signs of boredom and restlessness. Bormann sent the letters which she wrote to him, and copies of the letters he wrote to her, to his wife. From time to time, Gerda Bormann entertained M. or telephoned her in an effort to clarify her thinking about the war and stiffen her spirit.

Bormann's problem concerning "Uncle Heinrich" Himmler was not so easily solved. Himmler had, to all appearances, become the second most powerful figure in Nazi Germany by 1944. His SS empire embraced all police agencies from the Gestapo to the regular Order Police (Orpo). The SS ran the concentration and extermination camps and Himmler could thus literally decide between life and death for millions of people, more so than any single individual yet known to history. In 1944, Himmler also gained control of the Army's *Abwehr* (military counterintelligence service), the prisoner-of-war camps and the long-range rocket program, and became Commander in Chief of the Reserve Army. And under his personal command were thirty-eight combat divisions of the *Waffen* (Armed) SS. These highly trained, fanatically indoctrinated units numbering some half million specially selected men could be relied upon to fight to the death when required to do so.

No Nazi leader possessed greater tangible power than Heinrich Himmler. Had he chosen to use it to oust Hitler himself, he probably could have done so. As for Bormann, any struggle between him and the Reichsführer SS would have appeared to be heavily weighted in Himmler's favor. Except that Bormann had one thing in his favor that Himmler did not: He had the ear of the Führer.

Bormann and Himmler were bound to clash after Himmler had received still another appointment, Minister of the Interior, in August 1943. By then, Bormann controlled all internal affairs in Germany through the Nazi Party and the Gauleiter who were under his orders. Bormann did not intend to relinquish any of his power to Himmler and his SS, but he was prudent enough not to confront the Reichsführer SS openly. He set out to stalemate "Uncle Heinrich" by playing on his weaknesses. One of these involved Himmler's attitude toward money and children.

Where those whom he considered racially pure were concerned, Himmler did everything he could to encourage procreation. He had a genuine affection for children, especially blond children, and he was himself a good family man. The weakness that Bormann detected stemmed from the fact that the Reichsführer SS had two families.

Himmler had married Margarete Concerzowo, a nurse of Polish origin who was seven years his senior, when he was operating a small poultry farm outside of Munich in 1928. The following year, the daughter Gudrun, the only child of this marriage, was born. But as Himmler's prestige and power increased, he gradually became estranged from his wife. His official residence was in Berlin. Margarete lived with Gudrun at Gmünd on the shores of Lake Tegernsee in the Bavarian Alps.

During the war, Himmler's personal secretary became his mistress. She bore him a son and a daughter.* She was the great love of Himmler's life. But because of his affection for Gudrun and his desire to set a good example, the Reichsführer SS chose not to divorce his wife. Rather he maintained two households, one at Gmünd, the other in Berchtesgaden for his secretary and her two children. This arrangement presented the Reichsführer SS with a financial burden.

Heinrich Himmler was scrupulously honest in money matters. Reich Marshal Goering could spend millions of marks on his baronial estate of Carinhall. SS guards in the extermination camps could engage in a profitable black market in the gold teeth, jewelry, and other possessions taken from those going to the shower rooms. But Himmler made a point of living within his modest official salary of some $9,000 a year.

* Himmler formally acknowledged his paternity on September 12, 1944, and had himself legally appointed coguardian of the two children.

He could have solved the financial problem of supporting two households by taking the necessary funds from any one of his numerous SS economic organizations which controlled millions of marks. This was not Himmler's way.

"He therefore asked Bormann, his greatest opponent within the Party," Walter Schellenberg later recalled, "for a loan of eighty thousand marks [roughly twenty thousand dollars] out of Party funds—a completely incomprehensible action."

Bormann advanced the money. He also exacted a usurious interest rate. "It was a completely private matter and he [Himmler] wanted to act with meticulous rectitude," according to Schellenberg. "Under no circumstances did he want to discuss it with the Führer."

Bormann, who could discuss anything with Hitler, now had something on Himmler and he waited for another opportunity to sidetrack him. That Bormann should have thought that the game was worthwhile was unusual to the point of being bizarre. The future of the Third Reich and those who would wield major power in it depended on the present ability of the German Armed Forces to win the war. That this was no longer possible was evident to the generals, to Albert Speer, the intelligent Minister for Armaments and War Production, and even to Himmler after the Allied invasion of Normandy on June 6. Three weeks after D-Day, more than a million Allied troops were ashore in France and fighting cautiously toward the western borders of the Reich.

"The Americans show themselves to be lousy soldiers," Bormann informed his wife. His opinion of the German Army was not complimentary, either. He wrote to her from Wolf's Lair on July 15:

> Surprisingly, this war shows more and more clearly that it is the Führer and his Party followers who are imbued with a savage determination to carry on with the fight and the resistance, and not the military officers, among whom it should have been the more passionate and intense, the

higher their rank. The Führer had to come here in person to stiffen the—often disgustingly weak-kneed—attitude among the officers and hence among their men. . . .

Five days after this letter was written, Colonel Claus von Stauffenberg placed a briefcase holding a time bomb under Hitler's conference table during his noonday military conference. The bomb exploded at 12:42 P.M. Hitler narrowly survived the explosion. Because he did, the attempt of certain generals and other anti-Nazis to rid Germany of Hitler and the Nazi regime through a coup d'etat failed. Had it succeeded, one of the conspirators' first steps was to have been the paralyzing of the Nazi Party through the imprisonment of all Gauleiter by local military commanders. Instead, Bormann was able to inform his Gauleiter by teleprinter at 9:20 P.M. on the day of the abortive assassination that ". . . the miscarriage of this murderous attempt signifies Germany's salvation, for now the hopes placed in the traitorous generals have been destroyed."

The failure of July 20 completed the triumph of the Nazi Party over that once mighty and independent body, the German Army. The conspirators and their families were rounded up and brutally purged, although Bormann was obliged to rescind one of his early orders to his Gauleiter to arrest all Army commanders in their areas. The Nazis still had need of the Officer Corps to win the war. But henceforth the Nazi salute was to be compulsory "as a sign of the Army's unshakeable allegiance to the Führer and of the closest unity between Army and Party." And one of Bormann's long-sought goals was also achieved. Nazi political officers were attached to all military headquarters to insure the proper indoctrination of officers and men.

But October 7 found Bormann in a depressed mood. He wrote to his wife that he was looking forward to private life when he would be pensioned off after the war. Political life had proved disappointing. "I've come to know in excess all ugliness, distortion, slander, nauseating and false flattery, toadying, ineptitude, folly, idiocy, ambition, vanity, greed for money, etc., etc., in short, all unpleasant aspects of human nature. . . . No—only as long as the Führer Adolf Hitler needs me—and then I disappear from the political scene! An irrevocable decision!"

But before this happened, the war still had to be continued and Bormann continued his intrigues for power. On October 18, he was officially appointed political and organizational leader of the *Volkssturm*. Every able-bodied man between the ages of sixteen and sixty was called up to serve in this Home Guard. In the end, the only objective achieved by this motley crew of poorly trained and ill-equipped teen-agers and old men would be the slaughter of its members.

In December, Hitler, Bormann, and their entourage moved to "Eagle's Nest," a new headquarters at Bad Nauheim. Hitler was planning a massive counterattack on the western front through the Ardennes, to take place a few days before Christmas. Bormann was still thinking of ways to sidetrack Himmler. And on December 10, Himmler was made Commander in Chief of Army Group Rhine. Both by training and natural aptitude, Himmler was grotesquely unqualified for this post. In the opinion of General Heinz Guderian, Chief of the General Staff, Bormann influenced Hitler to make the appointment in order to expose Himmler's incompetence as a field commander. Himmler did botch his assignment.

The Ardennes offensive, though initially taking the Allies by surprise, failed, too. The men and supplies which had been wasted in the west left the eastern front dangerously exposed. On January 12, 1945, one hundred and eighty divisions of the Red Army opened an offensive in Poland. On January 21, Himmler was appointed Commander in Chief of Army Group Vistula. This was an improvised formation responsible for checking the advance of the Red Army east of Berlin. Bormann secured the appointment. The Reichsführer SS was thus kept far from Hitler's presence and once again was exposed as an incompetent commander. By January 30, Red Army spearheads reached the Oder River, fifty miles from Berlin. Himmler had to be replaced with a professional army officer, Colonel General Gotthard Heinrici.

On that same date, Albert Speer sent a report to Hitler which began: "The war is lost . . ." The Führer had it filed. In the middle of February, Speer decided to assassinate Hitler, Bormann, and Goebbels. The Propaganda Minister, having realized that the Führer would not seek a compromise peace, had also become the advocate of total war.

"I thought there was no other way out," Speer later said. "In my despair I wanted to take this step as it had been obvious to me since the beginning of February that Hitler intended to go on with the war at all costs, ruthlessly and without consideration for the German people. It was obvious to me that in the loss of the war he connected his own fate with that of the German people as well. It was also obvious that the war was lost so completely that even unconditional surrender would have to be accepted."

By this time, Hitler and his immediate entourage had moved into a series of bunkers underneath the Reich Chancellery in Berlin. No one could enter the Führer's bunker without first being examined for weapons or explosives by SS guards. But as an architect who knew the bunker intimately, Speer remembered that it had an air-conditioning plant. It was his plan to introduce poison gas into the ventilator, which was in the Reich Chancellery garden. But after Speer obtained the gas, he inspected the ventilator in the middle of March only to discover that it had recently been surrounded by a chimney four meters high on Hitler's personal order.

Speer had to abandon his assassination plan. But on March 18, he presented to the Führer another report. This emphasized that the war could not be continued for more than two months. "If the war is lost," Hitler responded, "the nation will also perish. This fate is inevitable. There is no necessity to take into consideration the basic requirements of the people for continuing a most primitive existence . . ."

The next day, Hitler issued his *Nero-Befehl* (Nero Order).

According to Speer, this called for the demolition of "all industrial plants, all important electrical facilities, water works, gas works . . . all food and clothing stores . . . the military authorities [were to] destroy all bridges, all railway installations, postal systems, communications systems in the German railway, also the waterways, all ships, all freight cars and all locomotives . . ." The destruction of everything not assigned to the military was to be carried out by Bormann's Gauleiter.

On March 23, Bormann himself issued a decree to his Gauleiter. All Germans, as well as foreign workers and prisoners of war, were to be brought from the East and the West to the still unoccupied central areas of the Reich. "These millions of people," Speer later said, "were to be sent on their trek on foot. No provisions for their existence had been made, nor was it possible to do so in view of the situation. The carrying out of Bormann's orders would have resulted in an unimaginable hunger catastrophe."

These orders, however, were not completely executed as the result of two factors. One was the quick overrunning of the areas in question by Allied troops. The other was Speer's action in gaining the cooperation of a number of local Army commanders in preventing Bormann's Gauleiter from carrying out the ordered destructions.

Speer was the only Nazi leader who dared, in the Führer's presence, to question the wisdom of his determination to continue the war. Bormann not only failed to do this, but did everything he could to ensure the continuation of the hopeless struggle.

"Bormann saw to it that Hitler was not kept informed of the real internal political situation," according to General Guderian, who was dismissed as Chief of the General Staff in March after a series of violent disputes over strategy with the Führer. "He [Bormann] prevented even the Gauleiter from seeing Hitler. Thus a grotesque state of affairs arose by which the Gauleiter . . . came to me, the representative of the military they so distrusted, and asked for help in arranging that they be allowed to see Hitler since Bormann consistently prevented them from obtaining interviews through normal Party channels.

"The sicker Hitler grew and the worse the military situation became, the fewer were the number of people who could reach the dictator. Everything had to be done through this sinister guttersnipe, Bormann, and his methods became increasingly successful.

"I had repeated angry altercations with him, because over and over again he would sabotage the taking of necessary military measures for the sake of the obscure political game that he was playing. . . ."

Guderian was not certain of what game Bormann was playing. But whatever his ultimate purposes, there was one mystery about Bormann that was easily solved. He had become the Führer's right-hand man and was able to influence him in some ways. But the secretary had never really gained the power to direct his master in making any major decisions. Bormann's power was derived from the Führer, who remained the absolute master of the Third Reich even now.

"They were all under his spell, blindly obedient to him, and with no will of their own—whatever the medical term for this phenomenon may be," Speer observed.

Bormann, in the face of oncoming disaster, certainly remained under Hitler's spell. On January 5, the Head of the Nazi Party Chancellery had written to his wife: "We must never cease to rejoice that we have our Führer, for our unshakeable faith in ultimate victory is founded in a very large measure on the fact that he exists—on his genius and rock-like determination." On February 2, he had described to her the condition of his Berlin offices: "The Party Chancellery buildings, too, are a sorry sight—all the tiles have gone, all the windows have been smashed and all the doors have been torn out. . . . All day long they have been busy clearing away glass and debris." But in a letter written the following day, Bormann refused to admit that defeat was inevitable: "Anyone who still grants that we have a chance must be a great optimist! And that is just what we are! I just cannot believe that Destiny could have led our people and our Führer so far along this wonderful road, only to abandon us now and see us disappear forever. . . ."

By April 2, however, the military situation had become so bleak that even the optimism of the Head of the Nazi Party Chancellery began to wane. On that date, he wrote in his last letter to his wife, "But we must not be downhearted; whatever comes, we are pledged to do our duty. And if we are destined, like the old Nibelungs, to perish in King Attila's hall, then we'll go to death proudly and with our heads held high! . . ."

Bormann would soon have the opportunity to live up to these words, if he stayed in Berlin. On April 16, at precisely four A.M., 20,000 Red Army guns erupted with an earsplitting, earthshaking roar at a bridgehead thirty-eight miles to the east. The bombardment signaled the beginning of the final assault on the capital of the Third Reich.

The next day, Hitler ordered a Nazi official* to go from Berlin to Bad Gastein in Austria. He was to arrange for the removal of the Nazi gold reserves from Bad Gastein to a salt mine in central Germany. Bormann then gave the official a sealed package for delivery to a place of safety. The package contained Hitler's private monologues from February 4 to April 2. As he had done with the earlier "table talk" given in East Prussia and the Ukraine, this last record of the Führer's private thoughts had been edited and annotated by Bormann for posterity. The valuable paintings, coins, and art objects intended for Hitler's museums in Linz had already been hidden in salt mines near Salzburg.

Toward midday of April 20, the British and American Air

---

* Fearing difficulties with the Allies, the official wished to retain his anonymity. His story, however, is accepted as authentic by H. R. Trevor-Roper in his introduction to *The Testament of Adolf Hitler—The Hitler Bormann Documents, February-April 1945. London, 1961.* This constituted an English translation of the documents, photographic copies of which were discovered in Germany after the war.

Forces bombed the center of Berlin for almost two hours in clear, sunny weather. Field Marshal Keitel observed the bombers "parading overhead in tight formation as though it were a peacetime air display, dropping the bombs in perfect unison." Red Army ground units reached the eastern suburbs, and began to encircle the city.

But as April 21 arrived, Hitler made no move to leave Berlin and Bormann, as usual, remained at the Führer's side. There was, despite the gravity of the situation, no reason for Bormann or any one else who was in the Bunker to believe that he would be trapped in it to suffer a violent death. On April 21, there were still ways out of Berlin, which was not yet completely encircled, and if it did become obvious that the Red Army was about to seal off the capital a plan would be put into effect. Hitler, along with Bormann, Keitel, and others, would go to Berchtesgaden. Resistance would then be continued by two separate commands. One would form around the Führer in the southern mountains, and the other in the northern coastal area around Kiel under Grand Admiral Karl Doenitz.

It was a feasible plan, and Bormann had every reason to believe that it would soon be executed. But here the secretary misjudged his master.

ELEVEN

The Executor

The Führer, in the face of all the evidence to the contrary, refused to admit that the fall of Berlin was inevitable. On April 21, he suddenly conceived a plan for the city's relief. Its success turned upon the ability of the 11th Panzer Army to strike immediately from north of Berlin and dislocate the Russian advance.

The 11th Panzer Army was commanded by SS Lieutenant General Fritz Steiner, a trusted holder of the Knight's Cross of the Iron Cross. All available personnel in Steiner's area were put at his disposal to reinforce his attack, which had the objective of joining up with other units coming to Berlin's relief from the southeast and southwest.

Throughout the morning of April 22, Hitler anxiously awaited news of Steiner's advance. The Führer learned that the Russians had now broken through the outer defense ring and entered northern Berlin. But no one could give him reliable news about Steiner.

There was still no word about Steiner at three in the afternoon, when the daily military conference began with Hitler on the verge of hysteria. During the conference, Hitler was told that Steiner had not launched his attack. To Steiner the reason was obvious. "I was a general," he later recalled, "without any troops."

Hitler had long ago lost confidence in the *Wehrmacht*. But now his own elite battle troops of the *Waffen SS* had, from his point of view, betrayed him. That this could happen, that Steiner could disobey a direct order, was the final blow.

The Führer went into a rage so violent that he seemed to have suffered a complete nervous breakdown. For the next five hours he shouted opinions which must have shocked Bormann and the others who heard them: the war was lost, treachery and incompetence surrounded him, his mission had failed, he would stay in Berlin and defend the city to the last and he wanted a radio broadcast made to that effect, he would shoot himself if Berlin fell.

But Hitler would not compel anyone to share his fate. Anyone who wanted to leave the Reich Chancellery, he said, was free to do so. He specifically ordered Bormann and Keitel to leave for Berchtesgaden.

Gerhard Herrgesell, one of the two stenographers assigned to the Supreme Headquarters staff, witnessed these scenes. "The really decisive conference," he later recalled, "took place late in the afternoon. It lasted only about fifteen minutes." Present for it were only Hitler, Bormann, Keitel, Jodl, Herrgesell and another stenographer named Hagen. According to Herrgesell, who preserved his transcription, "Hitler again expressed his determination to stay in Berlin, and said that he wanted to die there. He thought it would be the greatest service he could render to the honor of the German nation. In this conference his desire to stay in the Chancellery was violently opposed. Keitel spoke to him in really sharp terms, reminding him that his new attitude was contradictory to his former plans. Bormann supported Keitel no less strongly . . ."

But Hitler had meant what he said and once he had taken a fixed position there is no record of Bormann, Keitel, or any other man ever having dissuaded him from it. The Führer's decision confronted Bormann with a terrible personal dilemma. His family was in Berchtesgaden, and should the end come it would certainly be easier to escape and go into hiding from there than from an underground Bunker ringed by Red

Army troops. And of all the Nazi leaders, Bormann had the best chances of accomplishing a successful disappearance. "No one in the party or among the people knew him," Alfred Rosenberg later wrote. "Nobody could identify his name with a concept, an idea, an accomplishment, a personality."

Funds were available to finance Bormann's disappearance. His adviser for economic affairs, Dr. Helmut von Hummel, was given in Berchtesgaden a box containing 2,200 gold coins worth a considerable fortune. The gold coins had been requisitioned by von Hummel's agents from one of the salt mines near Salzburg, and would never be recovered.

But to go to Berchtesgaden without Hitler would mean abandoning the source of Bormann's power and the center of authority in the Third Reich. Isolated from reality in the Bunker, constantly exposed to the Führer's ability to awaken false hopes, Bormann might well have felt that this one man, who had survived so many crises before, could still find some way out of this one. Even if he did not, it was the Führer who would decide upon his successor and the future of Nazism.

Bormann's two principal rivals as the Führer's successor had seen Hitler for the last time during his fifty-sixth birthday celebration on April 20. Reich Marshal Goering, after being given an "icy farewell," had then left for Berchtesgaden. There, far from any battlefront, he was free to spin out any web of intrigue that he pleased.

Heinrich Himmler, still commanding the loyalty of his considerable SS forces, had gone to Hohenlychen, his retreat north of Berlin. There he resumed his peace negotiations, which he had begun in a hesitant way in February, with Count Folke Bernadotte, vice-president of the Swedish Red Cross and nephew of King Gustav V. The Reichsführer SS had now conceived a crazy idea of saving Germany from the Russians by offering to negotiate a separate peace with the British and American governments. Himmler also discussed with Norbert Masur, a representative of the Swedish section of the World Jewish Congress, the possibility of liberating those Jews still alive under SS control. The Reichsführer SS told Masur that he was willing "to let bygones be bygones." Himmler did not inform Hitler or Bormann of these undertakings.

Keitel, despite his protestations, Jodl, Speer, von Ribbentrop, and hundreds of lesser officials left the Reich Chancellery before the end. Goebbels, however, moved into the Bunker with his wife and six children at Hitler's request on the afternoon of the Führer's breakdown. As Gauleiter and Reich Defense Commissioner of Berlin, Goebbels could hardly flee the city as the battle for it approached its climax. And as the propagandist who had repeatedly assured the Berliners that the Russians would never conquer them, Goebbels found himself a prisoner of his own words. But he would have stayed despite this. For Goebbels had already begun to consider proving his devotion to the Führer by remaining with him and then killing himself if Hitler did the same.

Bormann entertained no such macabre thoughts. But as the man who had worked and intrigued to become Hitler's closest confidant, Bormann also found himself a prisoner of his previous actions. Nevertheless, he could have found an excuse to leave Hitler. Bormann saw that no attempt was made to prevent the flight of the other Nazi leaders and the bureaucrats from the various government ministries, and that Hitler did not reproach them for leaving. Moreover, Hitler had ordered Bormann to go to Berchtesgaden. To do this, which had seemed like the definite course that would be taken before the failure of the Steiner attack, or to stay, was now obviously a matter of personal choice.

The man who had once written to his wife that Hitler ". . . is really the greatest human being we know of. . . . Really, I was incredibly lucky to be called to his side," made his decision. Bormann stayed. He and Goebbels thus became the only leading Nazis to share the Führer's last days.

No more than 700 people were now with the Führer and most of them saw him rarely, if ever. These men and women were housed in a series of bunkers underneath the Old and

New Reich Chancelleries, buildings which had been turned
into fire-gutted wrecks by the bombings of the Allied Air
Forces. They were clerks, secretaries, chauffeurs, orderlies,
servants, and SS men attached to the Guard Commando, the
Führer's Escort Commando, and Battle Group Mohnke. The
latter unit, commanded by Major General of the Waffen SS
Wilhelm Mohnke, was charged with defending "Citadel," the
code name for the government quarter.

The Führer's personal Bunker consisted of eighteen small
rooms. Apart from the powerhouse, lavatories, telephone
exchange, and a single bathing room, there was a room for
Hitler's Alsatian bitch, Blondi, and Wolf, one of her puppies.
Hitler's personal valet of eleven years, Heinz Linge, occupied
another room. Eva Braun had come, at her own insistence,
from Berchtesgaden on April 15 and she occupied a combina-
tion living room and bedroom and a small dressing room. The
Führer himself had a bedroom and study, while his personal
surgeon, Dr. Ludwig Stumpfegger, was assigned a room next
to his first-aid station. Goebbels had a bedroom and an office;
his wife and six children lived in a connecting bunker of
twelve rooms which housed the kitchen, dining area, and servants' quarters. No one else was in constant personal contact
with Hitler, except Bormann.

Bormann did not sleep in the *Führerbunker,* but a short
distance away in the bunker of the Party Chancellery. He was,
however, assigned an office between that of Dr. Goebbels and
the powerhouse. This permitted him to remain close to Hitler
during the Führer's waking hours, which now comprised all
but two or three hours of each day.

Bormann's office was some fifteen feet square. Its walls of
cold gray concrete gave off a humid moldy smell typical of
new construction. Bormann also breathed the close, stale air
that pervaded the rest of the Bunker. From the powerhouse
next to him, he heard the constant clatter of the diesel engine
which supplied the power for the ventilation and electrical systems.

One of the three doors of Bormann's office opened onto Dr. Goebbels' office. Thus Bormann could keep an eye on the Propaganda Minister whom he had largely succeeded in keeping away from the Führer until recently, but with whom he was now obliged to conclude an uneasy alliance.

The second door opened onto the telephone exchange and communications center, enabling Bormann to screen all messages to the Bunker. The third door led to the conference room in which all of Hitler's staff meetings took place. And so, while his small office fifty feet below the ground was scarcely larger than the cell he had occupied twenty years before while serving sentence for his part in the Kadow murder, the Secretary of the Führer and Head of the Nazi Party Chancellery was nevertheless at the center of power of the Third Reich. That this power had shrunk to the point where its affairs were being directed from a hole in the ground was a grotesque irony which seemed to escape Bormann; he carried on business as usual.

Bormann maintained his close watch over all visitors who had business with the Führer. Most of them were minor personages who found themselves coming and going in the Bunker through an accident of fate rather than by choice. They included Hitler's two personal pilots and his chauffeur and valet; the detectives who had shielded him from assassination; secretaries; and numerous liaison officers to the Foreign Ministry and the various branches of the Armed Forces.

Hitler was content to let Bormann deal with these people. For the Führer, only the military situation was now of any importance. And to the conference room in the narrow central passage which divided the Bunker came a steady succession of military visitors. These were the last survivors of Hitler's rages at his generals, his constant shuffling of commands, and the purges which followed the July 20 anti-Nazi plot. Among them were General Wilhelm Burgdorf, Chief of the Personnel Office of the Army and Hitler's Army adjutant; Colonel General Gotthard Heinrici, commander of Army

Group Vistula, which was responsible for stopping the Red Army east of Berlin; General Hans Krebs, the last of many Chiefs of the Army General Staff; and General Helmuth Weidling, the last Commandant of Berlin.

The military situation which these officers discussed with their Führer was rapidly turning catastrophic. On April 23, Hitler had recovered his self-control after his breakdown of the previous day. He was then told that the eastern and western fronts were disintegrating and that three-fourths of Greater Berlin had been surrounded by Red Army units.

Constantly hovering at Hitler's side, Bormann listened to these reports which could mean only that the end of Nazi Germany was fast approaching. And yet he seemed much more interested in what had always been his principal concern: shielding Hitler from those who would supplant him as Führer and in so doing destroy Bormann's present position and, perhaps, future ambitions.

Goering was still Hitler's legally designated successor. And on the afternoon of April 23 Goering sent from the peaceful surroundings of Berchtesgaden a telegram to the besieged Bunker:

MY FÜHRER!—— Since you are determined to remain at your post in Fortress Berlin, do you agree that I, as your deputy, in accordance with your decree of June 29, 1941, assume immediately the total leadership of the Reich with complete freedom of action at home and abroad?

If by 10 P.M. no answer is forthcoming, I shall assume you have been deprived of your freedom of action. I will then consider the terms of your decree to have come into force and act accordingly for the good of the people and the Fatherland. You must realize what I feel for you in these most difficult hours of my life, and I am quite unable to find words to express it.

God bless you and grant that you may come here after all as soon as possible. Your loyal——HERMANN GOERING.

Goering undoubtedly felt that he had acted correctly in sending this telegram. He was well aware that Hitler was a physical and mental wreck and that Berlin could not be defended for more than another week. And around noon of April 23, General Karl Koller, Chief of Staff of the Luftwaffe, reported to Goering after having flown directly from Berlin. Koller described Hitler's collapse of the previous day, his decision to remain in Berlin and shoot himself if the city fell, and a remark that he had made, "There is no question of fighting now, there's nothing left to fight with. If it's a question of negotiating, Goering can do that better than I."

Presented with this report, Goering still did not act hastily. He conferred with a number of bureaucrats at Berchtesgaden, among them Reich Minister Hans Lammers, a legal expert, to determine if the decree of June 29, 1941, appointing Goering as the successor to Hitler was still valid. Goering feared that Hitler had changed this decree and made Bormann his successor. This was not the case, but Goering's apprehensions concerning Bormann caused him to delay action. "He is my deadly enemy," Goering said. "He's only waiting for his chance to liquidate me. If I act now, they'll call me a traitor. And if I don't act, I'll be reproached for having failed in the most decisive hour." Finally, Goering did act.

The Reich Marshal's telegram was first received by Bormann, as were most important messages addressed to Hitler. Bormann now went into action as though there was a future for Nazism and real power to be inherited from Hitler should he die. Above all, Bormann was determined that this power should not be inherited by Goering. As a precaution, the Reich Marshal had sent a parallel telegram to Hitler's Luftwaffe adjutant, Colonel Nicolaus von Below. Goering also requested von Below to make certain that Hitler's telegram was properly delivered and also to persuade him to fly to Berchtesgaden if this was still possible. Bormann relieved von Below of this communication and Hitler never saw it.

Bormann, wearing a look of righteous outrage, then

brought Goering's telegram to Hitler. Even before Hitler could digest and comment upon it, Bormann pointed out the passage: "If by 10 P.M. no answer is forthcoming, I shall assume that you have been deprived of your freedom of action . . ." Goering undoubtedly included this time limit because he felt that Berlin might be taken and Hitler killed at any hour; he wanted his instructions to come from Hitler himself before this happened.

Bormann, however, as always playing expertly upon the easily aroused suspicions of the Führer, branded the time limit as an ultimatum. And had not the Reich Marshal been suspected, six months before, of attempting to open peace negotiations? Now he had dared to send an ultimatum to the Führer, obviously in order to assume supreme power and capitulate while Hitler was still alive. The Reich Marshal, Bormann said, should be executed.

Thus guided, the Führer now studied the telegram. "Hitler was highly enraged," Speer later recalled, "and expressed himself very strongly about Goering. He said that he had known for some time that Goering had failed, that he was corrupt, and a drug addict." Surprisingly, Hitler added, "And yet he can negotiate the capitulation, not that it matters who does that."

Hitler would not follow Bormann's advice to have Goering shot. He did, however, authorize Bormann to draft and send the following telegram to the Reich Marshal:

YOUR ACTION REPRESENTS HIGH TREASON AGAINST THE FÜHRER AND NATIONAL SOCIALISM. THE PENALTY FOR TREASON IS DEATH. BUT IN VIEW OF YOUR EARLIER SERVICES TO THE PARTY THE FÜHRER WILL NOT INFLICT THIS SUPREME PENALTY IF YOU RESIGN ALL YOUR OFFICES. ANSWER YES OR NO.

This message was shortly followed by two more: the first rescinding Hitler's decree appointing Goering his successor, the second informing Goering that Hitler would ". . . ONLY

HAND OVER MY POWER TO WHOM AND WHEN I CONSIDER IT TO BE RIGHT. UNTIL THEN I SHALL BE IN COMMAND MYSELF."

Bormann had waited for years to ruin Goering. Now this had been accomplished, and the question of who would succeed the Führer was open. Still Bormann was not satisfied. The Reich Marshal, though stripped of all power, was still alive and at liberty. And so, on his own, Bormann radioed Lieutenant Colonels Bredow and Frank, the SS leaders in Berchtesgaden, to arrest Goering for high treason. "You will answer for this with your lives," Bormann informed the SS men.

By seven P.M. of April 23, an SS detachment had surrounded Goering's chalet on the Obersalzberg. Frank and Bredow then knocked on the door. It was opened by Robert Kropp, Goering's valet. Brushing by the valet with revolvers drawn, Frank and Bredow took Goering into custody. He was forbidden communication with his family, his staff, or the outside world. Thus the former Reich Marshal and successor to the Führer did not hear the Berlin radio next day announce that he had resigned from his offices for "reasons of health."

Field Marshal Keitel was "horrified" when he learned the facts behind Goering's resignation. These were related to him at the High Command Headquarters outside of Berlin through a telephone call from General Krebs in the Bunker. The Field Marshal protested that there must be some misunderstanding. At this, Bormann came on the telephone, shouting that Goering had been dismissed "even from his job as Chief Hunter of the Reich." The news depressed Keitel. To him, it underlined "the desperate mood in the Reich Chancellery and particularly the growing influence of Bormann."

In vain, Bormann kept urging Hitler to leave Berlin for the still untouched surroundings of Berchtesgaden. Then, on April 25, beginning at ten A.M., two successive waves of Allied bombers attacked Hitler's mountain retreat for the first time. His home, the Berghof, was destroyed during an unopposed raid lasting nearly an hour.

Goering sat in the air-raid shelter of his own nearby chalet as high explosives rained down and demolished it. He not only survived, but persuaded his SS guards to take him to an Austrian castle which he owned in Mauterndorf, a three-hour drive from Berchtesgaden.

The raid also destroyed Bormann's home. His wife then left Berchtesgaden in a bus painted with the emblem of the International Red Cross. She took her own children with her, as well as some local children she had decided to help. The entire party, dressed as ordinary refugees, reached a hiding place in a remote mountainous section of the Austrian Tyrol. This had been readied for Frau Bormann by agents of her husband.

When French and American soldiers entered the Berghof on May 4, they found a deserted, still smoldering wreck surrounded by a landscape of rubble. Intelligence officers who followed the combat troops searched the Obersalzberg area for traces of Hitler and Bormann. The agents were not certain, in the confusion of the time, that the two had not come there from Berlin. Hitler was not found. The search of Bormann's ruined Haus Göll near the Berghof yielded only a cache of rare wines, albums of classical music, and a large number of children's toys.

Later investigations also failed to discover Bormann in the Alps, but did turn up an interesting fact about him. He owned the Berghof, rather than Hitler. The entire complex of property on the Obersalzberg, consisting of eighty-seven buildings and worth over one and a half million marks, was legally registered in Bormann's name. So was Hitler's birthplace at Branau and his parents' house near Linz.

In Berlin on April 25, the day of the Obersalzberg air raid, Bormann learned around one P.M. that the Red Army had encircled the capital. Later that afternoon, Russian and American units made contact on the Elbe River seventy-five miles south of Berlin, thus cutting Germany in half. Now the only sure way to get out of Berlin and reach any of the small pockets of German forces that were still fighting was by air.

But Hitler would not go, and Bormann remained with him. The Führer carried on as usual with his daily military conferences, his moods of despair alternating with confidence. Poring over huge maps, he directed the movements of phantom armies and ordered counterattacks by forces too weak to undertake them. Hitler expressed his faith in the ability of the 12th Army commanded by General Walther Wenck to relieve Berlin, and prophesied a clash between British and American troops and their Soviet allies which could yet save Nazi Germany. A victory at the last hour was still possible.

Broken in health, his face white and his body trembling, his mental state bordering on lunacy, Hitler still retained his extraordinary ability to awaken false hopes in his remaining band of followers. And none, to all outward appearances, remained more of a believer than Martin Bormann.

Captain Gerhard Boldt, a young officer who had been wounded five times in the Russian campaign and who was now an aide to General Krebs, was approached by Bormann on the afternoon of April 27. Bormann talked to him about the early relief of Berlin by the 12th Army of General Wenck. Then Bormann said, "You, who have stayed here and kept faith with our Führer, together with him through his darkest hours, you shall, when this fight is victoriously ended, be invested with high rank in the State, and shall have huge estates in reward for your faithful service."

Boldt, who knew the true military situation, was aghast at this. "Could that stuff about 'the victorious fight' be really in his mind today, April 27?" Boldt asked himself. Did Bormann really believe what he said, or were his words "just a devilish mixture of dissimulation, megalomania, and fanatical stupidity?"

But even Bormann's faith must have begun to weaken that night. The Red Army, which had shelled the Reich Chancellery area at random the day before, now subjected it to a constant artillery barrage. Bormann could hear the massive masonry of the Reich Chancellery buildings splitting and crashing into the garden and courtyard above the Bunker. His nostrils filled with the stench of sulphur smoke and lime dust that was sucked into the Bunker through its ventilators, and he could see the thick concrete walls around him shaking. And he knew that during the day the Russians had taken Berlin's two airports, Tempelhof and Gatow. Now the only way that anyone could reasonably expect to get out of the city was a dangerous one: in a plane small enough to take off from an improvised flight strip and then elude Russian fighters and antiaircraft batteries.

Bormann remained where he was. He sat for the most part at the desk in his cell-like office, "recording the momentous events in the Bunker for posterity," according to one visitor, the test pilot Hanna Reitsch. Once compiled, Reitsch thought that Bormann intended to spirit them out so that they might take their place "among the greatest chapters of German history."

Around 2:00 A.M. of April 28, Captain Boldt, before going to bed, saw Bormann otherwise occupied. He was engaged in a drinking bout with Krebs and Burgdorf. This was surprising on two counts. Because Hitler never drank, neither did Bormann, at least when he was near the Führer. And the two generals were arguing with Bormann, even though both of them owed their present high status to Bormann's approval of their slavish fidelity to Hitler and Nazism.

Hans Krebs wore a monocle and was usually of an unperturbable nature. Before the war he had been deputy military attaché at the Embassy in Moscow, and he spoke Russian. He held his present job because of his talent for smoothing over the bleak facts of the military situation to Hitler. Wilhelm Burgdorf, as Hitler's Army adjutant, had abandoned his allegiance to the professional officer corps and thrown in his lot with the Nazis. It was Burgdorf who had personally delivered the poison to Field Marshal Rommel with which the latter had been obliged to kill himself after being incriminated in the July 20 plot.

Around 4:30 A.M., Boldt was awakened by a fellow officer to hear the climax of a noisy argument which had been going on while he slept. Boldt listened as Burgdorf, a florid-faced man who drank heavily, roared at Bormann:

"Nine months ago I approached my present task with all my strength and idealism. I tried again and again to coordinate the Party and the Forces. I have gone so far in this that I have been looked at askance, even despised by my comrades in the Forces. I have done the impossible to try to eradicate from Hitler and the Party leaders their mistrust of the Armed Forces. I have finally been called in the Forces a traitor to the officers' caste. Today I must confess that these accusations were justified, that my labors were for nought, my idealism was wrong, and not that only, but it was naïve and stupid."

Burgdorf paused, breathing heavily. Krebs attempted to calm him down, begging him to beware of Bormann. But Burgdorf told Krebs to let him alone, that all of this had to be said, that perhaps in another forty-eight hours it would be too late to do so. Burgdorf resumed railing at Bormann:

"Our young officers have taken the field with a faith and an idealism unique in the history of the world. By their hundred thousands they have gone to their death with a proud smile. But for what? For their beloved German Fatherland, for our greatness and future? For a decent clean Germany? No. They have died for you, for your life of luxury, for your thirst for power. In their faith in a good cause the youth of a people of eighty millions has bled to death on the battlefields of Europe. Millions of innocent people have been sacrificed while you, the leaders of the Party, have enriched yourselves with the property of the nation. You have feasted, have accumulated enormous wealth, have robbed estates, wallowed in abundance, have swindled and oppressed the people. Our ideals, our morals, our faith, our souls, have been trodden in the dirt by you. Man for you was nothing but the tool of your insatiable craving for power. You have annihilated the German nation. That is your terrible guilt!"

No one had ever dared to speak so harshly to Bormann,

and when Burgdorf had finished, his final sentences ringing "almost like a curse," there was a tense silence relieved only by the sound of Burgdorf's panting. Then Boldt heard Bormann, his voice "cool, premeditated, and oily", reply in a brief and uncharacteristically mild fashion: "My dear fellow, you ought not to be personal about it. Even if all the others have enriched themselves, I at least am blameless. That much I swear to you on everything that I hold sacred. Your health, my friend!"

Four days later, there would be no further toasts to Burgdorf's health; he would be found shot dead. But some seven hours after Burgdorf's diatribe against Bormann, Boldt saw them both again. The young captain went to Hitler's conference room to present a report and was greeted by the sight of Burgdorf, Bormann, and Krebs slumped in easy chairs and covered with cushions and wraps. They were asleep and snoring loudly; Hitler was obliged to pick his way over their outstretched legs to receive Boldt's report.

This report presented a bleak picture, as did all others throughout the remainder of April 28. The Red Army had fought its way into the center of Berlin, and some of its units had advanced to within a few blocks of the Reich Chancellery area. No news was received of Wenck's 12th Army, nor of any of the other exhausted, decimated forces which the occupants of the Bunker still hoped could break through the Russian ring and rescue them. General Weidling no longer believed that this was possible. He judged that the Bunker would be overrun in two days, for his battered and undermanned Berlin defense forces would then have run out of ammunition. Weidling planned to recommend to Hitler a breakout to the West at the military conference scheduled for later that evening.

Russian shells continued to explode over the Bunker, disrupting its communications network. That left as the only dependable channel of information to the outside world the radio-telephone to the headquarters of Grand Admiral Doenitz at Plön on the Baltic Coast, some 200 miles northwest of Berlin.

"The lack of fresh air became unbearable;" according to Boldt, "headaches, shortness of breath, and perspiration increased . . . the people . . . sank into a dull brooding mood." Martin Bormann, however, was not one of them. Once again active, he sent a radiogram to Doenitz at 8:00 P.M.:

INSTEAD OF URGING THE TROOPS FORWARD TO OUR RESCUE, THE MEN IN AUTHORITY ARE SILENT. TREACHERY SEEMS TO HAVE REPLACED LOYALTY. THE CHANCELLERY IS ALREADY IN RUINS.

Still there was silence about any relief forces, and Bormann sent Doenitz a second radiogram:

SCHÖRNER, WENCK AND OTHERS MUST PROVE THEIR LOYALTY TO THE FÜHRER BY COMING TO THE FÜHRER'S AID AS SOON AS POSSIBLE.

There was no reply to this. Doenitz' own command of the remaining armies in the north was rapidly being closed in upon by British and Canadian forces. Both Doenitz and the members of the Combined General Staff who had joined him knew that no German forces existed that were capable of relieving Berlin.

Hitler and Bormann could not know this for certain. Because of the communications breakdown, they had no true picture of what was going on outside the underground world of the Bunker. Since entering it, neither of them had even bothered to go out and inspect the fighting in Berlin itself.

Finally, at 9:00 P.M., sensational news from the outside world came. It did not concern any relief forces and it confirmed Hitler's earlier decision to kill himself. Nevertheless, the news must have given Bormann some moments of intense satisfaction. He was sitting in the waiting room before the Führer's conference room when Heinz Lorenz of the Propaganda Ministry appeared. Lorenz was responsible for monitoring foreign news media. He had with him copies of a British Reuters radio dispatch which he thought important enough to show to Hitler.

The Führer was busy in conference, so Lorenz gave translated copies of the dispatch to Bormann, Goebbels, and Walter Hewel of the Foreign Office. Bormann read that Heinrich Himmler had offered to surrender Germany unconditionally to the British and American governments, but not to Russia.

Goering had already been eliminated as Hitler's successor. Now, because of a leakage to the Press which gave away to the occupants of the Bunker for the first time Himmler's negotiations with Count Bernadotte, the Reichsführer SS, Minister of the Interior, and Chief of All German Police had also been eliminated. Bormann knew this and there was no need for him to interpret the meaning of the intercepted dispatch to Hitler. Bormann, however, did see to it that a copy was immediately given to the Führer by his valet, Heinz Linge.

Hitler's reaction has been variously described by surviving witnesses. Whether he "raged like a madman" or took the news with an almost stupefied resignation, there is no doubt that what was for him the unexpected treachery of "The Loyal Heinrich" signaled the end. He retired into private conference with Goebbels and Bormann. No record of it survives, but, judging from the events which now swiftly followed, the conference concerned the leadership of Nazi Germany after Hitler was dead.

Shortly before midnight, Goebbels, Bormann, and Hitler emerged for the evening military conference. General Weidling presented a carefully worked out plan for a breakout from the Bunker with the Führer protected by forty tanks. Hitler was not interested. "Your plan is good," he said to Weidling. "But what's the use of it all? Even if we succeeded we would only be going from one caldron to another. It is not my wish to be captured while running around in some woods or other."

There would be no breakout, and no capitulation. Hitler next went to visit Goering's replacement as Commander in Chief of the Luftwaffe, Ritter von Greim, who had been shot

in the right foot while flying into Berlin in a light plane. Now
Hitler asked von Greim to fly out again. He was to rally Luft-
waffe support for the ground forces which might still relieve
Berlin and also to make certain that Himmler was arrested.
"A traitor must never succeed me," the Führer said. Von
Greim did manage to fly out of Berlin, but to no purpose for
he lacked the means to discharge either of his assignments.

After leaving von Greim, Hitler defined his relationship of
thirteen years with Eva Braun to the extent of marrying her.
Sixteen years before, Hitler witnessed Bormann's marriage.
Now Bormann was one of the two witnesses to Hitler's marriage; the other was Goebbels. No one else was present, except
for one Walter Wagner, who performed the ceremony around
1:00 A.M. of April 29.

Wagner was a thirty-eight-year-old minor Nazi official in
the Berlin legal administration who was picked at random and
hastily summoned to officiate. He had never seen the Führer
before, nor heard of Eva Braun, and he was not invited to the
reception. Wagner left the Bunker to join a Volkssturm unit
and the next day was killed in action. His widow would later
read a copy of the marriage certificate and say, "Just look. It
was Walter who married Hitler. One can see from his handwriting how excited he was."

Champagne was served to those invited to the reception:
Bormann, Goebbels and his wife, and Hitler's secretaries,
Frau Christian and Frau Junge. Burgdorf, Krebs and a few
others from time to time dropped in on this bizarre celebration, during which the bridegroom reminisced about his past
life and spoke of his present plans for suicide. Around 2:00
P.M., Hitler excused himself and in an adjoining room began
dictating his political testament and personal will to Frau
Junge.

The documents were finished at 4:00 A.M. Bormann,
Goebbels, Krebs, and Burgdorf signed the political testament
as witnesses. In its first part, Hitler avowed that "international
Jewry and its helpers" were responsible for the war and the

troubles that had ensued from it. He also formally expelled
Goering from the Nazi Party and withdrew his rights to succes-
sion. Grand Admiral Doenitz was appointed President of the
Reich and Supreme Commander of the Armed Forces.

In the second part of the testament, Hitler expelled Himmler from the Nazi Party and from all of his offices. "Goering
and Himmler," the Führer dictated, "by their secret negotiations with the enemy, without my knowledge or approval, and
by their illegal attempts to seize power in the state have
brought irreparable shame on the country and the whole
people, quite apart from their disloyalty to my own person."

Hitler felt that he knew who had remained loyal. In the new
cabinet of Doenitz, he named Goebbels as Reich Chancellor.
As Party Minister, the man who would be most directly concerned with the future of Nazism, Hitler named Martin Bormann.

The Führer further noted that although a number of the
men whom he had appointed to the new cabinet, "like Martin
Bormann, Dr. Goebbels, etc. . . . stayed with me of their own
free will and under no circumstances wanted to leave the capital of the Reich, but rather were prepared to die here with me,
I must nevertheless ask them to obey my directions and in this
case put the interests of the nation over their own feelings."

In the brief personal will which followed the political testament, Hitler directed that: "My possessions, in so far as they
are worth anything, belong to the Party, or if this should no
longer exist, to the State. Should the State also be destroyed,
further instructions on my part will no longer be necessary . . ."

As his executor, Hitler would naturally select the man
whom he judged to be his most trusted and reliable disciple.
And the executor, by the nature of his function, would be
expected to survive the testator.

"As executor," the Führer directed, "I appoint my most
faithful Party comrade, Martin Bormann. He is given full
legal authority to make all decisions. He is permitted to hand

over to my relatives everything which is of worth as a personal memento, or is necessary to maintain a petty-bourgeois standard of living; especially to my wife's mother and my faithful fellow workers of both sexes who are well known to him. The chief of these are my former secretaries, Frau Winter, etc., who through their work gave me support through the years."

For Hitler, the end had come. In the last paragraph of his will, he explained why: "My wife and I choose to die in order to escape the shame of deposition or capitulation. It is our wish that our bodies be burnt immediately in the place where I have performed the greater part of my daily work during the course of a twelve-year service to my people."

Bormann signed the will as a witness. So did Goebbels and Colonel von Below. Hitler, having formalized his decision, retired to rest. This Bormann and Goebbels could not do. Both had their own decisions to make about the future.

TWELVE

"The Situation in Berlin Is More Tense"

Dr. Joseph Goebbels went to his own quarters to think, and then to compose his "Appendix to the Führer's Political Testament."

"The Führer has ordered me," he wrote, "should the defense of the Reich capital collapse, to leave Berlin, and to take part as a leading member in a government appointed by him.

"For the first time in my life I must categorically refuse to obey an order of the Führer . . . In the delirium of treachery which surrounds the Führer in these most critical days of the war, there must be someone who will stay with him unconditionally until death . . . I express an unalterable resolution not to leave the Reich capital, even if it falls, but rather, at the side of the Führer, to end a life which will have no further value to me if I cannot spend it in the service of the Führer, and by his side . . . ."

Bormann, too, decided to remain with Hitler until he was dead. But he was not going to kill himself. Hitler had directed him to survive and to carry on with the Nazi administration and policies, and this Bormann would attempt to do.

But first there was the matter of eliminating Goering. In the midst of the chaos surrounding him, Bormann took the time to send a telegram to his agents in Berchtesgaden:

THE SITUATION IN BERLIN IS MORE TENSE. IF BERLIN AND
WE SHOULD FALL, THE TRAITORS OF 23RD APRIL MUST BE
EXTERMINATED. MEN, DO YOUR DUTY! YOUR LIFE AND
HONOR DEPEND UPON IT!

Fortunately for Goering, he had been removed from
Berchtesgaden, which Bormann had no way of knowing, and
was thus spared execution there by the SS.

Bormann then took up the problem of delivering Hitler's
political testament and will to Doenitz. He summoned his personal assistant of many years, SS Colonel Wilhelm Zander,
and gave him copies of the documents with a scribbled
covering note:

> DEAR GRAND ADMIRAL,——Since all divisions failed to ar-
> rive, and our position seems hopeless, the Führer dictated
> last night the attached political Testament. Heil Hitler.
> ——yours, BORMANN.

Zander would be faced with making a hazardous journey of
200 miles on foot. Even if he did accomplish it, which was
doubtful, it would take him at least a week. Nevertheless,
though he could easily have done so, Bormann did not radio
the news of Doenitz' appointment to him immediately. It was
the first in a devious series of actions which Bormann now
undertook with the Grand Admiral.

Heinz Lorenz of the Propaganda Ministry was also given
copies as Goebbels' representative and told to find his way to
Doenitz. A third set of documents was entrusted to an army
major, Willi Johannmeier. He was instructed to deliver them
to the newly appointed Commander in Chief of the Army,
Field Marshal Ferdinand Schörner, whose army group in the
Bohemian mountains was still intact.

Around noon of April 29, Zander, Lorenz, and Johannmeier departed the Reich Chancellery. Before he left, Zander
telephoned Bormann's office to wish him good-bye. The gesture evoked only the testy question of why he had not left
already and he was ordered to do so at once.

Zander and Lorenz were unable to reach Doenitz, nor did Major Johannmeier reach Schörner. But all three messengers did manage to slip through the nearly two and one half million Russian troops who occupied all but a few square miles of Greater Berlin. Moving slowly through forests and across lakes and rivers, they survived a wild series of adventures and eventually found themselves in central Germany. In this area occupied by British and American troops, they succeeded in passing themselves off as foreign workers.

Zander wandered on foot to his native Bavaria. First he went to Munich and then forty miles south to the lakeside village of Tegernsee, where his documents were hidden. The personal assistant to Martin Bormann assumed a disguise and began a new life. SS Colonel Wilhelm Zander became a Bavarian market-gardener named Friedrich-Wilhelm Paustin.

In the Bunker itself, the end was fast approaching. Around 2:30 A.M. of April 30, about twenty members of Hitler's service staff, most of them women, were summoned to line up in the central dining passage. Accompanied by Bormann, Hitler emerged from his private quarters. His eyes glazed with a film of moisture, the Führer tottered down the line. With some he shook hands, to others he mumbled words that could not be understood. It was a farewell ceremony and after completing it, Hitler returned to his quarters.

For Bormann, who was plainly thinking of survival rather than death, there was work to do. Around 3:30 A.M. of April 30, he sent a radiogram to Doenitz:

> Fresh treachery afoot. According to enemy broadcast Himmler has made offer to surrender via Sweden. Führer expects you to take instant and ruthless action against traitors.

This was followed by another radiogram:

> DOENITZ!——Our impression grows daily stronger that the divisions in the Berlin theater have been standing idle for

several days. All the reports we receive are controlled, suppressed, or distorted by Keitel. In general we can only communicate through Keitel. The Führer orders you to proceed at once, and mercilessly, against all traitors.——BORMANN.

To this message, which still contained no word of Doenitz' appointment, Bormann added a postscript which seemed to deny the approaching end: "The Führer is alive, and is conducting the defense of Berlin."

At his headquarters in the quietly picturesque coastal village of Plön, Grand Admiral Karl Doenitz found himself puzzled by Bormann's messages.

"How could I be expected to 'take instant and ruthless action' against the Reichsführer," Doenitz wondered, "who had the whole of the Police and the SS at his disposal?"

Himmler was indeed in the northern coastal area, and he was accompanied by his sinister SS entourage. The Grand Admiral and his staff had no armed guards, and he had received no authority enabling him to take action against Himmler. Furthermore, Doenitz expected Himmler to be named head of state within a few days and had already offered his services to the Reichsführer SS if the latter were legally appointed. "That I myself might be entrusted with the task," Doenitz later recalled, "had never entered my head."

Doenitz' modesty was understandable. Since 1912, the Navy had been his whole life. He had served in U-boats in the First World War and, as an acknowledged submarine expert, had been appointed Commander in Chief of the Navy in January 1943. While Doenitz was not an ardent Nazi, he found much that was good in the party's aims, admired Hitler, and served him with unquestioning loyalty. But he had no experience whatever in either domestic or international politics.

To Hitler, this apparently surprising choice must have seemed completely logical. After he was dead, the Führer wanted the war to be continued and he knew that the Armed Forces would not continue to fight under the command of party civilians like Bormann and Goebbels. A respected senior officer could, however, command obedience. But the Luftwaffe and the SS were directed by traitors. For the officer caste of the Army, Hitler had only contempt. The relatively small Navy, however, had proved efficient and loyal, as had its Commander in Chief. The latter furthermore was in an area where he still possessed freedom of movement. Why not then Doenitz?

Bormann must have asked himself the same question and answered it easily. Cooped up in the besieged Bunker, he was hardly in a position to succeed the Führer himself. And it would be far better to burden Doenitz with continuing the war and, if it came to that, negotiating a peace settlement. The Grand Admiral was also a political neophyte. Once Hitler and Goebbels were dead, he would require the indispensable services of one experienced in political matters, one who would remain in the background while guiding the figurehead into the right Nazi channels. Under Doenitz, it would still be possible for Bormann to exercise the power to which he had grown so accustomed.

Even now Bormann was behaving toward Doenitz as though the Grand Admiral were a figurehead to be manipulated. The messengers had not reached Doenitz, nor did he even know of their existence. And by 3:00 P.M. of April 30, more than thirty-five hours after Hitler had completed his political testament, Bormann had still not bothered to radio any hint to Doenitz that he was the Führer's successor.

Bormann had apparently decided that Doenitz must wait until Hitler was dead. Then the Grand Admiral would learn of his elevation from his new Party Minister. Thus would Bormann's place in the new government be firmly established from the outset.

But time was running short. For Bormann's maneuvers to succeed, Hitler would have to kill himself before the Russians stormed the Bunker and eliminated any chance of Bormann's escape and survival.

Hitler began what would be his last military conference at noon, April 30. He was told that Red Army units were a block from the Bunker.

The Russians knew that Hitler was in Berlin, for this news had been broadcast over the German radio. But they did not know that he was in a Bunker underneath the Old Reich Chancellery. Had they known this exact location, they could already have taken it. Now, however, it was obvious that random units would come upon the Bunker the following day at the latest.

After the conference, Hitler quietly took his usual vegetarian lunch. Bormann ordered Colonel Otto Günsche, the Führer's six-foot-four-inch SS adjutant, to have as much gasoline as was available brought to the Bunker entrance. Günsche relayed the order by telephone to Erich Kempka, Hitler's personal driver of thirteen years, who was in charge of the motor pool. Kempka wondered why the gasoline was needed. He protested that a great deal of it would be difficult to obtain, but Günsche was insistent.

Hitler finished lunch around two-thirty. Accompanied by Eva Braun, he then began another farewell ceremony. The Führer shook hands with each of those people who would be the last to see him alive. Those who had remained to the end were few.

Bormann, Goebbels, Krebs, and Burgdorf were among them. So were Günsche; SS Brigadier General Johann Rattenhuber, chief of the detective bodyguard; his deputy, SS Colonel Hoegl; Hitler's secretaries, Frau Junge and Frau Christian; his cook, Fräulein Manzialy; and his valet, Heinz Linge. Also present were Werner Naumann, State Secretary in the Propaganda Ministry; Ambassador Walter Hewel, liaison to the Foreign Office; and Vice-Admiral Erich Voss, liaison to Doenitz.

The only other person present at the farewell was Bormann's secretary, Fräulein Else Kruger, a thirty-year-old native of Hamburg. As Head of the Nazi Party Chancellery,
Bormann had once required the services of four secretaries.
One was left, and she was not very busy, for Bormann had
taken to writing his own orders and wireless messages by
hand. "All I had to do," Fräulein Kruger later recalled, "was
to prepare myself mentally for my death."

Hitler had already done this. After completing his farewells,
he retired to his private suite with Eva Braun, leaving the
others to work out their own fates.

Bormann then ordered all but a few of the last visitors out
of the Bunker. The valet Linge went to his own small room.
Goebbels and Burgdorf waited in the central passage. Günsche and Bormann took up positions outside the closed door
of the anteroom leading to the Führer's suite.

"Where would we be without him?" Bormann had once
asked his wife.

The answer to that question came at 3:30 P.M. Bormann
heard a single pistol shot. He was the first person to rush
into Hitler's suite, according to Günsche, who followed with
Linge.

Bormann was nearly overpowered by the smell of cyanide
which Eva Hitler had used to poison herself. She was in the
right corner of a small sofa. Bormann saw Hitler sprawled on
its left corner, blood dripping from his shattered face. There
was a pistol on the table in front of him, and another one on
the rug beneath the table. Bormann, according to Günsche,
could find nothing to say. Nor did he issue any orders.

Günsche himself hurried out to the central passage. There
he saw Erich Kempka, who had just arrived to report that
jerricans containing some fifty gallons of gasoline had been
placed at the Bunker entrance. Günsche told a stunned
Kempka that Hitler was dead, and why the gasoline had been
so urgently needed.

Linge and Dr. Stumpfegger, Hitler's surgeon, carried his

body, which was wrapped in an army blanket to hide the face, upstairs to the Chancellery garden.

Bormann came next, carrying in his arms the unmarked body of Eva Hitler. The sight shook Erich Kempka. "Eva had hated Bormann," he later recalled. "He had caused her a lot of trouble. She had known for a long time about his intrigues for power. Now in death her greatest enemy was bearing her to her final resting place. She must not remain in Martin Bormann's arms for another step." Kempka went up to Bormann and, without a word being exchanged, took the corpse from him.

The bodies of Hitler and his bride were placed in shallow depressions just outside the Bunker entrance. Then they were drenched with gasoline by Günsche, Linge, and Kempka as Russian shells exploded in the garden.

From the Bunker entrance, Bormann, Goebbels, and Dr. Stumpfegger watched silently as Günsche flung a burning rag toward the graves. The bodies were embraced by a sheet of flame which mushroomed over them. As the flames rose higher in the April air, and the Russian barrage increased in tempo, Bormann and the five others stood to attention and thrust out their right arms in the Nazi salute.

Günsche, Kempka, and Linge continued to pour gasoline, so that the Führer might have his wish not to have his remains exhibited at a Russian freak show. Bormann and Goebbels did not linger at this macabre scene. They went downstairs to the conference room of the Bunker. It was up to them now to decide what should be done next.

Burgdorf, Krebs, Naumann, and a few others were in the conference room, as was Artur Axmann. He was the leader of the Hitler Youth which had been thrown into the defense of Berlin. Axmann was a pudgy fellow of thirty-two and a native Berliner. He had lost his right arm in Russia three years before. Looking at Bormann, Axmann noted that his face was flushed.

"Did this mean," Axmann wondered, "that he was inwardly

agitated for all his apparent self-control? His closeness to Hitler had been Bormann's power. Now, Hitler was dead, and so was Bormann's power."

Bormann himself apparently did not think so. He did not immediately scurry out of the Bunker in an attempt to reach Doenitz or some other more obscure destination, while time remained to do so. Rather, he and the new Reich Chancellor, Dr. Joseph Goebbels, began to concoct a plan.

But first, before putting the plan into operation, Bormann must send some clarifying word to Doenitz. And around six P.M., as the flames continued to consume Hitler, Bormann did send a radiogram:

> GRAND ADMIRAL DOENITZ——IN PLACE OF THE FORMER REICH MARSHAL HERMANN GOERING THE FÜHRER APPOINTS YOU, HERR GRAND ADMIRAL, AS HIS SUCCESSOR. CONFIRMATION IN WRITING IS ON ITS WAY. YOU ARE HEREBY AUTHORIZED TO TAKE ANY MEASURES WHICH THE SITUATION DEMANDS.——BORMANN.

"This took me completely by surprise," Doenitz later recalled. He sent a radiogram to the Bunker and addressed it to the Führer:

> MY LOYALTY TO YOU WILL BE UNCONDITIONAL. I SHALL DO EVERYTHING POSSIBLE TO RELIEVE YOU IN BERLIN. IF FATE NEVERTHELESS COMPELS ME TO RULE THE REICH AS YOUR APPOINTED SUCCESSOR, I SHALL CONTINUE THIS WAR TO AN END WORTHY OF THE UNIQUE, HEROIC STRUGGLE OF THE GERMAN PEOPLE.

Bormann took this message. On his own, he had deliberately neglected to inform Doenitz that Hitler was dead and that the Grand Admiral was therefore already the legal head of state. But this key omission was all part of the plan.

Goebbels and Bormann had decided that the time had come, not to capitulate to the Russians, but to negotiate with them. General Krebs, who spoke Russian, was selected as the negotiator. He was authorized to tell the Russian military authorities that Hitler was dead and to give them the names of those who had been appointed to the new government. He was also to deliver a letter written and signed by Goebbels and Bormann which contained the same information and was addressed to Stalin. Principally, Krebs was authorized to negotiate a truce so that the new government might form and undertake further negotiations.

The plan was fantastic. The Russians had nothing to gain from anything except an unconditional surrender. Goebbels and Bormann were trapped in the Bunker, and the Russians could capture them any time after they learned its exact location. But in going ahead with this final spasm of fantasy at the expense of reality, Goebbels had nothing to lose. If the truce proposal failed, he was prepared to carry out his earlier decision to kill himself.

The situation was different for Bormann. He was determined to live. If the plan succeeded, he would be recognized as an accredited member of the new government and perhaps be given a safe-conduct out of Berlin. Then he could undertake the journey to Doenitz as a privileged emissary.

But pending the reaction of the Russians to Krebs's mission, Bormann still had to withhold word of Hitler's death from Doenitz. The fear which Bormann had inspired, and the power which he had exercised, had issued from his unique proximity to the Führer. If Doenitz knew that Hitler was dead, he might not be willing to accept Bormann as his adviser. Doenitz might even enlist the services of Himmler to form a government which excluded Bormann.

The Russians were contacted by radio and agreed to receive a German representative. Around midnight, Krebs set out on foot across the ruins to enter the Russian lines at a point they had specified. He was accompanied by two soldiers, an interpreter, and Colonel Theodor von Dufving, Chief of Staff to the Berlin Commandant, General Weidling.

Krebs was a thickset man of middling height. His head was

shaved and his face was covered with freshly healed scars received during an air raid in March. He wore a leather overcoat, and around his neck an Iron Cross. But for this journey the last Chief of the Army General Staff did not wear his customary monocle.

Once Krebs had left, Goebbels and Bormann could do nothing but wait for some response to his mission. By dawn of the next day, May 1, they had heard nothing from Krebs or the Russians. At 7:40 A.M., Bormann, with understandable impatience, dispatched another of his cryptic messages to Plön:

> Grand Admiral Doenitz (Secret and Personal).
> Will now in force. Coming to you as quickly as possible. Pending my arrival you should in my opinion refrain from public statement.——Bormann.

Doenitz, of course, knew nothing about any will. He still had not been told that Hitler was dead. And Bormann, in fact, was not coming to him "as quickly as possible." For Bormann had decided to wait for some word from Krebs.

Word came in the middle of the morning, when Colonel von Dufving reappeared in the Bunker. He and Krebs had been received by Colonel General Vasili Chuikov, commander of the Eighth Guards Army, and Krebs was still negotiating with Chuikov. Krebs was not making much progress, for the Russian position was simple and adamant; they would accept only the immediate and unconditional capitulation of Berlin and of those in the Bunker.

Von Dufving looked at Goebbels and found him calm and without any outward sign of fear. In contrast, the Colonel had the feeling that Bormann was quivering and concerned only about his own life. But neither Goebbels nor Bormann would agree to a surrender. Krebs was recalled. When he reappeared in the Bunker around noon, he could only repeat what von Dufving had already reported.

This signaled the end for Goebbels. He began to make preparations for his suicide. Bormann began to plan his escape from the Bunker. But first Doenitz must at last be notified of the realities of the situation. There was no longer any point in withholding information from him, and so at 2:46 P.M., nearly twenty-four hours after Hitler's suicide, a radiogram was dispatched to Plön:

> GRAND ADMIRAL DOENITZ (Personal and Secret). To be handled only by an officer.
> Führer died yesterday, 1530 hours. In his will dated April 29 he appoints you as President of the Reich, Goebbels as Reich Chancellor, Bormann as Party Minister, Seyss-Inquart as Foreign Minister. The will, by order of the Führer, is being sent to you and to Field Marshal Schörner and out of Berlin for safe custody. Bormann will try to reach you today to explain the situation. Form and timing of announcement to the Armed Forces and the public is left to your discretion. Acknowledge.——GOEBBELS, BORMANN.

Now Doenitz at last knew that Hitler was dead and that he was free to act as his own man. Doenitz also read that Bormann was trying to reach him to "explain the situation." About this part of the plan, Doenitz had his own ideas. He began to disassociate himself from the more unsavory of the remaining Nazi paladins. The day before he had told Himmler that there was no way in which he "could make any use" of the further services of the Reichsführer SS. Now Doenitz ordered the arrest of Goebbels and Bormann should they appear in Plön.

"In the grave situation in which we found ourselves," Doenitz later recalled, "I could not afford to burden myself with interference from anyone."

Bormann was apparently determined to reach Plön. He was, of course, unaware of the reception which awaited him. None of the Bunker survivors can recall Bormann mentioning any other goal. But then Bormann had confided only in Hitler, and if he did have some other plan in mind he would not have jeopardized it by divulging its details.

This much was certain: Bormann wanted to get out of Berlin alive, and the last chance to do it had come. There had been one tangible result of Krebs's mission. The Russians for the first time had a good idea of where the Bunker was and who was in it. Their artillery fire into the Reich Chancellery area became furious and accurate. They were opposed only by Battle Group Mohnke, an improvised force of some 3,000 sailors, aged Volkssturm troopers, Hitler Youths, and SS men, all of whom were running out of ammunition.

There could be no question of a successful escape by daylight, so Bormann had to endure until nightfall the Russian cannonading and the possibility that they might overrun the Bunker at any moment. He was in nominal command of some six hundred soldiers, Party officials, government employees, and female secretaries who remained in the complex of bunkers. But with Hitler dead, Bormann no longer inspired unquestioned obedience. He was just another potential escapee like the others, most of whom were frantically milling around "like chickens with their heads off," according to one of their number.

The escape plan was the only one possible. The time had passed when flight in a small plane or by some other more exotic means was still feasible. There was a subway station opposite the Chancellery. Small groups would leave at intervals throughout the night and crawl through a series of tunnels and vaults into the subway station. Then they would walk along the tracks, unnoticed by the Russian troops on the surface above them, until they reached the Friedrichstrasse Station. Here they would emerge, hoping to find themselves in an area still held by the remnants of Battle Group Mohnke. A few hundred yards from the Friedrichstrasse Station, the Weidendammer Bridge spanned the Spree River. With the aid of Battle Group Mohnke, the escapees would force their way across the bridge and then strike out through the northwestern suburbs of Berlin toward Doenitz or any other place of personal safety they could find.

Bormann's only alternative to this plan would have been suicide. Four men would be important in guessing how successful he was: Artur Axmann, the one-armed Hitler Youth Leader; Erich Kempka; Dr. Ludwig Stumpfegger; and Werner Naumann.

Kempka was thirty-five years old. He had been born in the Rhineland, the son of a miner and one of nine brothers and sisters. At the age of fourteen, he had left school to become an apprentice electrician and mechanic. Since 1932, he had been Hitler's chauffeur. Kempka admired the Führer, but his attitude toward Bormann was different. "Those of us," he later recalled, "who had to work for long years in close proximity to this diabolical personality hated him."

Dr. Ludwig Stumpfegger was a competent orthopedic surgeon who specialized in the regeneration of bones. He came to his post as Hitler's last personal surgeon upon the recommendation of Himmler's own physician, Dr. Karl Gebhardt, in whose clinic he had worked. Stumpfegger was six and one half feet tall and held the rank of colonel in the SS. He, too, was an admirer of Hitler. Although he was not a quack as were many of the Führer's previous doctors, Stumpfegger had performed medical experiments on concentration-camp inmates. For the past few days, he had been supplying the inhabitants of the Bunker with poison capsules.

Werner Naumann, once State Secretary in the Propaganda Ministry, had been named to succeed Goebbels as head of that ministry by Hitler. Naumann had been a Nazi Party member since he was nineteen. He was now thirty-five, and a magnetic speaker whose eyes fixed his audiences with a fanatical stare.

Not everyone chose to escape with Bormann, Axmann, Kempka, Dr. Stumpfegger, and Naumann. Generals Burgdorf and Krebs stayed in the Bunker. The next day a Russian search party would find their corpses; presumably they had shot themselves.

Goebbels had remarked that he did not intend to spend the rest of his life "running around the world like an eternal refugee." He had also written of his resolve to "end a life which will have no further value to me if I cannot spend it in the service of the Führer, and by his side . . ."

To these words, at least, Goebbels remained true. Around 8:30 P.M., Joseph and Magda Goebbels walked unaccompanied up the Bunker stairs to the Reich Chancellery garden. Their six children were already dead of poison. In the garden, an SS orderly obeyed Goebbels' last order. It was to shoot Goebbels and his wife.

Bormann displayed no interest in Goebbels' demise. It was left to Günther Schwägermann, Goebbels' adjutant, to douse the corpses of the Reich Chancellor and his wife with gasoline and set them on fire. While the couple was being cremated, Bormann moved to another bunker under the New Reich Chancellery. From here the escape groups would depart, for an effort was made by SS Colonel Günsche to have the Führerbunker itself destroyed.

Erich Kempka, Artur Axmann and hundreds of others preceded Bormann before he began his own escape attempt around 1:30 A.M. In Bormann's small group were Dr. Stumpfegger, Werner Naumann, and Günther Schwägermann.

On this night of May 1, 1945, Bormann was forty-five years old. Despite the underground life he had been leading, this stocky, bull-necked man retained the robust physical health which had enabled him to work almost around the clock. There was a large mole on his left temple and a noticeable scar over his right eyebrow, but otherwise his appearance was in no way unusual. His teeth were sound and bore no marks that could later identify him. Certainly, no Russian soldiers or even German civilians would recognize him on sight because of the obscurity in which he had always preferred to work.

Bormann wore, not a disguise, but the uniform of an SS Lieutenant General and a leather overcoat. In one of the overcoat's pockets was the last copy of the will of which he was the executor; in the other, probably, was a poison capsule.

Fräulein Kruger met Bormann accidently before he left. *"Also dann auf Wiedersehen,"* Bormann said to his last secretary. "There is not much sense in it now, but I will try to get through. Very probably I shall not succeed."

Bormann headed for the subway station. Behind him the funeral flames of Dr. Goebbels were still rising into the night sky. The flames which had partially destroyed the Führer had died out.

THIRTEEN

Escape Attempt

Bormann emerged from the depths of the Friedrichstrasse subway station around 2 A.M. He had never visited the front lines during the war. Nor had he been outside the unreal world of the Reich Chancellery area in more than four months. Now he suddenly found himself at the eye of a hurricane of war.

Hundreds of refugees huddled apathetically on the stairs and platforms of the subway station as he came out into the night to see skeletons of buildings on both sides of the long Friedrichstrasse. There was no electricity in Berlin, but fires from all sections of the city brightened the sky. Bormann heard the constant rattle of small-arms fire and the roar of heavy artillery. But he saw that the area around the subway station was held by Battle Group Mohnke. The escape plan had been successful up to this point. But now he saw that there was a flaw in it.

The earlier escapees from the Chancellery bunkers were milling around before the Weidendammer Bridge. They had not been able to flee over it into the northwestern suburbs and Bormann could easily see why. Scores of bodies lay on the bridge like dark shadows. On its far side stood a tank barrier. Beyond this, Russian troops in ruined houses and cellars on both sides of the street were firing spasmodically into the German-held pocket.

Axmann and Kempka were among those who had been stopped by the tank barrier. Bormann told Kempka that he wanted to break through the barrier, but Kempka replied that this would be impossible without heavy weapons. And none was available. But shortly thereafter, a few German Tiger tanks accompanied by armored personnel carriers drove up. To Kempka, this appeared to be a miracle.

The possibility of escape existed on the other side of the river; not to cross it would mean certain capture. Bormann saw an opening in the middle of the tank barrier. He decided to push through it under the protection of the German tanks. And so small groups crouched around the tanks and began to move off with them over the bridge.

Kempka saw Bormann running close to the left side of the first tank, near its turret. Werner Naumann was directly in front of him. Behind Bormann jogged Dr. Stumpfegger and, next to the left rear wheels, Erich Kempka. Still further behind came Axmann and the members of other escape groups.

The first tank nosed through the opening in the barrier. It went a few yards further in the darkness. Then Kempka saw a flash like lightning and heard a deafening roar. The tank, heavily loaded with ammunition, exploded into pieces. Kempka thought it had been hit by a bazooka shell fired from a nearby window. He was flung aside by the force of the explosion and knocked unconscious to the ground. Before that happened, Kempka saw Bormann collapse in a sheet of flame.

Kempka regained consciousness, having suffered slight splinter injuries. Though temporarily blinded by the flash of the explosion, he managed to crawl back to the tank barrier. He was thinking that the Secretary of the Führer had certainly been killed by the blast. Later, Kempka recovered his vision, crossed the Spree River, and headed west.

Axmann, too, saw the flash, heard the deafening roar, and was smashed unconscious to the ground. When the Hitler

Youth Leader revived, he crawled into a shell hole. There he
saw Dr. Stumpfegger, Naumann, and Schwägermann. With
them, according to Axmann, was Martin Bormann. He was
alive and apparently unwounded.

The men in the shell hole abandoned all thought of making
another attempt to cross the Weidendammer Bridge and returned to the Friedrichstrasse Station. There Bormann took
charge. He led Stumpfegger, Naumann, Schwägermann,
Axmann, and the latter's adjutant, Weltzin, down a railway
embankment.

Bormann had removed his insignias of rank in an effort to
look like an ordinary Volkssturm trooper. So had those who
followed him. They crossed the Spree River on a railroad
bridge. This was part of the *Stadtbahn* (city railway) system
which, from the underground Friedrichstrasse Station,
changed to tracks above ground going to the Lehrter Station.
As the escapees continued down these tracks, random small-
arms fire was directed at them. Only the darkness, Axmann
felt, saved them from being hit.

After a walk of nearly a mile the escape party neared the
Lehrter Station. Bormann signaled a halt. The station was
occupied by Russian troops. To avoid them, the six men
climbed over an iron railing, jumped onto the ledge of a wall,
and let themselves down into a street.

They landed in the middle of a Russian sentry post. Russian
soldiers encircled them. *"Hitler Kaputt!* The war is over!"
Axmann remembers hearing. And the war was as good as over
for these Russians; only the cleaning up of a few still resisting
pockets and a formal German surrender remained.

The sentries showed no hostility to the men they took to be
beaten Volkssturm troopers. Cigarettes were offered and Axmann showed the Russians his mechanical right arm, which
they fingered with curiosity. While this was going on, the Head
of the Nazi Party Chancellery and Dr. Stumpfegger hurried
off in an easterly direction down the Invalidenstrasse.

The sentries eyed them suspiciously and gestured after
them. Axmann was frightened by the feeling that the Russians

would mow them all down. But nothing happened. So Axmann, Weltzin, Schwägermann, and Naumann wandered off
down the Invalidenstrasse in a westerly direction. Again, nothing happened.

Naumann and Schwägermann dodged under some trees and
bushes, parting company with Axmann and Weltzin who continued westward until they heard the clanking of approaching
Russian tanks. They turned and went back the way they had
come. On their left were the gray ruins of public buildings: an
old Prussian Army barracks, a Fire Department training
school, a post office. On their right was the grounds of the
Ausstellungs-Park (Exhibition Park). When they had nearly
passed a bridge over the tracks of the Lehrter Station, Axmann noticed two men lying on the bridge. Thinking that they
might need help, the Hitler Youth Leader knelt next to
them.

Axmann then realized that he was looking at Dr. Ludwig
Stumpfegger and Martin Bormann. Moonlight shone on their
faces as they lay on their backs with arms and legs slightly
outstretched. Axmann touched Bormann. There was no reaction. He leaned over Bormann's mouth. There was no trace of
breath. But there were no signs of blood or wounds either.

It was puzzling. Had Bormann taken poison, Axmann
wondered. For he certainly appeared to be dead. Or was he
merely unconscious? But it would have been a remarkable
coincidence for both Bormann and Stumpfegger to be lying
there unconscious in the same attitudes, Axmann thought.
Perhaps Bormann was feigning death? There seemed to be no
point at all in such a pretense, for he was lying near a Russian
sentry post in a hail of shell fragments and bullets, and Russian tanks were rattling toward his body.

Suddenly, the Russians began to direct a heavy fire at the
bridge. Axmann and Weltzin were obliged to flee into the
night. Thus, Axmann did not have time to determine with
clinical exactness that he had seen Bormann's corpse, although
he was convinced of it.

But Kempka and several others were equally convinced that

Bormann had been killed by the tank explosion. In any case, Weltzin would be of no help in corroborating Axmann's version of the events. The next day, Weltzin was captured by the Russians and later died in one of their prison camps; if he was interrogated by the Russians, they never divulged his testimony to their allies.

Artur Axmann, however, managed to get out of Berlin and make his way to the Bavarian Alps, where he joined up with a Hitler Youth unit and then went into hiding. Schwägermann and Naumann, after separating from Axmann, also got out of Berlin and reached an area of western Germany occupied by British and American troops.

But few who had attempted to escape from the Reich Chancellery were as successful as the members of Bormann's small group: Axmann, Kempka, Schwägermann, and Naumann. Members of the other escape groups ran into serious trouble. SS Colonel Hoegl, deputy to SS Brigadier General Rattenhuber, chief of the detective bodyguard, was killed at the Weidendammer Bridge. Rattenhuber himself was wounded and captured. SS Colonel George Beetz, one of Hitler's two personal pilots, was killed. The other pilot, Major General Hans Bauer, suffered a wound to his left leg which required its amputation in Russian captivity. Günsche, Mohnke, Linge and almost everyone else who had tried to escape from the Reich Chancellery were captured.

By the afternoon of May 2, 1945, when General Weidling surrendered Berlin, the Russians had found the corpses of Goebbels and Hitler. But they officially denied it. At a later press conference in Berlin on June 9, Marshal Zhukov said: "We have not identified the body of Hitler. I can say nothing about his fate. He could have flown away from Berlin at the very last moment. The state of the runway would have allowed him to do so." Zhukov was obviously acting as a mouthpiece for Stalin, who had his own strange ideas about the matter. Only after Stalin's death would the Russians confirm that they had found Hitler's charred body on May 2.

As for Bormann, the Russians would never acknowledge

that they had found either the man or his corpse on May 2 or
thereafter. In the still-smoking rubble of Berlin that was
strewn with wrecked airplanes and weapons and the bodies of
dead horses, soldiers, and civilians, Bormann appeared to
have vanished like the flames from the Führer's funeral pyre.
But if he was gone, in however mystifying a fashion, into an
unknown grave or alive into hiding, he was not forgotten.

Goering, for one, could not forget Bormann. The former
Reich Marshal was released from his SS captors in Mauten-
dorf Castle by a passing contingent of Luftwaffe troops on
May 5. The next day, Goering sent a message to Doenitz:

Are you, Admiral, familiar with the intrigues, dangerous to
the security of the State, which Reich Leader Bormann has
carried on to eliminate me? All steps taken against me
arose out of the request sent by me in all loyalty to the Führer, asking whether he wished that his order concerning his
succession should come into force. . . . The steps taken
against me were carried out on the authority of a radiogram
signed "Bormann." I have not been interrogated by anybody in spite of my requests and no attempt of mine to
justify my position has been accepted. Reichsführer SS
Himmler can confirm the immense extent of these intrigues.
I have just learned that you intend to send Jodl to Eisenhower with a view to negotiating. I think it important in the
interests of our people that, besides the official negotiations
of Jodl, I should officially approach Eisenhower, as one
marshal to another. . . .

To this, Doenitz, who was indeed preparing to negotiate a
surrender, did not bother to reply. An unconditional surrender was signed on the morning of May 7. The next day,
Goering was discovered by American troops in a traffic jam
on a Bavarian road and taken to their headquarters, where he
was initially treated as something of a celebrity.

Goering had wanted to surrender to the Americans. General Koller learned that the Reich Marshal and his entourage

arrived in captivity "much relieved, everybody in splendid humor. Goering is cracking jokes with the American soldiers."

Goering was made available for a mass press interview by Brigadier General William Quinn, Chief of Intelligence for the U.S. Seventh Army. One of the questions put to him was whether he believed that Hitler had named Doenitz as his successor.

"No!" Goering replied. "The telegram to Doenitz bore Bormann's signature."

"Why did so colorless an individual as Bormann have such a great influence on Hitler?" the questioner continued.

"Bormann stayed with Hitler day and night and gradually brought him so much under his will that he ruled Hitler's whole existence."

Such was Goering's firm opinion on this matter. On another, he was less certain.

"Do you know that you are on the list of war criminals?" he was asked.

"No," Goering said. "That surprises me very much, for I cannot imagine why."

Goering did not get his wish to talk to Eisenhower "as one marshal to another." On May 21, he was transferred to Bad Mondorf in Luxembourg, where he was held for later trial.

"When Goering came to see me at Mondorf," said Colonel Burton Andrus, the U.S. Commander of the hotel which served as a prison, "he was a simpering slob with two suitcases full of paracodeine pills. I thought he was a drug salesman. But we took him off dope and made a man of him."

Not every man wanted by the Allied War Crimes Commission was found and arrested as quickly after the May 7 capitulation as was Goering. The Doenitz government continued to function at Flensburg on the Danish border until it was dissolved by the Allies on May 23. Doenitz, Speer, Jodl, and Keitel were then taken into custody at Flensburg. But other prominent Nazis vanished in the stream of refugees, liberated Allied prisoners of war and foreign workers, and German ex-soldiers, which washed through the catacombs and ruins of the Third Reich.

"The greatest manhunt in history is under way from Norway to the Bavarian Alps," Foreign Minister Anthony Eden told the House of Commons. Nevertheless, the manhunt failed to locate at first many men who were wanted as major war criminals. Among them were Ernst Kaltenbrunner, Himmler, Baldur von Schirach, Von Ribbentrop, and Bormann. Plenty of time was left for a determined and imaginative man armed with sufficient contacts and money to go into hiding or even to get out of Germany itself.

Dr. Ernst Kaltenbrunner had succeeded Heydrich as head of the Reich Main Security Office, which embraced the Gestapo, the Security Service, the Criminal Police and other policing agencies. The end of the war found Kaltenbrunner in the Alpine tourist village of Alt-Aussee, at the foot of the Austrian *Totengebirge,* the Dead Mountains. He then set out for a hut in the Dead Mountains, armed with an Army paybook identifying him as a medical officer and bearing a false seal accrediting the officer to the International Red Cross. Only because Kaltenbrunner was betrayed by a guide who had led him through the snow to the hut was he captured by American troops on May 15.

It was not until May 23 that a man wearing a black patch over his left eye and carrying papers identifying him as one Heinrich Hitzinger appeared in the British 031 Civilian Interrogation Camp near Lüneberg. "He was small, ill-looking and shabbily dressed," recalls the camp commander, Captain Tom Selvester, who soon gained from Hitzinger an admission of his true identity: Heinrich Himmler, Reichsführer SS.

For a full sixteen days after the capitulation, Himmler and the remnants of his entourage had wandered south from Flensburg. Doenitz wanted no further part of them. At a bridge near Bremervörde, ninety miles from Flensburg, they were accidentally stopped at a British checkpoint set up to screen ordinary homeward-bound German troops.

Captain Selvester turned Himmler over to Colonel Michael
Murphy, Montgomery's Chief of Intelligence, for further interrogation. Colonel Murphy and an army doctor, Captain C.
J. L. Wells, began a routine physical examination of their
prisoner to determine if he had poison concealed on his person. Himmler, who had shaved off the small mustache he had
grown in imitation of Hitler's, was obliged to strip naked.
Suddenly, as Dr. Wells placed his fingers into Himmler's
mouth, the prisoner bit into a small black knob. It was sticking
out, as Murphy remembers it, "between a gap in the teeth on
the right-hand side lower jaw."

Despite the use of a stomach pump, emetics, and artificial
respiration, Himmler was dead in fourteen minutes. Thus the
riddle of the character of a man who had been in direct command of an organization which had destroyed at least six million human beings would never be solved by further interrogation. Himmler was buried in a grave whose location the British
have never disclosed, as the Russians have never disclosed the
location of Hitler's grave.

Baldur von Schirach had preceded Axmann as Hitler Youth
Leader before becoming Gauleiter and Reich Defense Commissioner for Vienna. When the Red Army entered the city,
he fled to Schwaz in the Tyrol, wearing a newly grown beard.
Under the name of Richard Falk, he boarded in a farmhouse
and, incredibly, managed to get a job as an interpreter for an
American unit. It was not until June 5 that Von Schirach
voluntarily disclosed his identity and gave himself up to the
American occupation authorities in Schwaz.

Joachim von Ribbentrop was not apprehended until June
14. The former Foreign Minister of the Third Reich, after his
services were rejected by Doenitz, wandered south to Hamburg. Under the name of Reiser, he tried to revive some of his
old business contacts from the days when he had been a wine
salesman. He took to strolling around Hamburg, the headquarters of British Military Government, wearing dark sun-
glasses, a black felt hat, and an elegant double-breasted suit.

Only when the son of a wine merchant from whom "Reiser" had attempted to gain employment notified the British authorities of his identity and location was the former Foreign Minister arrested. In his possession were letters addressed to Montgomery, Eden, and "Vincent" Churchill; a capsule of potassium cyanide; and several hundred thousand Reichsmark.

However tardily and haphazardly, all of the prominent Nazis were eventually accounted for, either through their arrests or having their deaths established. Except for Martin Bormann. His whereabouts remained a mystery. Stalin himself, on May 26, had told Harry Hopkins, President Roosevelt's emissary to the Kremlin, that he believed Bormann, among other Nazis, had escaped from Berlin and was alive and in hiding.

Then a man appeared who claimed to have seen Bormann alive. He was Heinrich Lienau, a sixty-two-year-old native of Flensburg and a minor writer who had been a prisoner in the Sachsenshausen concentration camp. He said that he had seen Bormann there on inspection visits. Lienau now told British Intelligence agents that he had seen Bormann again on July 26. Dressed in a green hunter's jacket, Bormann had climbed aboard a railroad train at Lüneberg. He and Lienau had ridden together in a crowded freight car as far as Flensburg. Then Bormann had vanished. British Intelligence could make nothing of this lead.

On August 31, the Russian-controlled Berlin radio announced that Bormann was "in Allied hands." No details were supplied for this statement. On September 1, it was officially announced by Montgomery's British Headquarters that Bormann was not in British hands. "We have not got him," the statement said. "That is definite, and it is not believed that the Americans have him."

The next day, a high-ranking officer on the staff of Associate Justice of the Supreme Court, Robert Jackson, the head of the U.S. staff for prosecuting international war criminals, said in Berlin that "Mr. Jackson does not know whether the Russians have Bormann."

Mr. Jackson's uncertainty was understandable. The Russians had taken Berlin. They alone were in a position to determine what had happened to those who were in the capital when it fell. But the Russians, in one of the first ominous indications that a cold war was beginning, did not cooperate with their Allies and divulge to them such information as they had gathered.

Stalin, for reasons of his own, persisted in misleading his allies about Hitler's death, which Russian investigators had established beyond any doubt. At the Potsdam Conference on July 17, Stalin had told James Byrnes, the American Secretary of State, that he believed Hitler to be alive, probably in Argentina or Spain.

In the middle of September, the Russian commission of inquiry submitted its verdict on the matter:

> No trace of the bodies of Hitler or Eva Braun has been discovered. . . . All witnesses have now admitted to our investigators that they saw neither the funeral pyre nor the bodies of Hitler and Eva Braun.
>
> It is established that Hitler, by means of false testimony, sought to cover his traces.
>
> Irrefutable proof exists that a small airplane left the Tiergarten at dawn on April 30, flying in the direction of Hamburg. Three men and a woman are known to have been on board.
>
> It has also been established that a large submarine left Hamburg before the arrival of the British forces. Mysterious persons were on board the submarine, among them a woman.

This was sheer fantasy, but fantasy inspired by the suspicions, prejudices, and incalculable moods of Stalin, who wanted the body of his greatest adversary for himself.

It was not until five months after the fall of Berlin that a British Intelligence team was permitted to conduct an inves-

tigation into the last days of Hitler. It was led by Hugh Redwald Trevor-Roper, an historian at Christ Church, Oxford,
who was commissioned for this job by British Intelligence. His
investigation established quite objectively, at least to the
satisfaction of the western allies, that Hitler and Goebbels
were dead. After Stalin's death, the Russians would at last
agree that the events had taken place much as Trevor-Roper
had described them.

Trevor-Roper, however, was unable to develop any conclusive answer to Bormann's fate, finding that "the evidence on
this question was conflicting and uncertain." Erich Kempka
had been taken into custody by American Army agents in late
May in Berchtesgaden. Kempka maintained that Bormann
had been killed by the tank explosion. So did Johann Rattenhuber, who was a Russian prisoner. But another Russian prisoner, Harry Mengerhausen, an officer of Hitler's SS bodyguard, was sure that Bormann had survived the blast. And
Günther Schwägermann, who was located in the American
Zone, said that he, Bormann, Axmann, and Werner Naumann
had walked to the Lehrter Bahnhof after the explosion. The
accounts of Axmann and Naumann could not be obtained as
of August, for at that time they appeared to have vanished as
completely as had Bormann.

These contradictory witnesses and the continued absence of
Bormann confronted the governments of the United States,
Great Britain, France, and also the Soviet Union with a
dilemma. The Allies had decided to indict and try before an
International Military Tribunal twenty-four Nazi officials as
major war criminals "whose offenses have no particular geographical location." This decision was reached only after a
great deal of haggling about the legal principles which the
judges were to observe, the form of the trial, and the duties
and rights of the participants. It was not, in fact, until August
8 that the four Allies had finally signed in London an agree-
ment on the Statute of the Court and on the International
Military Tribunal.

Bormann obviously had to be classified as a major war

criminal. But if he was dead, he could hardly be indicted and
tried, as Hitler, Goebbels, and Himmler were not. If Bormann
was not indicted, and was later found alive, this would create
complications for the Tribunal.

In Berlin on October 7, Sir Hartley Shawcross, the chief
British prosecutor, indicated what the solution to this dilemma
would be. He said that Bormann and Hess, who would be
brought from his captivity in England to stand trial, headed
the list of twenty-four war criminals. Bormann would be
named in the indictment and Hitler would not be, according to
Sir Hartley, because "there was less reason to believe that
Bormann was dead."

And indeed, as Sir Hartley spoke, none of the Allies would
admit to having found Bormann either alive or dead. The
International Military Tribunal was then obliged to take an
unusual step in regard to the missing Martin Bormann.

Beginning on October 22, 1945, a *Bekanntmachung* or Public Notice was read once a week for a month over Radio Hamburg and Radio Cologne, and printed during that same time in four Berlin newspapers. Two hundred thousand copies of it were posted throughout Germany. The Public Notice read:

ORDER OF THE TRIBUNAL REGARDING NOTICE TO DEFENDANT BORMANN

INTERNATIONAL MILITARY TRIBUNAL

THE UNITED STATES OF AMERICA, THE FRENCH REPUBLIC, THE UNITED KINGDOM OF GREAT BRITAIN AND NORTHERN IRELAND, and THE UNION OF SOVIET SOCIALIST REPUBLICS

——against——

HERMANN WILHELM GORING, *et al.,*

Defendants.

The International Military Tribunal having been duly constituted and an indictment having been lodged with the Tribunal by the Chief Prosecutors

AND one of the defendants, Martin Bormann, not having been found

IT IS ORDERED that notice be given said Martin Bormann in the following form and manner:

(a) *Form of Notice*
Take Notice:

Martin Bormann is charged with having committed
Crimes against Peace, War Crimes, and Crimes against
Humanity, all as particularly set forth in an indictment
which has been lodged with this Tribunal.

The indictment is available at the Palace of Justice,
Nuremberg, Germany.

If Martin Bormann appears, he is entitled to be heard in
person or by counsel.

If he fails to appear, he may be tried in his absence, com-
mencing November 20, 1945, at the Palace of Justice,
Nuremberg, Germany, and if found guilty the sentence
pronounced upon him will, without further hearing, and
subject to the orders of the Control Council for Germany,
be executed whenever he is found.

By order of
The International Military Tribunal
Harold B. Willey
General Secretary

If Martin Bormann read or heard this Public Notice, he did
not oblige those who had promulgated it by appearing at the
Palace of Justice. By November 17, the mystery concerning
his whereabouts had deepened. But the trial was about to
begin, and the Tribunal had to make a decision. And so its
President, the Right Honourable Lord Justice Sir Geoffrey
Lawrence of Great Britain, asked the Chief Prosecutors if they
wished to make any statement with reference to Bormann.

Sir David Maxwell-Fyfe, Deputy Chief Prosecutor for the
United Kingdom, who spoke also on behalf of France and the
United States, replied: "May it please the Tribunal, as the
Tribunal are aware, the Defendant Bormann was included in
the Indictment, which was filed before the Tribunal. There has
been no change in the position with regard to the Defendant
Bormann; nor has any further information come to the notice

of the Chief Prosecutors. . . . Three members of the party who were with Bormann in [sic] this tank have been interrogated. Two think that Bormann was killed, and the third that he was wounded. The position is, therefore, that the Prosecution cannot say that the matter is beyond probability that Bormann is dead. There is still the clear possibility that he is alive.

"In these circumstances I should submit that he comes within the exact words of Article 12 of the Charter:

> The Tribunal shall have the right to take proceedings against a person charged with crimes set out in Article 6 of this Charter in his absence, if he has not been found."

Sir David Maxwell-Fyfe moved that Bormann be tried in absentia. Colonel Pokrovsky of the Soviet Delegation concurred. After a recess, Sir Geoffrey Lawrence announced that Bormann would be tried in his absence and that counsel would be appointed to defend him.

This difficult job was given to Dr. Friedrich Bergold, a competent German lawyer, who thought that it was a miscarriage of justice for the Tribunal to try his client in absentia. To Dr. Bergold, this was a "quite novel procedure in the legal history of all times." Later, he remarked: "In Nuremberg, we have an adage which has come down to us from the Middle Ages, and which says: 'The Nurembergers would never hang a man they did not hold.' "

The trial began at 10:03 A.M., November 20, 1945. Two hundred and fifty reporters representing newspapers from all over the world sat in the press box of the courtroom. To their right, behind an oblong table on a raised dais, sat the judges from France, Great Britain, the United States, and the Soviet Union. They wore black judicial robes, except for the Soviet judge and his alternate, who wore military uniforms. There were places for the prosecutors, the defense attorneys, interpreters, stenographers, photographers, newsreel cameramen, and Sir Geoffrey Lawrence. For the benefit of the photographers and cameramen, twenty-two powerful floodlights lit up the courtroom.

Directly facing the judges was the prisoner's dock, consisting of two long wooden benches, behind which stood eight American soldiers carrying pistols and nightsticks. Observing the prisoners from the press box, William Shirer thought that they looked like "miserable little men."

The first day of the trial was entirely given over to rereading the indictment, which was divided into four main parts. The twenty-five thousand words of the indictment were later summarized by Robert Jackson, the head of the U.S. prosecution staff: "Count One charged the common plan or conspiracy to seize power, establish a totalitarian regime, prepare and wage a war of aggression. Count Two charged the waging of wars of aggression. Count Three charged the violation of the laws of war, and Count Four charged the crimes against humanity, the persecution and extermination."

Not all of the twenty-four men originally included in this indictment were present to hear it reread. The aged and senile Gustav Krupp von Bohlen und Halbach had been indicted as the representative of the German armaments industry. But the case against Krupp was dropped after an international medical commission found that he was unable "by reason of his mental condition, to follow the proceedings at a court of law." Robert Ley, the head of the Labor Front, had hanged himself in his cell on October 25. SS Lieutenant General Ernst Kaltenbrunner, whose Reich Main Security Office had controlled the Gestapo and most of the intelligence and police agencies in the Third Reich, suffered a cerebral hemorrhage and could not attend the trial's opening. Kaltenbrunner, however, did appear later.

There was a place for Bormann in the dock, but it remained empty. The trial nevertheless continued. So did the efforts to find the former Secretary of the Führer or some proof that he was dead. In December, American agents discovered Artur Axmann and Bormann's personal assistant, SS Colonel Wilhelm Zander.

Zander was found in Aidenbach, a small village near Passau on the Austrian frontier. The documents which he had brought out of the Reich Chancellery were located in a trunk in Tegernsee. Zander told the agents that he was disillusioned with Nazism. However, he could shed no light on Bormann's whereabouts, insisting that he had neither seen nor heard from his former chief since leaving the Reich Chancellery.

Axmann, the last head of the Hitler Youth, was apprehended in the Bavarian Alps. He said that he had seen Bormann alive in the shell hole after the tank explosion, accompanied him to the Lehrter Station, and later seen his corpse on the railroad bridge. Axmann thus became the only person to claim that he had seen Bormann's dead body in Berlin, a contention from which he would never waver.

"Whether we believe Axmann or not is entirely a matter of choice," Trevor-Roper later wrote, "for his word is unsupported by any other testimony. In his favor it can be said that his evidence on all other points has been vindicated. On the other hand, if he wished to protect Bormann against further search, his natural course will be to give false evidence of his death."

On January 16, 1946, Bormann was still missing. On that day, the case against him as an individual defendant was presented by Lieutenant Thomas F. Lambert, Jr., one of the assistants to Thomas J. Dodd, Executive Trial Counsel for the United States.

Lieutenant Lambert had a rather difficult time in establishing that Bormann was the unique creator and perpetrator of criminal acts. His role as the Führer's Secretary and closest confidant defied documentation. Who could state, with legal exactitude, what had been decided during the long private conversations between the two men? One was dead, the other missing. Lieutenant Lambert rested the prosecution's case with these remarks:

"May it please the Tribunal, every schoolboy knows that Hitler was an evil man. The point we respectfully emphasize is that, without chieftains like Bormann, Hitler would never have been able to seize and consolidate total power in Germany, but he would have been left to walk the wilderness alone.

"He was, in truth, an evil archangel to the Lucifer of Hitler; and, although he may remain a fugitive from the justice of this Tribunal, with an empty chair in the dock, Bormann cannot escape responsibility for his illegal conduct . . ."

Was Bormann's chair empty because he was dead, and buried in an unknown grave? Or because he was a fugitive? One answer came the first week in February. A radio broadcast from Montevideo, Uruguay, announced that Bormann was hiding in Misiones Province in northern Argentina.

This was the first of many reports that Bormann was alive in one of the Latin American countries ruled by dictators with Fascist sympathies. Argentine police searched Misiones Province. They did not admit to finding Bormann, or any trace of him. Later, it was determined that the Montevideo broadcast had been sponsored by Argentine exiles. Their object had been to embarrass the government of Juan Peron.

Meanwhile, as the prosecution's lengthy case against those indicted as major war criminals continued at Nuremberg, Bormann's wife died on March 22, 1946. She was thirty-seven years old. Her death was known to Allied Intelligence, which had discovered her whereabouts in an unusual fashion shortly after V-E Day. A distraught German national had then appeared at the Munich headquarters of the U.S. Counterintelligence Corps claiming that a child of his had been kidnapped from Berchtesgaden by Frau Gerda Bormann and that he knew where the wife of the Führer's secretary could be found.

C.I.C. assigned Alexander Raskin to investigate this lead, on the possibility that Bormann might be with his wife. Raskin was a thirty-one-year-old Belgian Jew who had escaped from a Nazi forced-labor unit and was later employed by C.I.C. In May 1945, he and the German national drove to a region of the Austrian Tyrol bordering the Italian city of Bolzano. They then searched this remote area on muleback. After four days, they came upon a villa at Wolkenstein in the Grödnertal in which a "Frau Bergmann" was operating a kindergarten.

Raskin questioned "Frau Bergmann," who readily admitted that she was Martin Bormann's wife. She said that she had taken the "kidnapped" child to Wolkenstein for safekeeping after the air raid on Berchtesgaden, as she had done with her own children. But Gerda Bormann would not admit that she knew what had happened to her husband. Nor were there any traces of him around the villa.

Frau Bormann appeared terribly sick to Raskin. He checked with a local doctor who informed him that she was dying from cancer. Raskin reported what he had learned to the Munich C.I.C. He was sure that his information reached General George Patton, for later an intelligence officer on Patton's staff told him, "The general feels that the woman should be left to die in peace."

Frau Bormann eventually went to the only place near Wolkenstein where competent medical treatment was available, a hospital in Merano, Italy, operated by the Americans for prisoners of war. Before dying there of cancer of the bowels, she became a Roman Catholic convert and consigned her nine children to the care of a guardian, the Reverend Theodor Schmitz.

From the time Raskin had found her in May 1945 until she died on March 22, 1946, C.I.C. agents kept Frau Bormann under surveillance on the chance that her husband might attempt to see or contact her. But nothing happened. Frau Bormann provided only one clue to her husband's fate. According to Raskin, she had shown him a telegram which Martin Bormann had sent to her in Berchtesgaden during the last days of the war. It read simply: "Everything is lost. I will never get out of here. Take care of the children."

But Bormann apparently had gotten out of Berlin. According to rumors which circulated in Nuremberg in April 1946, he was living in the village of Espirita Santu in Salamanca Province, Spain. However, when United Nations and Spanish authorities checked, Bormann was not there. Moreover, the

Spanish government announced that in the entire province of
Salamanca there was no village named Espirita Santu.

Bormann had still not been found, nor his fate conclusively
determined, when Dr. Bergold conducted his defense in July
1946. Before doing so, Dr. Bergold sought to prove that his
client was not willfully absenting himself from the proceedings. In Dr. Bergold's view, the Tribunal was trying a dead
man and should therefore dismiss the case against him.

To substantiate his argument, Dr. Bergold called Erich
Kempka to the witness stand on July 3 and elicited from him
this testimony:

Dr. Bergold: Witness, in what capacity were you employed
near Hitler during the war?
Kempka: During the war I worked for Adolf Hitler as his
personal driver.
Dr. Bergold: Did you meet Martin Bormann in that capac-
ity?
Kempka: Yes, I met Martin—Reichsleiter Martin Bor-
mann in this capacity at that time as my indirect superior.
Dr. Bergold: Witness, on what day did you see the Defen-
dant Martin Bormann for the last time?
Kempka: I saw the Reichsleiter, the former Reichsleiter
Martin Bormann, on the night of 1-2 May 1945 near the
Friedrichstrasse railroad station, at the Weidendammer
Bridge. Reichsleiter Bormann—former Reichsleiter Bormann—asked me what the general situation was at the
Friedrichstrasse Station, and I told him that there at the
station it was hardly possible . . .
The President [*Sir Geoffrey Lawrence*]: You are going too
fast. He asked you what?
Kempka: He asked me what the situation was and whether
one could get through there at the Friedrichstrasse Station. I
told him that was practically impossible, since the defensive
fighting there was too heavy. Then he went on to ask
whether it might be possible to do so with armored cars. I

told him that there was nothing like trying it. Then a few tanks and SPW [armored personnel carrier] cars came along, and small groups boarded them and hung on. Then the armored cars pushed their way through the antitank trap and afterwards the leading tank—along about at the middle of the left-hand side, where Martin Bormann was walking—suddenly received a direct hit, I imagine from a bazooka fired from a window, and this tank was blown up. A flash of fire suddenly shot up on the very side where Bormann was walking and I saw . . .

The President: You are going too fast. You are still going much too fast. The last thing I heard you say was that Bormann was walking in the middle of the column. Is that right?

Kempka: Yes, at the middle of the tank, on the left-hand side. Then, after it had got 40 to 50 meters past the antitank trap, this tank received a direct hit, I imagine from a bazooka fired from a window. The tank was blown to pieces right there where Martin—Reichsleiter Bormann—was walking. I myself was flung aside by the explosion and by a person thrown against me who had been walking in front of me—I think it was Standartenführer Dr. Stumpfegger— and I became unconscious. When I came to myself I could not see anything either; I was blinded by the flash. Then I crawled back again to the tank trap, and since then I have seen nothing more of Martin Bormann.

Dr. Bergold: Witness, did you see Martin Bormann collapse in the flash of fire when it occurred?

Kempka: Yes, indeed, I still saw a movement which was a sort of collapsing. You might call it a flying away.

Dr. Bergold: Was this explosion so strong that according to your observation Martin Bormann must have lost his life by it?

Kempka: Yes, I assume for certain that the force of the explosion was such that he lost his life.

The Tribunal did not share Kempka's assumption of certainty. Its members knew that both Artur Axmann and Günther Schwägermann claimed to have seen Bormann alive well after the tank explosion. Probably because their testimony would have contradicted Kempka's, Dr. Bergold did not call Axmann or Schwägermann to the witness stand. The Tribunal declined to suspend the proceedings against Bormann.

Dr. Bergold complained that this would only strengthen the growing legend that his client was still alive. Earlier, Dr. Bergold had commented, "Indeed, false Martin Bormanns have already made their appearance and are sending me letters which are signed Martin Bormann, but which cannot possibly have been written by him."

Nevertheless, on July 22, Dr. Bergold undertook his client's defense. "Your Lordship, Your Honours:" Dr. Bergold addressed the court, "The case of the defendant Martin Bormann, whose defense the Tribunal has commissioned me to undertake, is an unusual one. When the sun of the National Socialist Reich was still in its zenith, the defendant lived in the shade. Also during this trial he has been a shadowy figure, and in all probability, he has gone down to the shades—that abode of departed spirits, according to the belief of the ancients. He alone of the defendants is not present, and Article 12 of the Charter applies only to him . . ."

Dr. Bergold's main line of defense, and the only one he could take under the circumstances, was that the Tribunal had made an error in trying Bormann in absentia. "During the course of these long proceedings," he continued, "the man Bormann and his activity have remained shrouded in that obscurity in which the defendant, by his predisposition, held himself during his lifetime. The charges which many co-defendants have made against him, perhaps for very special reasons, and obviously in order to assist their own defense and exonerate themselves, cannot for reasons of fairness be taken as the basis for a judicial decision. The prosecution has stated on more than one occasion, through its representatives, that the defendants would seek to throw the chief blame upon dead or absent men for the acts which are now being judged by the Tribunal. . . .

"But nobody knows what the defendant Bormann could have said in answer to these men if he had been present. Perhaps he would have been able to show that his activities were not the cause of the happenings arraigned in the Indictment; also that he did not possess the influence which is imputed to him as the Secretary of the Führer and of the Party."

The heart of Dr. Bergold's long argument was this: "As long as Bormann does not appear and is not heard personally, the true part he played remains obscure. Nobody, not even the High Tribunal, could ever pass just sentence. The whole case remains dubious. . . . Unfortunately, a legend has already been woven around Bormann's personality, his activity, and his survival. But for the sober judgment of jurists, legends are not a valid basis for a sure verdict free from any doubt." Dr. Bergold closed by again asking the Tribunal "to suspend the proceedings against the defendant Bormann until he is personally heard and can personally state his case. . . ."

The day after the Tribunal rejected the defense attorney's request of July 22, Bormann was reportedly seen alive by Jacob Glas. He had been Bormann's personal driver in Munich and Berchtesgaden until late 1944. The Secretary of the Führer had then accused Glas of stealing vegetables from Bormann's private garden and discharged him. Glas told the C.I.C. that he was "absolutely certain" that a man he had seen riding in a car down a Munich main street was Bormann. He was dressed in ordinary, rather shabby civilian clothes. "I know Bormann," Glas insisted, "and the man I saw was Bormann."

The C.I.C. conducted an intensive house-to-house search in Munich, but Bormann was not found there, as he had not been found in Flensburg, in the Tyrol, in Spain, or in Argentina. He was still missing when the International Military Tribunal convened on September 30, 1946, to begin delivering its judgment on the twenty-two men who had been tried as major war criminals.

Bormann was found innocent on Count One of the Indictment, that of taking part in a common plan or conspiracy to seize power, establish a totalitarian regime, and wage a war of aggression. He had not been indicted on Count Two, which dealt with starting a war of aggression. Both of these actions stemmed from the recognition of the fact that Bormann had not played a significant role in the Nazi hierarchy until after the war had begun and Hess had flown to England. On Count Three, War Crimes, and Count Four, Crimes Against Humanity, he was found guilty.

In concluding its judgment, the Tribunal noted that Dr. Bergold had "labored under difficulties," and that "if Bormann is not dead, and is later apprehended, the Control Council for Germany may, under Article 29 of the Charter, consider any facts in mitigation, and alter or reduce his sentence, if deemed proper." On the afternoon of October 1, 1946, Bormann was one of twelve defendants sentenced to death by hanging.*

The death sentences were executed on the night of October 15, except in two cases. As noted earlier, Goering cheated the gallows by killing himself with poison. Bormann was not there to be hanged. Meanwhile, the reports that he was alive continued.

On November 1, 1946, one Joachim Borsburg was found marching down the main street of a town in Württemberg-Baden in the uniform of an SS Lieutenant Colonel. He was arrested and interrogated by C.I.C. agents. Borsburg told them that he had recently been promoted in a midnight cere-

* The other eleven were Goering; Keitel; Jodl; Kaltenbrunner; Rosenberg; von Ribbentrop; Hans Frank, Governor-General of Poland; Fritz Sauckel, boss of the slave-labor program; Arthur Seyss-Inquart, Reich Commissioner for the Netherlands; Wilhelm Frick, Reich Protector of Bohemia and Moravia; Walter Funk, head of the Reichsbank; and Julius Streicher, Gauleiter of Franconia. The other defendants received sentences ranging from life imprisonment (Hess) to acquittal (Hans Fritzsche of the Propaganda Ministry).

mony conducted in a graveyard by Martin Bormann. Upon further investigation, C.I.C. determined that Borsburg had been taken prisoner in Saxony at the end of the war as a simple private soldier. He escaped from a hospital and was now mentally unbalanced.

Was everyone who thought he had seen Bormann mistaken, or, like Joachim Borsburg, mad? Or was the Secretary of the Führer in hiding? This last possibility deeply troubled Allied intelligence agents, for a resurgence of Nazism was not easy to discount in 1946. A living Bormann could be seen as a potential Führer of a Fourth Reich. Hitler had singled him out as the executor of his will and the future leader of the Nazi Party. Now Bormann was the only member of the Nazi hierarchy who could not be accounted for, and this unsettling fact held true through 1947.

As the mystery grew, so did the number of reports which attempted to explain Bormann's fate. Some of the reports were fantastic, some were plausible, and one in particular was startling. This was offered early in 1948 by a man who was in a better position to know what he was talking about than the previous informants. He was SS Lieutenant General Gottlob Berger.

FIFTEEN

"Death Not Completely Established"

The "Wilhelmstrasse Trial" began on January 6, 1948, in Nuremberg. This was one of twelve war-crimes trials known as the Subsequent Proceedings because they followed those of the International Military Tribunal against the major war criminals. The Subsequent Proceedings were all held before the Nuremberg Military Tribunal, which was entirely of American composition.

The twenty-two defendants at the "Wilhelmstrasse Trial" were former high officials of the German Foreign Office and other ministries with offices on the Wilhelmstrasse in Berlin. One of the defendants was Gottlob Berger, once a village schoolmaster, the director of a gymnastics institute, and an early enthusiastic Nazi.

During the war, Berger became an SS Lieutenant General and Head of the *SS Hauptamt* (Main Office), which administered the domestic affairs of fifteen Armed SS divisions fighting outside the Reich. He was responsible for SS personnel, and recruited into the Armed SS natives of Holland, Belgium, France, Finland, Denmark, Norway, and the Ukraine who were of suitably "Nordic" appearance and anti-communist sympathies.

Berger was also Himmler's per-

sonal liaison to Alfred Rosenberg's Ministry for the Eastern
Occupied Territories and managed to take over Rosenberg's
Main Political Department. *Der Untermensch,* the notorious
illustrated brochure which defined Russians as subhumans,
was issued in 1942 by Berger's SS Main Office. He knew Bormann well and considered him to have been a sinister figure
whose intrigues harmed the Nazi war effort, the SS, and
Himmler.

"I thought, and still think, that Bormann did the greatest
harm of anybody in all those years, apart from a few smart
guys in uniform," Berger* said on the stand at Nuremberg.
"For the rest, this judgment concerning Bormann will, I think,
be confirmed in the course of the next years."

In Berger's opinion, the Secretary of the Führer had been a
Soviet agent. When the Russians took Berlin, he simply joined
them. Bormann was now in the Soviet Union and would reappear at the proper moment as the Soviet-backed commissar
of a communist Germany.

But Bormann could not have been in Russia in 1948, if
another informant was correct about having seen him that
year in Chile. This was Pablo (Paul) Heisslein, a sixty-two-
year-old native of Bavaria. During the 1920's, Heisslein had
been mayor of a Saxon town, a Catholic Center Party deputy
to the Reichstag, and press chief for the Federation of German
Civil Servants. He lost these posts when the Nazis came to
power. After years of harassment by the Gestapo, he emigrated in 1938 to Chile and supported himself there by writing
newsletters on politics and economics.

In February 1948, Heisslein was the guest of another Ger-
man refugee, Count Jean Ulrich von Reichenbach, at the
Count's property in the virgin tropical forest of Chile near the
Argentine border. While there, Heisslein decided to visit
Ranco Sur, one of Chile's most beautiful lakes. To do this, it

---

* Berger was sentenced to 25 years in prison by the Nuremberg Military
Tribunal. After serving three years he was released by an American
clemency board.

was necessary to walk for about three hours through the tropical forest. For protection, Heisslein brought with him some of
Count von Reichenbach's dogs and a revolver, for the former
Reichstag deputy knew that pumas and hostile Indians lived in
the area. He was also aware of the rumors that Nazis had
settled near Ranco Sur. Supposedly, they were put ashore on
the west coast of Chile from two submarines after the fall of
the Third Reich.

At midpoint in Heisslein's journey, three horsemen wearing
ponchos and sombreros suddenly appeared and rode to within
a few feet of him. The dogs became agitated. Heisslein pulled
out his revolver. Then he recognized the rider in the middle as
Martin Bormann.

"It's Heisslein!" Bormann murmured, then added in a
commanding tone, "Gallop!" The three horsemen rode toward the Argentine border and vanished. Heisslein was absolutely certain that it was Bormann, whom he remembered well
from prewar Berlin. He told Chilean authorities of his forest
encounter, but they requested him to remain silent until their
own investigations into Bormann's whereabouts were completed. Later, Heisslein read newspaper reports that the Secretary of the Führer had left Argentina and gone to Spain.

However, Bormann did not appear in Spain or anywhere
else in 1948, 1949, or 1950. But in 1950 another missing
Nazi, and a close friend and protégé of his, was found in West
Germany. This was Erich Koch, Gauleiter of East Prussia and
Reich Commissioner for the Ukraine.

Self-characterized as a "brutal dog," Koch regarded the
Ukrainians, by his own admission, as "niggers," and handled
them "with vodka and the whip." When the Red Army retook
the Ukraine, Koch fled to Pillau in East Prussia. As the Russians approached Pillau on April 23, 1945, Gauleiter Koch
and his staff boarded an icebreaker named *Ostpreussen.* The
Gauleiter barred ordinary refugees from *Ostpreussen,* thus
abandoning them to the advancing Russians.

Ostpreussen cruised the Baltic until Koch heard Doenitz'

radio broadcast of the Führer's death. Directing the ice breaker to dock at Flensburg, Koch debarked there bearing papers identifying him as Major Rolf Berger, and wearing a newly grown moustache of enormous proportions. He then spent nearly a year undetected in an East Prussian refugee camp in Schleswig-Holstein.

In May 1946, Koch left the camp and became a day laborer in a village in the British Zone seventeen miles from Hamburg. Still successfully posing as Major Berger, he attended meetings of East Prussian refugees and at them frequently announced his belief that the hated Gauleiter Erich Koch had drowned when *Ostpreussen* was sunk by Russian planes. Koch remained a free man until he was recognized by a former German army officer whose family the Gauleiter had refused to evacuate from East Prussia. The vengeful officer reported Koch's whereabouts to Hamburg police. Koch was arrested and turned over to British occupation authorities, who agreed to his extradition to Warsaw by the Polish Government in February 1950.*

No postwar connection between Erich Koch and his strongest supporter, Martin Bormann, was established by Hamburg police or British occupation authorities. But the belated apprehension of Koch did indicate that it was possible for a prominent Nazi to remain at liberty for five years after the end of the Third Reich. Even after Koch's arrest, a number of them continued to remain unaccounted for, including Werner Naumann and Adolf Eichmann.

Dr. Naumann, of course, had been named by Hitler to suc-

---

* Eight years passed before Koch was tried. In March 1959, a Warsaw court sentenced him to death, but there is no evidence that this sentence has been executed. Although he was the leading Nazi official in the Ukraine, the Soviet government displayed no public interest in his trial, which dealt solely with his relatively minor depradations in that part of East Prussia which came under Polish administration after the war. That the Soviet Government did not want to try Koch and thus publicize his Ukrainian nationalist victims, who were also opponents of the Kremlin, must remain one speculation among many until the facts in this curious affair are available.

ceed Goebbels as head of the Propaganda Ministry. He was also in the group which attempted to escape from the Reich Chancellery with Bormann on May 1, 1945. After that night, Naumann disappeared. But in 1950 he was living, undetected, in West Germany. In that same year, a man bearing a refugee passport identifying him as Ricardo Klement arrived in Buenos Aires, Argentina, on a ship from Italy. "Klement" was Eichmann. If he and Naumann could evade capture as late as 1950, it was at least possible that the Secretary of the Führer was doing the same thing, had he indeed survived the war.

Bormann's chances of remaining at liberty were strengthened by circumstances unique to his case. In 1945, he had been the target of manhunts by the military intelligence agencies of the Soviet Union, the United States, Great Britain, and France. He was tried, convicted, and sentenced in his absence by the International Military Tribunal, whose charter was never dissolved. Therefore the responsibility for finding Bormann and executing the Nuremberg sentence rested solely with the signatories to the charter. However, the urgency of discharging this responsibility had faded by 1950 because of the cold war.

The former Allies against Nazi Germany were now enemies. The Soviet Union was primarily interested in securing its hold over East Germany. The United States, Great Britain, and France wanted to establish a democratic, western-oriented state in their zones of influence. As a result, the finding of missing Nazis was replaced by other priorities.

By 1952, none of the members of the International Military Tribunal was making a determined effort to solve the continuing mystery of Bormann's fate. Even if they had wanted to, the occupied Germans had no authority to act in the matter. To the Israeli Secret Service, Bormann was of much less interest than Adolf Eichmann, who had been exclusively involved in the Final Solution. Interpol's targets were bank robbers, counterfeiters, embezzlers, ordinary murderers and the like. The international detective agency had no jurisdiction over the new type of criminal produced by the Third Reich. This was the man who had committed none of the traditional crimes and who would never have thought of doing so, but who, from behind a desk, executed the murderous orders of the Führer which were yet perfectly legal in Nazi Germany.

These circumstances favored Bormann's chances of successfully hiding in some country tolerant of Nazi fugitives. And the rumors and reports persisted that he had not been killed in Berlin and was still alive in 1952.

In January 1952, the former Italian partisan leader Luigi Silvestri told newspaper reporters that he had seen Bormann in Bolzano, Italy, on May 10, 1945. Bormann was then getting out of a large black Mercedes-Benz to enter a Dominican monastery which served as Italian Red Cross Headquarters. He posed as the leader of a humanitarian German organization responsible for the exchange of Italian and German war prisoners. Bolzano was on the sunny south side of the Alps, just across from that part of the Austrian Tyrol where Frau Gerda Bormann was living in May 1945, after she had left Berchtesgaden.

One month after Silvestri's report, Eberhard Stern, a former official in the Nazi Ministry for Armaments and War Production, saw a monk in the Franciscan monastery of San Antonio in Rome and recognized him as Bormann. A photograph of a "Brother Martini" who bore a striking resemblance to Bormann was widely published in the world press. However, the San Antonio monastery denied that it had ever sheltered Bormann, and "Brother Martini" proved to be Father Romualdi Antonuzzi, a Franciscan monk.

On February 17, 1953, there was another newspaper report that Bormann had survived. This came from the West Berlin grain dealer, and former SS major, Joachim Tiburtius. As a staff officer of the SS Nordland Division, Tiburtius commanded a group of some 400 people attempting to escape from the Reich Chancellery on May 1, 1945. He saw Bormann jogging next to the tank when it was blown apart on the

Weidendammer Bridge. But the blast had not killed the Secretary of the Führer, according to Tiburtius, who saw him shortly thereafter near the Hotel Atlas on the far side of the bridge. He was dressed in civilian clothes.

"We pushed on together toward the Schiffbauerdamm and the Albrechtstrasse," Tiburtius maintained. "Then I finally lost sight of him. But he had as good a chance to escape as I had."

Two days before the former SS major's statement, a startling event had given further credence to the possibility of Bormann's escape from Berlin. On February 15, 1953, the High Commissioner of the British Zone of West Germany announced the arrest of seven men in Hamburg and Düsseldorf on suspicion of engaging in a conspiracy to overthrow the Federal Republic and replace it with a Nazi regime.

The British claimed the confiscation of four tons of material which would provide evidence to support an indictment for high treason and conspiracy of the seven suspects. Their backgrounds were undoubtedly disturbing. Among the seven were Karl Kaufmann, once Gauleiter of Hamburg; Dr. Gustav Scheel, Gauleiter of Salzburg; and Dr. Heinrich Haselmeyer, former head of the Nazi Students League and an expert on "racial science" and the sterilization of the unfit.

As ringleader of the conspiracy, the British named Dr. Werner Naumann. It developed that he had reached the Black Forest after escaping from Berlin on the night of May 1, 1945. Naumann worked in the Black Forest and in Frankfurt as a manual laborer for five years without being detected by American occupation authorities. He then went to the British Zone and obtained employment in a Ruhr export-import firm owned by a former colleague in the Propaganda Ministry. Still undetected, he forged a circle of former Nazi Gauleiter, SS officers, and bureaucrats. Their apparent aim was to establish links with Nazi cells abroad and to capture control of respectable West German right-wing parties, such as the Free Democrats, by infiltrating them. The British regarded Werner

Naumann as the instigator of the most serious neo-Nazi threat to the Federal Republic which had yet developed.

The Federal Republic was close to being granted complete sovereignty by the occupation powers. And so, in March 1953, the British High Commissioner agreed to Chancellor Konrad Adenauer's request that the Federal Republic be given responsibility for the investigation and eventual prosecution of Dr. Naumann and his associates. Later, West German authorities released the seven men after deciding that there was no real evidence of a serious Nazi conspiracy. Dr. Naumann himself was penalized only by being barred for life from political activity.

The West Germans could find no evidence that Bormann was in contact with the alleged conspirators. But Naumann was able to throw some light on Bormann's fate. Naumann told West German investigators that he, with Bormann, Axmann, Kempka, Dr. Stumpfegger and a number of other men, tried to cross the Weidendammer Bridge on the night of May 1, 1945. The tank they were using as a shield was blown apart by a Soviet bazooka shell. But the blast did not kill Bormann. He, Naumann, Axmann, and some others walked on to the Lehrter Station. There the last Propaganda Minister of the Third Reich parted company with Bormann and struck out for the west. Naumann did not know what had happened to him after that. However, Bormann was still alive when he left him between three and four A.M., Naumann maintained. He was not wounded and he did not appear exhausted and desperate.

But Bormann did not escape from Berlin, according to two German legal bodies which in 1954 ruled him legally dead. The Berchtesgaden *Amtsgericht* (County Court) conducted an investigation in order to settle his personal estate. On January 30, 1954, the Berchtesgaden court ruled that the Head of the Nazi Party Chancellery had died in Berlin and even fixed the date and hour: May 2, 1945, midnight. The county court was not required under German law to make public the evidence which led to its decision and did not do so.

On July 24, 1954, the Registrar's Office of the City of West Berlin, Bormann's last known place of residence, followed the Berchtesgaden ruling and declared the Secretary of the Führer legally dead. The Registrar's Office published annually a "Book of Death Notices," which announced the deaths of Berlin residents confirmed during the year. In this volume for 1954, Bormann was listed as Death Number 29,223. However, the listing carried a qualifying note: "Death not completely established."

After the actions of the Berchtesgaden court and the Registrar's Office, the West Berlin *Spruchkammer* (Denazification Court) was legally enabled to confiscate Bormann's estate for purposes of restitution to Nazi victims. But the *Spruchkammer* could only find property worth about $8,300. Not all of this was confiscated. Some $450 was set aside for Bormann's children to pay the costs incurred by the Denazification Court in settling their father's estate.

It can be doubted that the investigation of the Berchtesgaden court was definitive and had any other motive than the final settlement of Bormann's estate, for it was concluded more than a year before five eyewitness accounts of his fate became available in the west.

In 1955, the West German Federal Republic obtained the release of a number of war prisoners from the Soviet Government, some of whom had been captured by the Russians while attempting to escape from the Reich Chancellery with Bormann. Among those released after ten years spent in Soviet prisons was Hitler's valet, Heinz Linge.

"I tell you, Bormann is dead," Linge assured West German reporters who questioned him upon his return from Russia in October 1955. The valet had last seen the Secretary of the Führer near the tank as it exploded into flame on the Weidendammer Bridge.

Another returnee, Johann Rattenhuber, chief of the Führer's detective bodyguard, was sure that the blast had killed Bormann. So was Hans Bauer, Hitler's personal pilot, who was unable to obey the Führer's order to fly Bormann out of Berlin from a nearby airfield. Otto Günsche, Hitler's SS adjutant, was also convinced of Bormann's death. But in Günsche's version, the Reichsleiter had been inside the tank when it exploded.

Linge, Rattenhuber, Bauer, and Günsche had been extensively interrogated concerning Bormann's fate by their Soviet captors. To them, they told the same story they now told western reporters. Though the versions of the four returnees varied slightly in details, all agreed that Bormann had died on the Weidendammer Bridge. But none had seen his corpse.

This was not the case with another returned prisoner, the Spaniard Juan Roca-Pinar. Once a member of the Spanish Blue Division on the eastern front, Roca-Pinar found himself attached to a small SS unit near the Weidendammer Bridge on the night of May 1, 1945. There he saw an immobilized tank and heard an SS officer order him to "get Bormann out of it."

Roca-Pinar and another soldier jumped onto the tank, tore open its hatch, and peered inside. The Spaniard saw two dead men. He recognized one of them as Martin Bormann. According to Roca-Pinar, he dragged Bormann out of the tank. But the mounting intensity of the Russian fire forced Roca-Pinar to abandon Bormann's corpse on the street.

The returned prisoners, while apparently confirming the death of the Head of the Nazi Party Chancellery, actually added to the mystery. For their statements were in direct conflict with those of Naumann, Axmann, Schwägermann, and Tiburtius. These four claimed to have seen Bormann alive long after the tank explosion. Were all or some of them mistaken, or were they part of a conspiracy to protect the missing man? What had happened to the Führer's closest confidant?

None of his children, all of whom were raised by various foster parents, supplied a satisfactory answer. However, Bormann's eldest son appeared briefly in the news in 1958. Hitler was the godfather of Adolf Martin, who had once been a prize pupil at the elite Nazi school for teenagers in Feldafing. After his flight from Berchtesgaden and the death of his mother when he was fifteen, the homeless boy was raised as "Martin Bergmann" by a family named Hohenwärter. They were Austrian peasants and devout Catholics.

Martin Bormann had instructed his wife to "make sure that none of our children get depraved and diseased by the poison of Christianity, in whatever dosage." Nevertheless, his eldest son became a Catholic convert. Moreover, young Martin Bormann (he had dropped his godfather's name) was ordained a Roman Catholic priest in the order of the Missionaries of the Sacred Heart at the Jesuit Church in Innsbruck, Austria, on August 20, 1958.

"We know of the heavy load that rests on his shoulders," one of the Jesuit Order remarked after the ordination. "For us, he is new confirmation that even among the Godless evolved by totalitarianism there is a way back."

Father Martin Bormann, S.J., later became a missionary in the Congo and remained there after the Belgian colony attained independence. From time to time, European investigators asked him if he could shed any light on his father's fate. Like the eight other Bormann children, he could not. An American writer once interviewed Father Bormann at his primitive mission station in an immense tropical forest three hundred miles south of Kinshasa, the Congolese capital. The writer asked if he had any idea of where his father might be.

"I'm almost completely sure he's dead," Father Bormann replied. "I don't believe the stories that he's been seen alive since his disappearance in Berlin. He never contacted my mother or any other member of my family. He died in Berlin, I think."

"If your father should be alive," the writer asked, "and if he should ever come here to the Congo—would you protect him, give him a place to hide?"

"Yes."

"How—after all that has happened—could you?"

"Because he is my father. In spite of everything he has done, he is my father. There is no law of man or God or of the Church which says I must deliver my own father to the hangman."

"But you entered the priesthood—and came here—to expiate for him."

"If you wish," Father Bormann said, concluding the conversation.

In the year of young Father Bormann's ordination, 1958, the West German Federal Republic opened a new agency in Ludwigsburg, a small town near Stuttgart. It was called "Center for Preparation and Coordination for the Prosecution of Concentration Camp and War Crimes," and was headed by a former district attorney, Dr. Erwin Schuele.

The Allies controlled the discovery and trial of Nazi war criminals when West Germany was occupied, but now it was a sovereign state with jurisdiction in these matters and Dr. Schuele's office dealt with them. He was eventually successful in bringing to trial many Nazis the Allies had overlooked, including twenty-two staff members of the Auschwitz extermination camp. But in 1959 and 1960, Dr. Schuele was no more successful in finding Martin Bormann than anyone else had been.

The world gradually lost interest in the Head of the Nazi Party Chancellery. Even in the more sensational European illustrated magazines the articles about his being seen alive ceased. It just did not seem possible that Bormann, or any other important Nazi, could have survived for fifteen years without being discovered. The idea was too fantastic.

Then, on May 11, 1960, at a bus stop near his home in a Buenos Aires suburb, Israeli agents picked up Adolf Eichmann.

SIXTEEN

"The Search Is Narrowing Down"

Martin Bormann was alive. Adolf Eichmann told his pre-trial interrogators this in Jerusalem. However, the Israelis never made the details of Eichmann's assertion public.

After he went on trial, Eichmann received numerous letters. Some were threatening, some obscene, and a few were encouraging. One read only "Courage, Courage." It was signed "Martin." Handwriting experts believed that this letter was written by Martin Bormann, according to the Israeli prosecutor Gideon Hausner.

The capture and trial of Eichmann sharply revived interest in Bormann's fate. For if Eichmann could have worked undetected as a common laborer in West Germany until 1950, then gone to South America via Italy with the help of some SS veterans and survived in Argentina as "Ricardo Klement" for another ten years, there was no apparent reason why Bormann could not have done something similar. Attempts to answer the question of what had happened to the head of the Nazi Party Chancellery resumed their appearance.

In June 1960, the Israeli newspaper *Haolam Hazeh* reported that Bormann owned a large house in a Buenos Aires suburb. Finding himself in need of medical treatment, he sought it from a doctor who happened to be Jewish. The doctor recognized his patient, despite the obvious plastic surgery to his face. He then killed Martin Bormann with a heart injection.

But in September 1960, Vitolo, the official Argentine news agency, reported the capture of Bormann by Argentine police in the industrial city of Zárate, eighty miles northwest of Buenos Aires. The captured man did indeed resemble Bormann, but he turned out to be a one-armed German immigrant named Walter Flegel. He was released and Vitolo announced that the Argentine police would continue looking for Bormann because they had no evidence that he was dead.

The sudden activity of the Argentine police was undoubtedly spurred by the furor caused by Eichmann's capture. It was embarrassing to the Argentine Government that the Israelis had found Eichmann in Argentina. More embarrassing still would have been the discovery of Martin Bormann by anyone but the Argentines themselves.

The West German government was also roused to action by the Eichmann case. West Germany was now enjoying the prosperity engendered by its "economic miracle," its new army was a major force in NATO, and, in contrast to East Germany, it symbolized the efficacy of free enterprise and democratic institutions. But Eichmann released a flood of ghastly memories. As a sovereign, democratic nation, West Germany could not afford to let it be said that it was not doing everything possible to bring missing Nazis to justice. To this purpose, Dr. Erwin Schuele's "Center for Preparation and Coordination for the Prosecution of Concentration Camp and War Crimes" had previously been opened near Stuttgart. Now another West German official joined Dr. Schuele in the search for Bormann, who was the most important missing Nazi of all.

In April 1961, in Frankfurt, Dr. Fritz Bauer publicly entered the Bormann case and opened an active file on it. Dr. Bauer was a fifty-seven-year-old German Jew. He had twice been imprisoned in Nazi concentration camps, but managed to escape to Sweden in 1940. Nine years later, Dr. Bauer returned to Germany. In 1961 he was District Attorney for the State of Hesse and connected with *Abteilung VI der Frankfurter Staatsanwaltschaft der hessischen Zentrale für die Verfolgung nationalsozialistichen Verbrechen* (Department VI of the Frankfurt District Attorney's Office of the Hessian Center for the Pursuance of National Socialist Crimes).

Dr. Bauer collected eight thick files filled with 1300 pages of documents concerning Bormann's fate. On April 13, he told a news conference that he was convinced that Bormann was alive, adding that a secret international Nazi organization might have sent him abroad through an elaborate underground system.

One of Dr. Bauer's hundreds of informants was Eichmann's eldest son, Horst Adolf. During a visit to West Germany in February 1961, Horst Adolf Eichmann had told the District Attorney of his many recent conversations with Bormann in South America.

Shortly after Dr. Bauer's Frankfurt press conference, another reputable public official held one in Tel Aviv. He was Dr. Gregory Topolevsky, a former Argentine ambassador to Israel. On May 9, 1961, Dr. Topolevsky said that Bormann had recently fled from Argentina and was hiding in Brazil. But the next day the Ambassador qualified his statement; he had only been quoting from Argentine press reports and had no knowledge from official sources of Bormann's whereabouts. And there the matter stood until June 1962. Then a press attaché at the Spanish Embassy in London, Angel Alcazar de Velasco, told newspaper reporters that he had met Bormann in Madrid in May 1945 and later boarded a German submarine with him. After a voyage of twenty-one days from Spain, Bormann and Alcazar de Velasco debarked in Argentina. The Spaniard said that he saw Bormann again in 1958 in Ecuador. He then looked prematurely old and was totally bald. His cheeks were completely sunken and he had undergone three facial plastic surgery operations. But as was the case with all the other Bormann informants, there was only Alcazar de Velasco's word for what he maintained was true.

By 1963, the "Center for Preparation and Coordination for the Prosecution of Concentration Camp and War Crimes," was making a systematic effort to find missing Nazis. This joint undertaking of the eleven states of West Germany, located in a former women's prison just a few hundred feet from a picturesque baroque castle in Ludwigsburg, had a staff of 115 investigators. The center maintained a master list of 160,000 names. Bormann's name, of course, headed the list, followed in importance by that of Heinrich Mueller.

SS Lieutenant General Heinrich Mueller, a cold, secretive personality, was Chief of the Gestapo. One of his underlings, SS Lieutenant Colonel Willi Hoettl, described him as "a man with an imposing head and sharp features, curiously disfigured by a thin gash of a mouth that had no lips." Mueller was in Berlin as the Red Army encircled the city. From his office in Kurfürstenstrasse he reported every day to the *Führerbunker*. He was last seen there on April 29, 1945. Since then, it had been assumed that he was killed in the Berlin street fighting at the age of forty-five and buried in the garrison cemetery in the West Berlin district of Kreuzberg. His family placed a marker to that effect on the grave.

However, the Ludwigsburg Center was not convinced that the Chief of the Gestapo, or Martin Bormann, had been killed in Berlin. The Center felt that Mueller might have escaped and tried to cover his flight by the burial of another corpse in what was supposed to be his grave. The evidence that led to this belief could not, of course, be made public. But as part of its continuing secret project to determine Mueller's fate, the Center requested the West Berlin District Attorney's office to open the grave. This was done in the early morning hours of September 25, 1963. The grave did not yield a complete skeleton, but the bones of three different men. Pathologists determined that none of the bones could have belonged to Heinrich Mueller. Now to the mystery of what had happened to Martin Bormann was added the puzzle of the Chief of the Gestapo.

The Ludwigsburg Center continued its systematic efforts to solve both mysteries. So did Dr. Fritz Bauer.

A break in the Bormann case appeared to take place in March 1964. One Richard Bormann then gave himself up to police in São Paulo, Brazil, because he was "tired of living in the underground." Richard Bormann told the Brazilian police that his brother Martin was living in the state of Mato Grosso (Thick Forest), a wild, undeveloped section of Brazil's interior nearly twice as big as Texas and inhabited mostly by Guarani Indians.

Brazil was an ideal country for wanted Nazis to hide in. It borders seven other Latin American countries, permitting easy entry and exit. Foreigners cannot be deported or extradited if they have Brazilian dependents. There is no capital punishment, and prison terms cannot be longer than thirty years. There are large German populations in the states of Santa Caterina, Paraná, and Rio Grande Do Sul.

Dr. Fritz Bauer was already investigating reports that the Secretary of the Führer had died in Paraguay in 1959 and was buried in a village near its capital, Asunción. When the grave in question was opened it was found to contain the remains of a Paraguayan named Hormoncilla. So Dr. Bauer gave serious consideration to the new report from São Paulo, Brazil.

Bormann, it developed, did have a younger brother. The Reichsleiter had once gotten him a job as one of the Führer's adjutants. This was nothing new, although the brother had been forgotten since the war. Dr. Bauer's investigators found him again. His name was Albert and he was living in the village of Icking in Upper Bavaria.

"I have no brother named Richard," Albert Bormann said. "None of my relatives had that name. The man who reported himself in Brazil under the name of Richard Bormann must be either an egotist or a swindler." The man then turned out to be a fifty-two-year-old SS veteran who had made his way to South America with false papers; he was now suffering from a mental disturbance.

Despite false alarms such as the one involving "Richard" Bormann, the West German government took the accumulating reports of Martin Bormann's survival seriously enough to post a $25,000 reward in November 1964 for information leading to his capture. Mindful of the strong diplomatic protests lodged by Argentina against Israel for its abduction of Eichmann, the Federal Republic cautioned that if the Secretary of the Führer were found, kidnapped, and returned to West Germany, the reward would be paid only if the country in which he had been hiding approved of his return.

Months passed and the reward went unclaimed, although the reports that Bormann was alive continued. In March 1965, São Paulo Interpol representatives arrested a man carrying an Argentine passport in the name of Carlos Rodrigues and a West German passport in that of Alfred Trenker. He was really a former SS officer, Detlev Sonnemberg, who had made his way to Guaraja, Brazil, from Egypt in 1953. Interpol was not interested in Sonnemberg because of his SS past, but because he was on its wanted list for six cases of armed robbery in West Germany. According to Sonnemberg, former Nazis living in South America had formed a self-protection organization after Eichmann's capture. Bormann was one of them and he was living in Brazil.

Nothing came of Sonnemberg's contention. But in West Germany, Dr. Bauer continued his investigation. Among the hundreds of people interviewed by his staff was Artur Axmann. Now a businessman in the Ruhr, the former Hitler Youth Leader repeated the story he had told Allied intelligence officers about the night of May 1, 1945, in Berlin. Axmann remained the single authoritative eyewitness to Bormann's death. And yet he had been a prominent Nazi, and no one could prove or disprove his insistence that he had seen the corpses of Bormann and Dr. Stumpfegger on the Invalidenstrasse railroad bridge. But if it did develop that he was right, Bormann's fate would be solved.

The persistent Dr. Bauer then discovered that on August

14, 1945, the Berlin Post Office 40, Lehrter Railroad Station, had officially notified Frau Gertrud Stumpfegger in writing of her husband's death. Post-office employees buried a corpse bearing Dr. Ludwig Stumpfegger's identification on May 8, 1945, after finding it on the Invalidenstrasse railroad bridge. The burial place was a few hundred yards from the bridge, in the *Ausstellungs-Park* (Exhibition Park), an amusement area where summer art exhibitions had been held.

Dr. Bauer also discovered a sixty-seven-year-old retired Berlin mailman named Albert Krumnow, who said that he and three other Lehrter Post Office employees had buried two bodies found on the railroad bridge. They had done this at the direction of the Russians, who wanted to forestall the possibility of an epidemic. On May 8, 1945, Krumnow and his three fellow mailmen buried a tall man bearing Dr. Stumpfegger's identification in the Exhibition Park and next to him a shorter, thickset man. His helpers had since died and after twenty years Krumnow could not be certain of the exact burial places. But his testimony and the official notice to Dr. Stumpfegger's widow appeared to corroborate Axmann's story.

Was the answer to a question that had apparently baffled the intelligence and police agencies of numerous countries for two decades to be found buried in the ground of West Berlin? Dr. Bauer intended to find out, and he took an obvious step that no one had taken before. On July 19, 1965, West Berlin policemen, armed with picks and shovels and assisted by a bulldozer, began to turn up the earth of the former Exhibition Park. It now served as a lot and storage yard for a shipping company and was close to the Berlin Wall.

For two days, the policemen patiently and methodically dug up hundreds of square yards of earth. They uncovered rocks, tree stumps, beer bottles, old weapons of German and Soviet manufacture, but not a trace of any human bones. The digging was abandoned.

Another Nazi-hunter, Tadek Tuvia Friedman, could have told Dr. Bauer that he was wasting his time looking for Bor-

mann's remains in Berlin. He should have been searching for
the living man in Argentina. Friedman, as a young Polish Jew,
had been a Nazi slave laborer in a weapons factory in Radom,
his home town. After the war, he went to Vienna and on his
own began to trace missing Nazi criminals. In the summer of
1952, Friedman emigrated to Israel. Lacking any professional
training or skill, he had a rather difficult time in the new
nation. He obtained work as a newspaper reporter and,
briefly, as a minor government employee. But hunting Nazis
remained his chief concern and he opened his own small, private Institute for the Documentation of Nazi War Crimes in
Haifa. Friedman collected considerable information about
missing Nazis and in particular became something of a gadfly
to Israeli government officials in urging them to do something
about Eichmann.

In October 1965, Friedman came to New York City to
attend an auction at which a letter written to him by Eichmann from his prison cell was sold for $1,000. Friedman was
now forty-two years old. A reporter from the New York *Post*
described him as "a short round man with stubby fingers and
the distinct air of a shopkeeper." He was still privately active
in hunting Nazi criminals and his principal target was Martin
Bormann.

"For a $50,000 reward we could get him overnight," Fried-
man told the *Post* reporter who interviewed him. "We know
he is in Argentina. We know exactly where. But the trouble is
nobody wants him. You see, he is an international criminal
and it would be up to Germany or England or the United
States to punish him, and after the Eichmann trial they want
none of this trouble, none of this heartache. But, as for me, I
still keep an eye on him, yes."

Friedman spoke for himself as a private investigator of
missing Nazis and not for the Israeli Government. He might
have been wrong in his belief that Bormann was in Argentina.
But he was certainly right in implying that the Israeli Government had no official motive to search for him. Bormann

had already been tried at Nuremberg as a major war criminal "whose crimes have no particular geographical location." By this definition, Bormann was not specifically a Jewish problem. Eichmann was, which is why the Israelis had found and tried him.

The Soviet Union was one of the four charter members of the International Military Tribunal who still shared the responsibility for finding Bormann if he were alive. The Russians, of course, possessed an intelligence apparatus of no small expertise. The location of any individual was a routine job for Soviet Intelligence. But after Nuremberg, the Russians maintained official silence regarding Martin Bormann. In 1965, however, a book was published in East Berlin called *Auf den Spuren von Martin Bormann** (On The Trail of Martin Bormann). Its author was Lew Besymenski, a former major in Soviet Intelligence.

Besymenski devoted several years to interviewing Russian and German officers and officials who might have firsthand knowledge of Bormann's fate. He also researched relevant documents in West German, East German, and Soviet archives. As a product of his extensive research and interviews, Besymenski offered his version of Bormann's fate. Because his book had to be approved by Soviet and East German censors before publication, it could be taken as the official line on Bormann.

The Secretary of the Führer had not been killed in Berlin, according to the Soviet author. After escaping from the city, he made his way as an unknown civilian to Wolkenstein in the Tyrol, where his wife was living. Somewhere in the Nazi "Alpine Fortress" he collected the hidden box of gold coins originally meant for the Führermuseum in Linz. The coins were turned over to Bormann's adviser on economic affairs, Dr. Helmut von Hummel, in Berchtesgaden at the end of the war and were worth about five million dollars. Thus financed,

* The original Russian edition of this book was published in Moscow in late 1964.

Bormann went to the naval base at Kiel in northwest Germany to find a submarine to take him out of the country.

However, since the entire submarine fleet of Grand Admiral Doenitz had been captured by the Allies, Bormann hid in Schleswig-Holstein and later in neighboring Denmark until the Nuremberg Trial ended. He then made contact with *ODESSA**, a clandestine organization of SS veterans which organized escape routes for wanted Nazis leading over the Alps into Italy. The *ODESSA* network was aided by Italian aristocrats, princes of the Roman Catholic Church, and American intelligence agents.

With *ODESSA's* help, Bormann crossed into Italy on a dark August night in 1947 from Nauders, a village at the head of the Inn Valley where the Austrian, Swiss, and Italian frontiers meet. Italian sympathizers suggested that he place himself under the protection of the Roman Catholic Church. He agreed and was sheltered first in a monastery on Lake Garda and then in a Franciscan monastery in Genoa.

Eventually, the Secretary of the Führer met Bishop Alois Hudal at the Via della Pace in Rome. He was the leader of the Christian Welfare Foundation and also the tutor of Bormann's eldest son, Adolf Martin, who was already preparing for the priesthood. Bishop Hudal placed two possibilities before Hitler's closest confidant. He could either go to Spain, where Otto Skorzeny, the Nazi commando leader, and Leon Dégrelle, the former head of the Belgian Fascists, were living or to Argentina, like Eichmann. Argentina was the more suitable choice.

But this was only a "working hypothesis," Besymenski wrote. It was what "could have happened." The Soviet author had no thought of supporting his hypothesis with specific names and addresses. He did not want to proceed "like Sherlock Holmes," but to point out that the trail of Martin Bormann led into the political life of those western countries where it was possible for him to have gained refuge. Whether

* *Organisation der ehemaligen SS-Argehörigen* (Organization of former SS members).

or not the man himself was alive, his spirit certainly was. This particularly was true in West Germany, whose postwar government was riddled with Nazis. Besymenski devoted half of his book, which was subtitled *Truths About German Imperialism,* to advancing this thesis.

Klaus Eichmann was more positive than the former Soviet Intelligence major in contending that Bormann was literally alive in South America. In January 1966, the thirty-year-old son of Adolf Eichmann wrote an open letter to Bormann. This was published in *Quick,* a popular West German illustrated magazine. Klaus wanted to clear his father's name. In Klaus' view, Adolf Eichmann had been made a fall guy for crimes for which Bormann was responsible.

"I am waiting for you to give yourself up," Klaus wrote. "I am waiting for you to come forward for that part of the guilt for which you are responsible and for which my father stood in your place during the trial in Israel . . . You still live on in your South American hiding place. You rub your hands over every report of your death in Berlin in 1945 . . ."

At about the same time that this open letter appeared, Horst Adolf Eichmann, Klaus's older brother, was interviewed in Buenos Aires. Horst Adolf had already told Dr. Fritz Bauer in February 1961 of his frequent conversations with Bormann in South America. Now he said that he believed the Secretary of the Führer had been killed in Berlin, after all. Asked to explain the contradiction between his belief and that of his older brother, Klaus Eichmann told *Quick:* "When one lives in South America, where there are still influential Nazi circles, one must take into account that these Nazi circles will one day strike out at anyone who makes things uncomfortable for them."

Nothing whatever came of this incident. Eichmann's sons retired into obscurity, along with their memories and whatever useful evidence they possessed. But in Germany, Dr. Fritz Bauer pressed on. The West Germans had a motive for finding Bormann. Even though he was tried at Nuremberg as an in-

ternational war criminal, West Germany could try him for his
actions as a German citizen against other German citizens.
Only one instance of this was his order of March 23, 1945, to
destroy all food reserves in Germany and to herd the entire
population, on foot and by force if necessary, to the center of
the country.

On April 16, 1966, Dr. Bauer said at a press conference in
Bonn that he had "fresh evidence" concerning Bormann. "The
search is narrowing down," the investigator said. "We have
sifted reports from all over the world and now I am hopeful
that we are hot on his trail." Dr. Bauer was convinced that
Bormann was in South America, but he declined to divulge
details of his new evidence. The year 1966 passed without
Bormann being apprehended.

Simon Wiesenthal, too, thought that Bormann was alive.
Wiesenthal, an architect and engineer before the Nazi invasion of his native Poland, had been gathering information
about missing Nazis since his liberation from the Mauthausen
concentration camp in Austria by American troops in February 1945. He continued his private investigations because
he felt that the cold war caused the official police and intelligence agencies in the East and West to ease up on the prosecution of Nazis who had committed crimes against the Jews.
This was done "to sweeten the West Germans" or "when
Nazis recanted and joined the Communists."

Wiesenthal was not a professional detective and he did not
personally hunt down wanted Nazis, but he did amass a large
amount of valuable material from private informants and
from careful study of his dossiers. He then passed on his information to official government agencies for action. Leads
which he gave to the Israeli Government were helpful in the
capture of Adolf Eichmann. After this event, he became interested in Bormann, who was on the list of more than 22,000
Nazi war criminals in Wiesenthal's Jewish Documentation
Center in Vienna. The center, with a staff of sixteen, was
supported by modest contributions from Jews.

In February 1967, magazine excerpts from a then forthcoming book by Wiesenthal, *The Murderers Among Us,*
began to appear in the United States. In these excerpts, Wiesenthal told of some of his more important cases. One concerned Franz Stangl. From March through August 1942 he
was commandant of the Sobibor extermination camp. In
August and September 1942, Stangl commanded the Treblinka extermination camp. In these camps located in Poland,
Wiesenthal estimated that 700,000 people, all but a few of
them Jews, were gassed to death.

Like Adolf Eichmann, Stangl was interned in an American
prisoner-of-war camp after the war. Intelligence officers were
unable to discover the true identity of either man. Both escaped from the POW camps without great difficulty. Wiesenthal maintained that Stangl had made his way to Brazil in
1951, was now working in an automobile factory in São
Paulo, and that he knew Stangl's address.

Another of Wiesenthal's cases was "the biggest unsolved
Nazi mystery," as he described it. From a study of information
given to him by a variety of people who had seen Bormann or
heard that he was alive, Wiesenthal deduced that the Secretary
of the Führer was "most probably" living near the frontier
between Chile and Argentina. But no country was really interested in apprehending him. Since Bormann was sixty-seven
years old, the mystery surrounding him would "degenerate
into a simple biological equation."

"He is well protected," Wiesenthal wrote. "No country will
want to attempt a second Eichmann case. Bormann will come
to his end some day, and the reward of 100,000 marks
[posted by the West German government] will never be paid.
Death needs no money."

Then, on March 2, 1967, the Department of Political and
Social Order of the State of São Paulo, Brazil, detained Franz
Stangl. The Brazilians acted at the request of the Austrian
government, which in turn had acted on information supplied
by Wiesenthal. Stangl was employed as a maintenance inspec-

tor in the Volkswagen of Brazil plant in São Paulo, a sprawling industrial city of 5.25 million people. He lived modestly in Brooklyn, a São Paulo suburb, with his Austrian wife and three daughters.

Stangl denied any complicity in the mass murders which had taken place at Sobibor and Treblinka. Jailed in the disciplinary cells of the First Antiaircraft Battery in Brasilia, he told his Brazilian interrogators that his job had been to take down the names of the victims as they were marched to the gas chambers. Stangl made this statement: "I only obeyed orders, which at times came from the Führer himself, for I was an *Oberleutnant* [first lieutenant] in the Gestapo." However, Austria, West Germany, and Poland formally requested his extradition from Brazil.

The Austrian Foreign Ministry had asked Brazil to arrest Stangl. He was born in Austria in 1908, and had been a police officer there before joining the SS. Poland wanted to try Stangl because Sobibor and Treblinka were located in that country. West Germany based its claim on the fact that both Poland and Austria were under Nazi occupation at the time of Stangl's activities as a German functionary. While the legal merits of these conflicting petitions were considered by the Brazilian Supreme Court, Stangl remained under arrest and was interrogated about his knowledge of other missing Nazis who might be in South America.

On March 5, 1967, Simon Wiesenthal was interviewed by Dutch newspapermen while visiting his married daughter in Utrecht. He said that another important suspected war criminal, whom he would not identify, would be arrested soon in South America. Wiesenthal maintained that most of the war criminals in South America were assisted by "a very influential and dangerous organization," the *Kameradenwerk* (Action for Comrades).

Then, on May 11, Eduardo Garcia Gomez, Secret Police Chief of Guatemala, announced the arrest of a balding, gray-bearded man in his late sixties in Mariscos, a village 155 miles

from Guatemala City. The man identified himself as Juan
Falero Martinez, an itinerant carpenter born in Uruguay.
His face bore what appeared to be the marks of plastic sur-
gery. Guatemalan police suspected that they had found Mar-
tin Bormann, although the man who called himself Juan
Falero Martinez said that this idea was "crazy."

Dr. Fritz Bauer requested that the suspect's fingerprints be
flown to West Germany. Five days after the arrest, a waiting
police squad picked up the fingerprints at Rhein/Main Airport in Frankfurt and brought them to the Crime Bureau in
nearby Wiesbaden. There, experts compared the fingerprints
to those of Bormann in their files. They did not match.

On June 7, the Brazilian Supreme Court finally settled the
legal squabble concerning Franz Stangl by agreeing to ex-
tradite him to West Germany. Sixteen days later, he stepped
from a plane at Düsseldorf and was handcuffed to two West
German policemen. No date was then set was for his trial in a
Düsseldorf civil court. But he would be accused of responsibility for the extermination at Treblinka of 400,000 Jews from
the Warsaw ghetto and charged with twenty-three individual
charges of murder.

While awaiting trial, Stangl was questioned by Dr. Fritz
Bauer concerning the whereabouts of Martin Bormann. And
on July 4, the Supreme Court of Brazil received a formal
request from the West German Ministry of Justice for the
preventive arrest and extradition of the Secretary of the Führer. But this apparently did not mean that the Ministry of
Justice believed that Bormann was in Brazil, for Dr. Bauer
described the action as routine and nothing more than a "reminder" that the West German government had lodged a
permanent request with almost all Latin American countries
for the arrest and extradition of missing Nazi war criminals.
On July 7, Dr. Bauer told the press of the results of his interrogation of Stangl.

"Stangl knows nothing of Bormann's whereabouts," Dr.
Bauer said. "Even if he did, he certainly would not tell us."

Thus faded the most promising recent possibility of solving the mystery of Martin Bormann's whereabouts. Was there no solution to it? The military intelligence agencies of Great Britain, France, the United States, and the Soviet Union had searched for the Secretary of the Führer or some proof of his death in the postwar years, without apparent success. A definitive answer to the question of his fate later eluded Simon Wiesenthal, Dr. Fritz Bauer, the Soviet author Major Lew Besymenski, and the investigators of the West German Center for Preparation and Coordination for the Prosecution of Concentration Camp and War Crimes, who had uncovered sufficient evidence for 796 criminal proceedings in other cases since the Center's founding in 1958.

Could Bormann not be found because he was killed in Berlin, after all? But if this was true, why was his body never discovered? And what of all the witnesses who, since 1945, claimed to have seen him alive in West Germany, Spain, Italy, and Latin America? Had Bormann really escaped from Berlin and, aided by Nazi funds and perhaps plastic surgery, been more clever and resourceful at evading detection for more than two decades than, for example, Naumann, Eichmann, and Stangl?

Was there no satisfactory answer to the question of the fate of the Head of the Nazi Party Chancellery and Secretary of the Führer?

One had existed since 1953, although this answer was as fantastic as Martin Bormann's rise from convict to the closest confidant of the man who had nearly conquered Europe.

The location of missing Nazis and the prosecution of war-crimes trials had been superseded as major objectives of the United States and the Soviet Union in 1953 by newer problems created by the cold war, which was then at its height. North Korean and Chinese forces fighting United States and other United Nations troops in Korea were being supplied with arms and other essentials by the Soviet Union. There was almost no tourist exchange, trade, or other normal relations between the two major powers which had been allied against Nazi Germany.

There was an atmosphere of terror within the Soviet Union itself at the beginning of 1953 due to the "doctor's plot." Stalin, seventy-four years old but still very much in command, had instigated an accusation against a group of doctors, most of them Jews, of plotting to kill Soviet leaders. Those in the west who specialized in trying to understand the workings of Stalin's mind interpreted the "doctor's plot" as a signal for the start of a new purge of men who sought to modify the dictator's policies.

Eight years after Hitler's death, West Germany had become one of the most prosperous and economically powerful countries in the world. The West German Federal

Republic, created in 1949, was on its way to complete sovereignty, although Great Britain, France, and the United States retained some controls under the Occupation Statute. West German rearmament, encouraged by the western allies as a counterforce to the East German People's Army and the Soviet Army, had become an accepted fact of realistic politics. So had the return of some former Nazis to government positions.

Dr. Konrad Adenauer, the West German Federal Chancellor, favored a policy of absorbing minor and repentant Nazis into the mainstream of West German life. To treat them forever as pariahs would only unify them as a disgruntled and dangerous threat to the democratic aspirations of the Federal Republic. The western allies agreed with this policy. The Federal Republic appeared stable. The facts did not seem to warrant a serious concern over a resurgence of Nazism. This view received a jolt on January 15, 1953. As noted earlier, the British High Commissioner for Germany then announced the arrests of seven Germans on suspicion of engaging in a conspiracy to overthrow the Federal Republic and restore a Nazi regime. Dr. Werner Naumann was named as the ringleader of this suspected conspiracy.

The Berlin Headquarters of the United States Central Intelligence Agency was located in January 1953 somewhere in the suburb of Dahlem. The British action against Naumann and his associates came as a surprise to the Chief of the Berlin CIA, a man who shall here be called Dr. John Broderick. It also intrigued him. For there appeared to be some merit in the British charges, and they caused Dr. Broderick to ask himself two questions: Had Martin Bormann escaped from Berlin with Naumann, and was he behind the Naumann plot?

In 1953, there was no conclusive evidence that Bormann was dead. This was not the fault of the CIA, which had never investigated the matter. The CIA was not created until 1947, well after the International Military Tribunal concluded its proceedings, and the operations of the new civilian agency were directed in Europe against the Soviet Union and her eastern satellites. Then as now, the finding of missing Nazis as such was not one of CIA's responsibilities, which is why the agency had not looked for Naumann. What had been done in the extermination camps or on the battlefields of a war that was over did not concern CIA.

What did concern CIA were individuals in foreign countries who constituted a present or future threat to the security of the United States. Bormann would certainly qualify as such a threat if he had survived and was now masterminding the neo-Nazi Naumann group in a conspiracy against one of the leading anti-communist allies of the United States. And so, in January 1953, Dr. Broderick asked for and received approval from his superiors in Frankfurt and Washington to undertake an investigation of Bormann's whereabouts. Previously, such investigations had been conducted by military intelligence agencies which possessed neither the funds nor the talent commanded by CIA.

Dr. Broderick maintained a personal interest in the investigation, but to conduct it on the day-to-day working level he chose the writer of this book, who was then employed as a case officer by the Berlin CIA. Like most espionage work, this was not glamorous or exciting, but instead required the drudgery of checking out evidence and coordinating the work of different individuals and organizations.

The first step in the investigation was to call upon the services of the staff psychiatrist of the Berlin CIA and its principal "scenario writer." The psychiatrist's assignment was to review Bormann's life and to compose a psychological profile of him. This would then be turned over to the "scenario writer," who would assemble the known facts of Bormann's last days, mix them in with the psychological profile, and write plausible scenarios of what might logically have happened to him. This was a recent and sophisticated technique designed to stimulate the thinking of case officers who might find themselves "locked in" or inhibited by conventional thinking and a mass of information.

Next, CIA offices throughout Latin America, the Arab states, and Europe were requested to check out the authenticity of the many reports of Bormann's appearances and to investigate whether he was alive in any of those areas. Since Bormann was in Berlin when the Red Army took the city, I next turned to an organization which was capable of penetrating official Soviet circles and discovering what had really happened in Berlin in May 1945. This was the South German Industrial Development Organization, the cover name for an intelligence operation headed by Reinhard Gehlen, financed by the CIA and headquartered in a closely guarded twenty-five acre compound in Pullach, south of Munich.

Gehlen had served as the German Army's intelligence chief in certain sectors of the Russian front. As such, he had provided accurate information to Hitler about the intended moves of the Red Army. The Führer disregarded most of this information. After the war, Lieutenant General Gehlen put himself, his files, and his apparatus at the disposal of American occupation authorities, who bought his package.

The price to the CIA for Gehlen's services in 1953 was around six million dollars. This sum bought the expertise of some 4,000 German intelligence specialists, many of them experienced former Army and SS men with unique contacts and knowledge of eastern, and especially East German and Soviet, affairs. I asked the Bureau Gehlen to develop whatever information it could about what had happened to the Secretary of the Führer after he left the Reich Chancellery.

As the various phases of the investigation continued, Joseph Stalin died in March. This caused some relaxation of his inflexible policies and also shifts in the Soviet hierarchy. In the same month, the British High Commissioner, at Dr. Adenauer's request, turned over to West German authorities the responsibility for the investigation and eventual prosecution of Dr. Naumann and his associates. Later, of course, they were released without being tried because the West Germans concluded that there was no serious evidence against them.

I was told by the CIA's liaison officer to the West German Ministry of Justice that the Ministry had satisfied itself that Bormann had nothing whatever to do with the Naumann group. This news, whose credibility there was no reason to doubt, seemed to remove Bormann's possible connection with Naumann. Nevertheless, the investigation was now so far along that the CIA decided to take the precaution of learning for itself whether Bormann was alive or dead.

By early June 1953, I had completed a report for Dr. Broderick. The first item in it was a summary of the findings of CIA offices in Latin America, the Arab states, and Europe. None of these offices had been able to find Bormann. All of them doubted the accuracy of those who claimed to have seen him after the war. There were different speculations on the eyewitnesses' motives; they were honestly mistaken, or publicity seekers, or the kind of persons who see flying saucers.

The Bureau Gehlen reported that Bormann was not in East Germany or the Soviet Union. The Bureau also had been unable to discover what had happened to him after he left the Reich Chancellery. However, it did provide one specific fact. Bormann's *Tagebuch* (daily log or calendar of events) had been found by Russian soldiers in Berlin in May 1945 and sent to Moscow. The last two entries in it read: "April 30. Adolf Hitler X, Eva B. X. May 1. *Ausbruchsversuch* [Attempt to escape]."

The principal scenario writer for the Berlin CIA offered four scripts as a stimulus to thinking. His first suggested that Bormann was an informer. Always the opportunist, he placed himself at the service of Soviet Intelligence when it became obvious that the Nazi cause was lost. He funneled invaluable information about the Führer's intentions and the strategy of the German Armed Forces High Command to the Soviets, thus insuring the latter's victory. Bormann's reward was obvious. At the time of General Krebs's mission to them, the So-

viets arranged for Bormann to reach the bridge over the Invalidenstrasse and there to feign death. He was then picked up
by a Soviet patrol and taken to Russia, where he now lived in
comfortable surroundings as the Soviet Union's leading resident expert on German affairs. If suitable conditions arose, he
would return to Germany as its Commissar.

The second scenario suggested that Bormann was a British
informer. Realizing that Germany could not win a long war,
Bormann persuaded his eccentric chief, Rudolf Hess, to fly to
Scotland. Though Hess's peace mission failed, he succeeded in
putting Bormann in contact with British Intelligence. The Secretary of the Führer remained a British agent throughout the
war. He was not killed on the Weidendammer Bridge, nor had
he died near the Lehrter Station. Those who claimed that he
died in Berlin were lying and part of a conspiracy to protect
Bormann. He made his way, as many of the others had, to
western Germany. Bormann went toward Plön, which would
be taken by British forces. This explained his expressed determination to reach Grand Admiral Doenitz. Bormann actually had a prearranged rendezvous with British agents, who
took him to some remote spot in the British Isles. He functioned as an adviser to British Intelligence and the Foreign
Office on German affairs, especially on questions relating to a
revival of Nazism. Eventually, when the ill feelings engendered by the Nazi period subsided, Bormann's true role would
be made public and he would be allowed to return to Germany. There he could live out his days in peace on a modest
pension, a misguided idealist who followed the Führer only to
the point where he realized that to do so further would bring
catastrophe to his beloved Fatherland.

The third scenario, too, relied on the premise that those
who said that Bormann was killed in Berlin were part of a
conspiracy to protect him. How else could the contradictions
in their testimony be logically explained? Wouldn't Bormann
have followed Hitler and Goebbels and committed suicide if
he indeed believed that his position was hopeless? The answer

was that he knew it was not hopeless. He had a carefully planned escape route. He reached a German submarine somewhere on the Baltic coast and escaped in it to Argentina. There, protected by the Fascist dictator Peron, financed by millions of marks taken from the Nazi Party treasury, Bormann gathered about him a band of SS men and Nazi Party officials. In a secret and closely guarded compound somewhere between Tierra del Fuego and the Tropic of Capricorn, the Andes and the Atlantic, the Secretary of the Führer directed a worldwide Nazi conspiracy whose ultimate aim was to establish a Fourth Reich with Bormann as its Führer.

None of these three scenarios seemed very promising to me. They were supposed to stimulate thinking, but the stimulus had to be based on facts. However, the fourth scenario appeared to have merit. It presented the idea that Bormann had no real escape plan. If he really wanted to escape from Germany, he would not have stayed with Hitler in the Bunker. He would have gone to Berchtesgaden when the opportunity presented itself. Bormann did reach the Friedrichstrasse Station. Those who thought he was killed by the tank explosion were honestly mistaken. He did unwittingly descend upon a Russian sentry post near the Lehrter Station with Axmann, Stumpfegger, Weltzin, Naumann, and Schwägermann. He hurried off in an easterly direction down the Invalidenstrasse with Stumpfegger. But the two men ran into heavy Russian fire and retraced their steps to the bridge over the Invalidenstrasse. They were now caught in a crossfire, with no place to go.

At this point, the staff psychiatrist's contribution appeared important. Bormann lived for years in close proximity to Hitler. He gained his power from the Führer and exercised it through him. Now Hitler was dead. Bormann's life work had turned out to be worthless. Psychologically, he was completely disoriented. There was no way out. Within minutes, he was going to fall into the hands of the Russians, whom he always despised and whose vengeance he had good reason to fear. So he and Dr. Stumpfegger swallowed poison capsules. Artur

Axmann was right. He did see the corpses of Bormann and Stumpfegger on the railroad bridge. In a final irony, the Russians did not even recognize the Secretary of the Führer. They had him buried, along with scores of other bodies lying in the area, in an unmarked mass grave.

This last version of Bormann's fate was, of course, speculation. But coupled with the failure of the Bureau Gehlen and the CIA offices to discover any other evidence, it seemed to be the most likely thing to have happened. When I presented my complete report to Dr. Broderick, he did not appear disappointed by its inconclusive nature. He had recently received information of his own from a high-level source in the Soviet government, some of whose members were advocating hesitant cooperation with the west now that Stalin was dead.

Dr. Broderick agreed that Bormann had taken poison on the railroad bridge. But according to Dr. Broderick's Soviet source, whose accuracy he did not question, Russian officers identified Bormann. He was carrying his *Tagebuch,* or daily log, in his pocket. They had him buried by the employees of the Lehrter Post Office. After notifying Moscow of this, and then receiving further instructions, Russian officers returned to the grave, dug Bormann up, took his body to an isolated spot in East Germany and reburied him in an unmarked grave.

If this seemed pointless, there was really a kind of shrewd logic behind it. Stalin had caused difficulties over Hitler's death. He would not admit to his Allies that a Russian search party found and identified the Führer's corpse. As for Bormann, Stalin wanted it to be thought that the Secretary of the Führer was still alive. This could be used as a stick to beat the West with. As long as it could be thought that a leading Nazi was alive in some western country, the West could be accused of sheltering a Nazi revival.

The CIA had no intention of making public this story of Bormann's death, according to Dr. Broderick, for three reasons. First, now that Stalin was dead the United States government did not want to do anything that would be of no real advantage to the United States and might embarrass Russia. Rather, the idea was to explore certain avenues of cooperation with the new rulers in the Kremlin in an age of possible nuclear war. Second, it would be embarrassing to have it known that the International Military Tribunal tried a dead man. Finally, Stalin's curious idea was not really such a bad one. Let the suspicion linger that the second most powerful Nazi leader was still alive as a reminder not to forget the horrors of the Third Reich.

Sources

Because Martin Bormann preferred anonymity, there is today much less source material available about him than there is about Hitler and such other leading members of the Führer's court as Goering, Goebbels, and Himmler.

There is one biography: *Martin Bormann—Hitlers Schatten* (*Martin Bormann—Hitler's Shadow*), written by the specialist in the Nazi era Joseph Wulf. Published in West Germany in 1962, this book has not yet appeared in English. Nor has *Das Gesicht Des Dritten Reiches* (*The Face of the Third Reich*) by Joachim C. Fest, which was published in West Germany in 1963. Fest's study contains, among other chapters on the personalities of the Third Reich, a perceptive chapter entitled *"Martin Bormann—Die braune Eminenz* (*Martin Bormann—The Brown Eminence*)."

An American writer, Eugene Davidson, has attempted to define Bormann's personality and activity in "The Party in Action and Theory," the fourth chapter of Davidson's massive study: *The Trial of the Germans—An account of the twenty-two defendants before the International Military Tribunal.* New York, 1966.

The British historian and author of *The Last Days of Hitler,* Hugh Redwald Trevor-Roper, provides a study of Bormann in his introduction to *The Bormann Letters*. These private letters which Bormann and his wife wrote to each other between January 1943 and April 1945 were not intended for publication. However, they survived the war and were published by Weidenfeld and Nicolson, London, in 1954. Trevor-Roper edited this volume and, as noted, introduced it.

Bormann was head of the Nazi Party Chancellery. The records of the Nazi Party are on microfilm in the National Archives, Washington, D.C.

In addition to the sources noted above, I have studied the testimony and documentary material published in connection with the trial of the major war criminals at Nuremberg, where Bormann was tried *in absentia* and much material about him presented both by his prosecutor and defense counsel. The full text of the documents presented in evidence during the entire trial and the complete version of the trial proceedings has been published in forty-two volumes as: *The Trial of the Major War Criminals before the International Military Tribunal.* Nuremberg, 1947–49. The first twenty-three volumes contain the text of the trial testimony. The remaining volumes contain the text, mostly in German, of the documents accepted in evidence. This publication is cited in the chapter notes as *IMT*.

English translations of most of the documents used by the United States and British prosecutors, together with English translations of some defense documents, pretrial interrogations, and affidavits, have been published in ten volumes, with two supplementary volumes A and B, as: *Nazi Conspiracy and Aggression.* United States Government Printing Office. Washington, 1946–48. This is cited in the chapter notes as *NCA*.

A verbatim record of the trial testimony has been published in twenty-three parts, or volumes, as: *The Trial of German Major War Criminals.* His Majesty's Stationery Office. London, 1946–50. This is cited as *TGMWC*.

United States military tribunals conducted twelve trials in Nuremberg subsequent to the trials of the major war criminals. Some of the testimony and documents presented at these trials has been published in fifteen volumes as: *Trials of War Criminals before the Nuremberg Military Tribunals.* United States Government Printing Office. Washington, 1951–52. This is cited as *NMT*.

In addition to these principal sources, I gathered information and quotations from many historical studies, diaries, memoirs, and biographies. Only those which are relevant to Bormann and the events described in this book are listed in the bibliography. Some of these sources are cited again in the individual chapter notes, where this seems called for, along with citations from *IMT, NCA, TGMWC, NMT,* and pertinent magazine and newspaper reports.

I have also drawn upon my own experiences in postwar Germany for certain information. It should be noted, however, that I left the employ of the CIA in 1954 and have had nothing whatever to do with that agency since then. This book is my responsibility alone.

J. McG.

Selected Bibliography

Adenauer, Konrad: *Memoirs 1945-1953*. Chicago, 1966.
Arendt, Hannah: *Eichmann in Jerusalem*. Revised and enlarged edition. New York, 1965.
Bauer, Hans: *Hitler's Pilot*. London, 1958.
Bernadotte, Folke: *The Curtain Falls*. New York, 1945.
Besymenski, Lew: *Auf den Spuren von Martin Bormann*. East Berlin, 1965.
Boldt, Gerhard: *In The Shelter With Hitler*. London, 1948.
Bormann, Martin: *The Bormann Letters, The Private Correspondence Between Martin Bormann and His Wife from January 1943 to April 1945*. Edited with an introduction and notes by H. R. Trevor-Roper. London, 1954.
Bullock, Alan: *Hitler, A Study in Tyranny*. New York, 1952.
Byrnes, James F.: *Speaking Frankly*. New York, 1947.
Carell, Paul: *Hitler Moves East, 1941-1943*. Boston, 1965.
Churchill, Winston S.: *The Second World War, Closing the Ring*. Boston, 1951.
———, *The Second World War, Triumph and Tragedy*. Boston, 1953.
Ciano, Count Galeazzo: *The Ciano Diaries, 1939-1943*. New York, 1946.
Clark, Alan: *Barbarossa: Russian-German Conflict 1941-1945*. New York, 1965.
Crankshaw, Edward: *The Gestapo, Instrument of Tyranny*. London, 1956.
Dallin, Alexander: *German Rule in Russia, 1941-1945*. New York, 1957.
Davidson, Eugene: *The Trial of the Germans—An account of the twenty-two defendants before the International Military Tribunal*. New York, 1966.
Doenitz, Karl: *Memoirs: Ten Years and Twenty Days*. Cleveland and New York, 1959.
Fest, Joachim C.: *Das Gesicht des Dritten Reiches*. Munich, 1963.
Fitzgibbon, Constantine: *20 July*. New York, 1956.
Francois-Ponçet, André: *The Fateful Years*. New York, 1949.

Frank, Hans: *Im Angesicht des Galgens.* Munich, 1953.

Frieden, Seymour and Richardson, William, editors: *The Fatal Decisions.* New York, 1956.

Friedman, Tuvia: *The Hunter.* New York, 1961.

Frischauer, Willy: *The Rise and Fall of Hermann Goering.* Boston, 1951.

————, *Himmler.* London, 1953.

Gilbert, Felix, editor: *Hitler Directs His War: The Secret Record of His Daily Military Conferences.* New York, 1950.

Gilbert, G. M.: *Nuremberg Diary.* New York, 1947.

Gisevius, Hans B.: *To The Bitter End.* Boston, 1947.

Goebbels, Joseph: *Vom Kaiserhof zur Reichskanzlei.* Munich, 1936.

————, *The Goebbels Diaries, 1942-1943. Edited by Louis P. Lochner.* New York, 1948.

Guderian, Heinz: *Panzer Leader.* New York, 1952.

Gumbel, E. J.: *Vier Jahre politischer Mord.* Berlin, 1922.

————, *Les Crimes Politiques en Allemagne, 1919-1929.* Paris, 1931.

Halder, Franz: *Diary.* Office of the Chief of Counsel for War Crimes. Nuremberg, 1946.

————, *Hitler als Feldherr.* Munich, 1949.

Hassel, Ulrich von: *The von Hassel Diaries, 1938-1944.* New York, 1947.

Hausner, Gideon: *Justice in Jerusalem.* New York, 1966.

Heiden, Konrad: *Der Fuehrer.* Boston, 1944.

Heydecker, Joe J. and Leeb, Johannes: *The Nuremberg Trial.* Cleveland and New York, 1962.

Hilberg, Raul: *The Destruction of the European Jews.* Chicago, 1961.

Hitler, Adolf: *Mein Kampf,* Boston, 1943.

————, *Hitler's Table Talk 1941-1944.* Edited and introduced by H. R. Trevor-Roper. London, 1953.

————, *The Testament of Adolf Hitler: The Hitler-Bormann Documents February-April 1945.* With an Introduction by H. R. Trevor-Roper. London, 1961.

Hoess, Rudolf: *Commandant of Auschwitz.* New York, 1960.

Hoettl, Wilhelm (Walter Hagen): *The Secret Front—The Story of Nazi Political Espionage.* New York, 1954.

Hoffmann, Heinrich: *Hitler Was My Friend*. London, 1955.

Horne, Alistair: *Return to Power*. New York, 1956.

Jackson, Robert A.: *The Nürnberg Case*. New York, 1947.

Keitel, Wilhelm: *The Memoirs of Field-Marshal Keitel*. Edited with an Introduction and Epilogue by Walter Görlitz. New York, 1966.

Kelly, Douglas M.: *22 Cells in Nuremberg*. New York, 1947.

Kempka, Erich: *Ich habe Adolf Hitler verbrannt*. Munich, 1950.

Kersten, Felix: *The Kersten Memoirs*. London, 1956.

Koller, Karl: *Der letzte Monat*. Mannheim, 1949.

Kuby, Erich: *Die Russen in Berlin 1945*. Munich-Bern, 1965.

Leasor, James: *The Uninvited Envoy*. New York, 1962.

Lerner, Daniel: *The Nazi Élite*. Palo Alto, 1951.

Luedde-Neurath, Walter: *Die letzten Tage des Dritten Reiches*. Goettingen, 1951.

McRandle, James H.: *The Track of the Wolf: Essays on National Socialism and its Leader, Adolf Hitler*. Evanston, 1965.

Manvell, Roger and Fraenkel, Heinrich: *Dr. Goebbels*. New York, 1960.

——, *Hermann Goering*. New York, 1962.

——, *Himmler*. New York, 1965.

Naumann, Bernd: *Auschwitz: A Report on the Proceedings Against Robert Karl Mulka and Others Before the Court at Frankfurt*. New York, 1966.

Neumann, Franz: *Behemoth* (revised edition). New York, 1944.

Oven, Wilfred von: *Mit Goebbels bis zum Ende*. 2 vols. Buenos Aires, 1949.

Payne, Robert: *The Rise And Fall Of Stalin* (paperback edition). New York, 1966.

Pearlman, Moshe: *The Capture and Trial of Adolf Eichmann*. New York, 1963.

Prittie, Terence: *Germany Divided: The Legacy of the Nazi Era*. Boston, 1960.

Recktenwald, Johann: *Woran hat Hitler gelitten?* Munich, 1963.

Rees, J. R.: *The Case of Rudolf Hess: A Problem in Diagnosis and Forensic Psychiatry*. London, 1947.

Reitlinger, Gerald: *The Final Solution*. New York, 1953.

——, *The House Built on Sand—The Conflicts of German Policy in Russia 1939-1945*. New York, 1960.

Rosenberg, Alfred: *Memoirs*. Chicago, 1949.

Rossbach, Gerhard: *Mein Weg durch Die Zeit*. Weilburg/Lahn, 1950.

Roxan, David and Wanstall, Ken: *The Rape of Art*. New York, 1965.

Ryan, Cornelius: *The Last Battle*. New York, 1966.

Schellenberg, Walter: *The Labyrinth*. New York, 1956.

Schlabrendorff, Fabian von: *They Almost Killed Hitler*. New York, 1947.

Schmidt, Paul: *Hitler's Interpreter*. New York, 1951
———, *Statist auf diplomatischer Bühne, 1923-1945*. Bonn, 1949.

Schneider, Franz and Gullans, Charles, editors and translators: *Last Letters from Stalingrad*. New York, 1961.

Schwerin von Krosigk, Lutz: *Es geschah in Deutschland*. Tuebingen, 1951.

Semmler, Rudolf: *Goebbels—The Man Next to Hitler*. London, 1947.

Sherwood, Robert: *Roosevelt and Hopkins*. New York, 1948.

Shirer, William L.: *End of a Berlin Diary*. New York, 1947.
———, *The Rise and Fall of the Third Reich*. New York, 1960.

Smoydzin, Werner: *Hitler Lebt*. Pfaffenhofen/Ilm, 1966.

Stein, George H.: *The Waffen SS: Hitler's Élite Guard at War 1939-1945*. Ithaca and London, 1966.

Steiner, Felix: *Die Freiwilligen: Idee und Opfergang*. Goettingen, 1958.

Tauber, Kurt: *Beyond Eagle and Swastika—German Nationalism Since 1945*. volume I. Middletown, Connecticut, 1967.

Taylor, A. J. P.: *The Origins Of The Second World War*. London, 1961.

Thorwald, Juergen: *Flight in Winter: Russia, January to May 1945*. New York, 1951.

Toland, John: *The Last 100 Days*. New York, 1966.

Trevor-Roper, Hugh Redwald: *The Last Days of Hitler*. Third edition with a new preface by the Author. New York, 1962.

Warlimont, Walter: *Inside Hitler's Headquarters 1939-45*. New York, 1964.

Wheeler-Bennett, John W.: *The Nemesis of Power: The German Army in Politics 1918-1945*. New York, 1953.

Wiesenthal, Simon: *The Murderers Among Us: The Simon*

Wiesenthal Memoirs. Edited and with an Introductory Profile by Joseph Wechsberg. New York, 1967.

Wighton, Charles: *Heydrich*. London, 1962.

Wulf, Joseph: *Martin Bormann—Hitler's Schatten*. Guetersloh, 1962.

Zoller, A., editor: *Hitler Privat*. Düsseldorf, 1949.

Chapter Notes

ONE: "The Biggest Unsolved Nazi Mystery"

The description of the Nuremberg executions is based on *The Nuremberg Trial* by Heydecker and Leeb and on articles in *Life* and *Time*. The quotations of Keitel, Frank, Schwerin von Krosigk, Guderian and Rosenberg are taken from their books which are listed in the bibliography. The sources of other quotations are: Goering, *NCA;* Fritzche, *TGMWC;* Speer, *The Last Days of Hitler;* Klaus Eichmann, *Quick;* Bauer and Wiesenthal, *New York Times;* Friedman, *New York Post.* Wiesenthal describes the whereabouts of Martin Bormann as "the biggest unsolved Nazi mystery" in chapter twenty-five, "Where Is Bormann?" of his book *The Murderers Among Us.*

TWO: The Convict

Based on the listed books by Wulf, Rossbach, Gumbel, Wheeler-Bennett, and Besymenski.

THREE: The Unknown Reichsleiter

The quotation of Goebbels is taken from his *Vom Kaiserhof zur Reichskanzlei.* The sources of other quotations are: Goering, *Hermann Goering,* by Manvell and Fraenkel; Hoess, *Commandant of Auschwitz,* by Rudolf Hoess; Bormann on Jewish physicians, *NCA;* Bormann on the "gang of fairies" around Roehm, *Der Führer,* by Konrad Heiden; Bormann to his wife on avoiding notoriety, *The Bormann Letters.* The description of Bormann as looking like a boxer is given by Walter Schellenberg in his *The Labyrinth,* and as looking like a wrestler is given by Boldt in his *In The Shelter With Hitler.* Boldt is also the source of Bormann's comment: "It is not my habit to have relations with idiots." This chapter is also based on the listed books by Wulf, Lerner, Bullock, and Francois-Ponçet.

FOUR: Chief of Staff to the Deputy Führer

Particularly helpful were the books by Bullock, McRandle, Schellenberg. *The Rape of Art* by Roxan and Wanstall is the source of Hitler's interest in obtaining artistic masterpieces for Linz and Bormann's involvement in Special Mission Linz. The source of Funk's remark to Kempka and Kempka's observations of Bormann's behavior is *Ich habe Adolf Hitler verbrannt* (I Burned Adolf Hitler) by Kempka. The quotations of Alfred Rosenberg are from his *Memoirs*. Bormann's description of Hitler as "the greatest human being" is from *The Bormann Letters*.

FIVE: Obstacles to Power

Hitler's remark about the destruction of Poland is from *IMT*. The Warlimont quotations are from his book *Inside Hitler's Headquarters 1939-45*. Bormann's record of the conference of October 2, 1940, is from *IMT*. Other material is from books by Ciano, Von Hassell, Schellenberg, and Kersten and the three biographies *Dr. Goebbels; Hermann Goering;* and *Himmler* by Manvell and Fraenkel as well as the two biographies *The Rise and Fall of Hermann Goering;* and *Himmler* by Frischauer. Bormann's comment to his wife that Hitler "towered over the rest of us like Mount Everest" is from *The Bormann Letters*. IMT document 872-PS is the source of Hitler's comment that "the world would hold its breath" concerning Barbarossa.

SIX: The Opportunity

The material concerning Hess's flight is largely based on *The Uninvited Envoy* by Leasor and *The Case of Rudolf Hess,* edited by Rees. Other material is from books by Keitel, Bullock, Schmidt, Schellenberg, as well as *Mein Kampf* by Hitler and *Closing the Ring* by Churchill. Keitel's description of Hitler's reaction to Hess's flight is from *NCA,* as is Bormann's views on the "Relationship of National Socialism to Christendom." Bormann's letter to Himmler speculating on the reasons for Hess's flight is printed in *The Nuremberg Trial* by Heydecker and Leeb.

SEVEN: Brown Eminence

Useful here were *German Rule in Russia* by Dallin; *Hitler Moves East* by Carell; *Barbarossa* by Clark; and *The House Built on Sand* by Reitlinger. Dallin's book gives a long, detailed and interesting account of the struggle between Rosenberg and his opponents, Bormann and Koch. Other sources for background material and quotations in this chapter were the diaries of Ciano, Halder, and Goebbels; *Justice in Jerusalem* by Hausner; *The Fatal Decisions*, edited by Frieden and Richardson, and *Hitler's Table Talk 1941-1944*.

EIGHT: Rumors About the Position of the Jews

Bormann's decree is one of the documents published in an English translation in *NCA*. I also drew upon Halder's diary; Keitel's *Memoirs; The Labyrinth* by Schellenberg; *Heydrich* by Wighton; *Auschwitz* by Naumann; *The Bormann Letters; Last Letters from Stalingrad* edited and translated by Schneider and Gullans; *The Final Solution* by Reitlinger; and *The Destruction of the European Jews* by Hilberg.

NINE: Secretary of the Führer

The diaries of Ciano, Goebbels, and Semmler were drawn upon here, as were the books by Bullock, Wulf, Schellenberg, Naumann, Recktenwald, Zoller, Hoffmann, Churchill's *Triumph and Tragedy*, and *The Bormann Letters*. Gottlob Berger's observation about Hitler's distrust is from *NMT*.

TEN: "Our Unshakeable Faith In Ultimate Victory"

Books by Schellenberg; Guderian; Fitzgibbon; Bullock; and *The Bormann Letters; The Testament of Adolf Hitler*; and *Himmler* by Manvell and Fraenkel. Speer's observations are from *TGMWC*.

ELEVEN: The Executor

Most of the events in this chapter are described in *IMT, NCA,* and *TGMWC*. I have drawn upon these official publications and also found the following books particularly helpful as source material: *The Last Days of Hitler* by Trevor-Roper; *The Last Battle* by Ryan; *The Last Hundred Days* by Toland; *The Waffen SS* by Steiner; *Die Freiwilligen* by Steiner; *In The Shelter With Hitler* by Boldt; *Memoirs* by Keitel; *The Bormann Letters.*

TWELVE: "The Situation in Berlin Is More Tense"

IMT, NCA, TGMWC. Also the books by Kempka and Doenitz, and *The Last Days of Hitler* by Trevor-Roper.

THIRTEEN: Escape Attempt

Erich Kempka has given his version of the events in which he was involved in pretrial interrogations printed in *NCA,* trial testimony printed in *IMT,* and his book. Axmann, of course, did not testify at Nuremberg. However, he was interrogated by Allied intelligence officers after being located in the Bavarian Alps. Twenty years later, Axmann retold his story in a magazine article *"Meine Flucht mit Bormann [My Flight with Bormann]"* in the West German magazine *Stern* (Number 19/1965). I have used this article as source material. Zhukov's statement appeared in *Soviet War News,* June 11, 1945. The Goering quotations are from *Hermann Goering* by Manvell and Fraenkel and *The Nuremberg Trial* by Heydecker and Leeb. Eden's statement is from *Justice in Jerusalem* by Hausner. The account of Himmler's death is derived from *Himmler* by Manvell and Fraenkel. Other material is from *IMT; The Last Days of Hitler* by Trevor-Roper; *Roosevelt and Hopkins* by Sherwood; *Speaking Frankly* by Byrnes; and newspaper reports in *The New York Times.* The verdict of the Soviet commission of inquiry is printed in *The Rise and Fall of Stalin* by Payne.

FOURTEEN: In His Absence

The *Bekanntmachung* or public notice and the statements by Maxwell-Fyfe, Bergold, Kempka, and Lambert are all printed in *IMT.* Other material is from *The Last Days of Hitler* by Trevor-Roper; *End of a Berlin Diary* by Shirer; *The Nürnberg Case* by Jackson; and newspaper reports in *The New York Times.*

FIFTEEN: "Death Not Completely Established"

Berger's testimony is printed in NMT. His statement that Bormann had been a Soviet agent is from *Martin Bormann—Hitlers Schatten* by Wulf. Heisslein wrote of his forest encounter with Bormann in *Le Figaro*, December 29, 1950. Koch's adventures are related in *The House Built on Sand*, by Reitlinger. The Naumann affair is described in *Germany Divided* by Prittie and *Beyond Eagle and Swastika* by Tauber. Material on Silvestri, Stern, Tiburtius, Linge, Rattenhuber, Bauer, Günsche, Roca-Pinar, Schuele, the Berchtesgaden County Court and the Registrar's Office of the City of West Berlin is from newspaper reports in *The New York Times* and various West German newspapers. For the material about Bormann's son, I drew upon a magazine article about Father Bormann, "In the Forest of Fear," by Edward R. F. Sheehan, which appeared in *The Saturday Evening Post*, August 12, 1967.

SIXTEEN: "The Search Is Narrowing Down"

Justice in Jerusalem by Hausner; *The Capture and Trial of Adolf Eichmann* by Pearlman; *The Secret Front* by Hoettl; *Auf den Spuren von Martin Bormann* by Besymenski; and *The Murderers Among Us* by Wiesenthal. Also various newspaper and magazine reports in *The New York Times, The New York Post, Quick,* and *Der Spiegel.*

SEVENTEEN: A Reminder

As noted earlier, the Naumann affair has been described in *Germany Divided* by Prittie and *Beyond Eagle and Swastika* by Tauber. For most of the material in this chapter I have drawn upon my own experiences in postwar West Germany.

INDEX

231

A Note About the Author

James McGovern was born in New York City. He served for three years in the United States Army during World War II, specializing in cryptanalysis, and was graduated from Harvard College in 1948. From 1949 to 1954, Mr. McGovern worked in Frankfurt and Berlin, Germany, first for the State Department and then for the Central Intelligence Agency. Since leaving the CIA in 1954, Mr. McGovern has previously published four books. He lives in New York City and Stonington, Connecticut, with his wife and two children, and works for Rumrill-Hoyt, an advertising agency.